CREATING THE EUROPEAN COMMUNITY

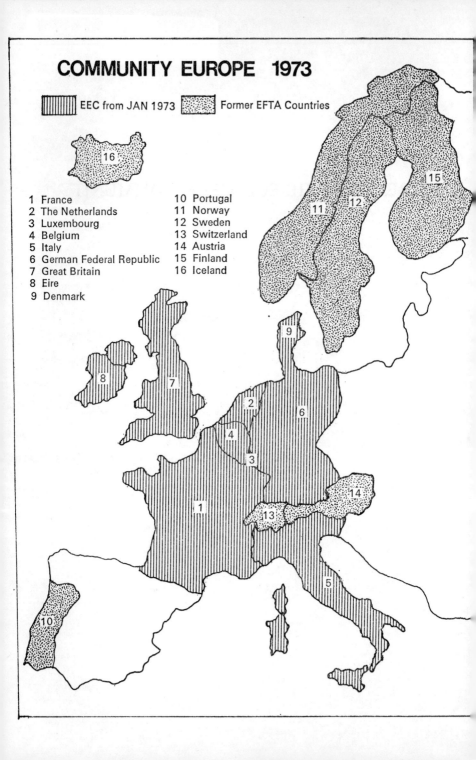

COMMUNITY EUROPE 1973

EEC from JAN 1973   Former EFTA Countries

1 France
2 The Netherlands
3 Luxembourg
4 Belgium
5 Italy
6 German Federal Republic
7 Great Britain
8 Eire
9 Denmark
10 Portugal
11 Norway
12 Sweden
13 Switzerland
14 Austria
15 Finland
16 Iceland

Creating the
European Community

R. C. Mowat, M.A., D.Phil.

BLANDFORD PRESS
LONDON

First published in 1973
© 1973 Blandford Press Ltd
167 High Holborn, London WC1V 6PH
ISBN 0 7137 0636 8

Printed in Great Britain by
Tonbridge Printers Ltd,
Tonbridge, Kent

Contents

CONTENTS

Foreword

Since 1 January 1973, Great Britain, together with Denmark and Ireland, has been a member of the European Community.

This significant event in the history of Britain and of the European continent has been awaited for twenty-two years, from the declaration of Robert Schuman in May 1950 to the end of the negotiations in 1972. Curiously enough, this long period can be divided into two equal parts. For the first eleven years—from 1950 to 1961—Great Britain was reluctant to join the enterprise, and for the next eleven—from 1961 to 1972—the British government, headed successively by Mr. Harold Macmillan, Mr. Harold Wilson and Mr. Edward Heath, was obliged to wait at the door of the Community till the Six had settled their lack of unanimity, their vetoes and their internal crises. It follows that the responsibilities for the delay are equally divided, and the time has come to go forward together.

Problems, of course, lie ahead. But, to solve them, to understand what is at stake, to know what since the very beginning have been the aims of the 'Founding Fathers' of the Community, it is important to look at the past.

Dr. R. C. Mowat's book is of great interest in this respect. Not only has the author displayed a considerable and very accurate knowledge of the history of Europe, the efforts towards unity and the place which the creation of the three Communities (now combined) occupies in these events, but he has gone deeper in his analyses than the day-to-day life and the political action, towards what I may call the spiritual thinking which animated the creation of the Community.

For the enterprise of the Six, as he very clearly demonstrates, is not merely a concerted economic enterprise, an effort of six countries to pool their interests for the sake of profit, as might have been decided by a multi-national company. The founders, Schuman, Adenauer, de Gasperi and Spaak were motivated by the conviction that the time had at last come, after centuries of wars, invasions and destruction, to build a continent reconciled, united, strong and generous. The idea of reconciliation, let us repeat, has played and still plays a decisive part in the whole enterprise. The forces at work have been not only of an economic nature, but also political and spiritual, and it is the achievement of Dr. Mowat to have underlined them. All these elements have played their part in the concept and creation of this great ensemble, which since the very beginning has not been called a league or an association, but a community, involving besides institutions, a common faith: faith in the essence, the future, and the responsibilities of Europe in the world.

Jean Rey
President of the Commission
of the European Communities, 1967–70.

Preface

This book began as an inquiry into the motives and ideas of those who played leading parts in the reconstruction of Western Europe after the war, and into the climate of opinion which made their actions fruitful. It is evident that with the defeat of the dictators and the eclipse of their ideologies a new type of leadership arose on the Continent, typified by men of Christian conviction, such as Robert Schuman, Konrad Adenauer and Alcide de Gasperi, along with others who, if not churchgoers, belonged like Jean Monnet to the same tradition, as well as Socialists who were also of Christian background or inspiration, like André Philip. It seemed the logical antithesis that, in the place of men whose ideologies were anti-Christian, after they had brought Europe within an ace of total destruction, leaders should come forward whose values and guiding ideas were those on which European civilisation has been essentially based. The extent to which this was the case is the subject of this inquiry, with a further investigation into the way in which these men, with the ideas which inspired them, were able to create something entirely new in Western Europe, the Community. The last chapter speculates as to the significance of this development, with its possibilities of organic growth capable of trans--forming economic and political relations on a planetary scale.

The direction of this inquiry has indicated certain aspects of the origins and development of the European Community which have needed examination in depth, and some of these, notably the antecedents of the Schuman Plan, I have been able to research into with the aid of private archives and of the memories of some of the personalities involved. Since official archives are for the most part closed to the contemporary historian, these sources have been particularly valuable, and my obligations are great to those who have assisted me in this way. I would like to thank especially M. Jean Monnet, M. Jean Rey, Mr. J. W. Beyen, Dr. Joseph Luns, M. Henri Beyer, Baron Snoy et d'Oppuers, His Excellency J. V. M. van der Meulen, Minister van Staat A.-E. de Schryver, Mr. Tony Rollman, M. Maurice Lagrange, M. François Vinck, Dr. Henri Brugmans, Professor Henri Rieben, Professor Max Beloff, Mr. Uwe Kitzinger, Mr. Richard Mayne, M. Bernard Zamaron and M. Georges Micholet-Coté. To the last three of these my debt is doubly great, since besides giving me information and understanding concerning the intricacies of the Brussels arrangements, they have kindly read the book in draft form, or certain chapters of it, and have given me corrections and advice—and this also applies to Mr. Roy Pryce, Mr. Garth Lean, M. Philippe Mottu, Mr. Peter Hintzen, Mr. Steve Dickinson and last, but very much by no means least, Professor Douglas Johnson.

Besides expressing my gratitude to these and others for their help, I should apologise for any shortcomings in the use of their information or advice. For these shortcomings and any other blemishes the fault is clearly mine, as is also the responsibility for the interpretation of the facts or the conclusions which I have drawn.

I would also like to express my thanks to members of the Association des Amis du Président Robert Schuman, who have helped me with information and who have kindly escorted me on my visits to Metz; to Chevalier Professor Emmanuel Coppieters de ter Zale, for putting at my disposal the library of the Institut Royal des Relations Internationales at Brussels, and for arranging for me to meet many of the aforementioned personalities; and to Mr. Max Kohnstamm and Dr. Wolfgang Hager of the European Community Institute of University Studies, who gave me much of value at the final stage.

Finally I would like to thank Mrs. Jane Clitheroe, Miss Sally Raven and Miss Lindsey Stevenson for typing various drafts; and members of my family for help and encouragement at all stages, particularly my son, David, for his work on the Index, and my wife for her constant support and forbearance.

Oxford, January 1973.

R.C.M.

1

Unity and Division in European History

Since the Roman Empire, Europe has evolved into two areas with
distinct civilisations: that of the East based on Constantinople and
that of the West derived from the Roman Catholic Church. Within
Western Europe (with the exception of Moslem Spain) cultural
unity began to be attained in the eleventh century, when at last the
raids of Huns, Magyars, Arabs, Vikings and other marauders virtually ceased, and the infant civilisation (which had got through this
crucial phase by 'the skin of its teeth')[1] was able to grow and
prosper. Freed too were the people from the fear that their world
would end—the event that was anticipated for A.D. 1000—for the
fateful year came and went, and Europe took on a new lease of
life. In architecture and sculpture the new spirit was dramatically
expressed in those romanesque abbeys and cathedrals, in whose
building an entire population, as at Chartres, sometimes took part,
hauling stone from the quarries as a labour of love.

But apart from the earlier transitory sway of Charlemagne—and
Charlemagne's empire did not include the British Isles, Scandinavia
and the Iberian Peninsula—there was little political unity, even in
Western Europe. Such unity as Western Europe had (apart from
the Moslem part of Spain) came from its religion. The Gospel
message was sometimes translated into reality in a monastery or
even a city where the fruits of the Spirit, noted by St Paul as love,
peace and joy, were to be found. A saint like Francis of Assisi
could live in reality a life close to that of Christ, and so keep alive
faith that the ideal and the real could become one. Politically,
where this influence reached, as happened through St Francis in
Assisi itself, bitter conflicts could be ended, in this case with a
treaty between the patricians and the plebeians.

The wars of Popes against Emperors, and the harrying of here-
tics and Jews which sometimes reached the proportion of military

1

campaigns—these conflicts foreshadowed the fragmentation of the continent, both spiritually and politically, at the end of the Middle Ages. The crisis came when a succession of Popes in the fifteenth century practically abandoned their role as representing Christendom's spiritual authority, and took on that of an Italian prince playing power-games with the other rulers in the peninsula. Since in private life several Popes were notoriously grasping and immoral, the prestige of their office sank low, and the Papacy was unable to maintain the spiritual unity of the West in the face of the challenge which came first from Hus and Wycliffe and later from Luther and Calvin.

Even the Turkish threat in the fifteenth and sixteenth centuries was not enough to restore the unity of Christendom. Constantinople fell without the West coming to its help, and at the moment when the pressure of Suleiman the Magnificent was at its strongest, contention as fierce as any that had gone before broke out over the Reformation, culminating in the long ordeal of Germany in the Thirty Years War. Its ending with the Treaty of Westphalia marked the emergence of a system of sovereign states, with a degree of stability precariously maintained by a balance of power.

With the French Revolution of 1789 ideas labelled 'liberal' or 'radical' became the vogue among progressives, but liberalism was never strong enough to stand up against nationalism, because it lacked ideological content. The religious elements, such as they were, in the ideas of 1789 had been devalued by the extremism of Robespierre and his fellow-Jacobins, and Christianity on the continent after 1814 tended to be identified with reactionary clericalism. The alternative to Christianity as the ideological element in liberalism was a laissez-faire philosophy, tolerant and inclining to scepticism: the prevailing attitude of the Viennese, which they had inherited from forebears who had been bullied into abandoning their Protestant convictions and had adopted a tongue-in-cheek conformism. However much this attitude was reinforced by discontent which, economic as much as political in origin, built up to the explosion of 1848 in Vienna and elsewhere, it lacked the force of nationalism. This extension of primeval tribalism, rooted in the elemental instincts of man, was capable of developing passion more powerful and aggressive than liberalism.[2] Though capable of bringing together in Germany and Italy larger and more cohesive units than had existed before, it could only do this at the cost of deeper divisions such as those which came to separate Germany from France, with consequent spiritual fragmentation.

Prussia's strength, as the state which unified Germany, lay as much in her economic power as in her military efficiency. Her advantage in possessing two rapidly developing industrial areas, Silesia and the Ruhr, had been enormously increased by her pioneering and extension of the Zollverein. This customs union became a tool of the nationalism which Bismarck—though no nationalist himself—perforce made use of, to exclude Austria from Germany. The National-Liberals of Prussia, proponents of free trade, began as opponents of Bismarck, but came to support his methods after his success over Schleswig-Holstein. Having accepted that the Zollverein be used as a bludgeon against Austria in the fifties, they went on to acclaim Bismarck's successful use of force against her in the sixties. Finally they lost what liberalism was left in their programme when Bismarck abandoned free trade in 1878–79. Nationalism was the gainer, the Zollverein itself serving merely to harden, not loosen, the frontiers of Germany against the rest of the world.

Bismarck's abandonment of free trade meant the end of those high hopes which, in Britain and elsewhere, Cobden and his followers had cherished for bringing the nations together. The idealistic creed which he and Bright had propagated with evangelical zeal had been largely a British phenomenon: the creed had been created in the light of Britain's interests at that particular stage of her economic development. It looked to the lowering or elimination of tariffs as a means of making the whole world a free trade area, and—with the application of other principles such as laissez-faire and disarmament—of bringing about an era of peace and prosperity when the world would be truly one. The 'Cobden' trade treaty between Britain and France in 1860 was hailed at the time as a practical application of this creed. In fact, the tide on the Continent shortly after turned against free trade, indicating the failure of Cobdenism as a world ideology for bringing the peoples together, and the success of nationalism, and particularly German nationalism, with its effects of keeping nations apart.

This apartness of the states of Europe which shaded into rivalry, both within Europe and throughout the globe, was only prevented

3

from breaking into war by the exercise of skilful diplomacy, of which Bismarck was one of the greatest masters. Sometimes indeed diplomacy gave way to war—Bismarck himself contrived his three wars at the times he thought most suitable.

Bismarck's ascendency, first in Prussia, then over Germany as a whole, reinforced that doctrine which had first become accepted in Prussia and other countries at the end of the Thirty Years War, of 'the right of the prince to raise himself above religion and morality in order to serve only the superior interest of the state'.[3]

This separation of the sphere of religion and personal ethics from that of politics marked a stage in Europe's development which may be termed 'schizoid'. The inner spiritual life of a person, and of people as individuals, was regarded as having little or no relation to political activities: these were governed by 'reason of state'. The consequence of this approach was to aggravate the element of competition, rivalry and friction between the component elements of Europe, both as a geographical entity and as a civilisation; the sense of unity, harmony and the complementary nature of the nations, classes and occupational groups which composed it diminished. These elements increasingly asserted themselves against each other, claiming their own autonomy and laws of being, in the same way that artists repudiated their social function and embraced the concept of 'art for art's sake'.

The most radical nineteenth-century critic of Christianity, Kierkegaard, ruthlessly dissected the formal Christianity of his day and the establishments which the adherents of that 'Christianity' supported. Its lack of relevance was, he indicated, due to its bearing little relation to the teaching of its founder. Politics had to do with men 'in droves', with 'the compact mass', of which mediocrity is the principle—mediocrity which 'egoistically wants a materially good and enjoyable life, and does not want to hear of the Absolute: for the Absolute is sheer unrest and effort and torment'.[4] 'Politics consists of never venturing more than is possible at any moment, never going beyond what is humanly probable. In Christianity, if there is no venturing farther out beyond what is probable, God is absolutely not with us'.[5]

Kierkegaard, a Dane who wrote in his native tongue, was little heeded at the time in his own country, and little known outside it, and he scarcely affected the powerful trend of thought, which

Bismarck, as a contemporary statesman, reflected. For Bismarck had been converted to Christianity—he was already thirty-one when this event took place—but it was a Christianity which was personal and had little to say in those matters where 'reason of state' operated. Inspiration might help to make effectively those moves in 'the game of political chess' which he came to regard as his life's work: he could spend days, weeks and even months ruminating, walking with his dog in the woods—for, as he said 'a man who doesn't believe in God has only got to walk for two hours in a wood, and he'll find God'.[6] Then he might hear 'God's footsteps in events' and 'leap forward to catch the hem of his garment',[7] but this made no difference to his belief that the realm of politics operated according to its own laws on principles which were not those of the Gospel; to be swayed by any principles other than that of serving the interests of the state, no matter what one's personal predilections, smacked of disloyalty to the ruler and country which one served.[8] He never accepted the pietism of conservative fellow-Junkers like Ludwig von Gerlach, who warned against 'the hideous and mistaken doctrine that God's holy ordinances do not apply to the sphere of politics, of diplomacy and war ... as though these spheres were governed by no higher law than that of patriotic egoism'.[9]

Bismarck's triumph over Ludwig von Gerlach marked the failure to find a unifying idea for Europe on a Christian basis. It meant the rejection of any belief, such as Gladstone's, that there was a divine order which was being progressively realised among men—a divine order which, in European terms, was to be perceived in the 'Concert' of the powers—'the highest and most authentic organ of modern Christian civilisation' (as Gladstone called it) supported by an enlightened public opinion which he believed was coming into existence. Bismarck sneered at 'Professor' Gladstone and his ideas of the Concert; he did not agree with Gladstone that there was a 'public law of Europe' which reflected the divine ordinances of society, and which it was the business of the powers working in concert to promote. The most that Bismarck's pallid version of Christianity did for him was to 'confirm his belief that the best one could do was to prevent disorder from gaining ground'.[10]

This, after achieving control not only of Prussia but of Germany, Bismarck proceeded to do. During his last two decades of

5

power he devoted himself to limiting conflicts and creating a system in which the existing order would be maintained. But peace was not Bismarck's main objective. It was power, and this was what he bequeathed as his legacy. Power became increasingly the preoccupation of his successors, to the exclusion of any greater creative idea—such as seeking the well-being of other peoples for their own sakes—which an acceptance of Christian values would have involved.

The other dangerous aspect of Bismarck's approach was precisely that in which he might be regarded as being most 'spiritual', in his waiting for the inspired moment to 'catch the hem of God's garment' as he planned his next move in the political field. Granted that Bismarck was often inspired in his moves and timing, whence did his inspiration come? It may not have come from God any more than did the inspired hunches of Hitler, who as Bismarck's successor set himself to commune with Bismarck and other great ones of the German past in making those decisions which unleashed the most terrifying forces of destruction which Europe had ever seen.[11]

Bismarck cannot alone be blamed for the fact that the nineteenth-century trends towards internationalism and free trade, and towards customs unions of increasing amplitude, failed to achieve a basis on which the integration of Europe could go forward as the growing-point of a world-order of prosperity and peace. The improvements in communications and the ease of travel, the mobility of people and of capital in search of work and profits, the common elements in the outlook of the educated élite from Russia to Ireland and from Scandinavia to Spain, concealed fundamental rifts which no unifying idea was strong enough to overcome. Each country remained to some extent an island, geography only emphasising in the case of Britain a fact of mass-psychology apparent elsewhere.

No reaching back to a Catholic past which had endowed Western Europe with a certain unity in the Middle Ages could achieve this end. The Calvinist international had failed in the seventeenth century, as had the democratic idealism of the French revolutionaries, Napoleon's conquering genius, the romantic aspirations which had culminated in 1848, and the international political evangelism of Cobden, Bright and Gladstone—all these had left Europe little more united than before. The maintenance of a precarious order depended on the will to peace of a Germany which, overtaking Britain as the strongest industrial power, held the central position in Europe, and on a degree of restraint and co-operation by the other leading states.

Bismarck's cynical playing along with nationalism, and his obsession with power, contributed to the growth of irrationality in the European outlook of these decades: a perversion of passions and enthusiasms which had been denied a fully creative outlet. The tragedy lay in the failure of statesmen of the calibre of Bismarck, Gladstone and Salisbury to join in building a Europe which could unitedly carry out the task of bringing the best which the advanced nations had to offer to their poorer neighbours and to peoples overseas.

In Germany itself, when Bismarck's rule was over, the government became increasingly fragmented. Its authority diminished as rival foci of power militated against each other, particularly the Kaiser, the Chancellor and the leaders of the armed forces. The Kaiser himself, William II, failed to maintain the authority of his position and manifested in himself many of the characteristics of a divided personality. His enthusiasms were rootless, he was a dilettante in art, literature, history, even in politics, and the impression he made on the perspicacious was of vanity and falseness. Among the rulers of Germany there is a progressive deterioration in the trio, Bismarck, William II and Hitler, symbolising the increasing fragmentation of the European personality and of its body politic—Bismarck with his deliberate separation of religion from politics; William II, playing several different roles, always maintaining a false front; and finally Hitler, a man of schizoid and paranoiac tendencies, who imposed his fantasies upon his adopted country and Europe as a whole, bringing them to the nadir of disintegration and chaos.

REFERENCES

[1] Kenneth Clark: *Civilisation* (London, 1969), 17.

[2] See G. Barraclough: *European Unity in Thought and Action* (Oxford, 1963), 43.

[3] René Alleau: *Hitler et les Societés Secrètes* (Paris, 1969), 96.

[4] Søren Kierkegaard: *The Last Years: Journal 1853-1865,* ed. and translated by Ronald Gregor Smith (London, 1968), 354–356.

[5] Ibid., 162–4.

[6] A. O. Meyer: *Bismarck* (Stuttgart, 1949), 13.

[7] Werner Richter: *Bismarck* (London, 1964), 31.

[8] Bismarck: *Memoirs* (English edition 1898), I, 171 (letter to Ludwig von Gerlach, 2.5.57.).

[9] W. H. Simon: *Germany in the Age of Bismarck* (London, 1968), 124–5; Richter, 123.

[10] Simon, 39.

[11] Alleau, 185.

2

The Fragmentation of Europe

The war of 1914–18 was the outward and visible expression of inner and psychological divisions. With the peace treaties of 1919 the further fragmentation of Europe was marked by the splitting-up of Austria-Hungary and the splitting-off from Germany and Russia of territories which formed a number of states, of which the largest was Poland and the smallest those of the Baltic littoral.

The frontiers of the new, or in some cases enlarged, states (like Rumania) were not only political: they were fiscal as well, and the barriers which they erected with tariffs were amplified by the imposition of quotas. The tariff which Austria-Hungary had formerly imposed on ten German finished goods was more than doubled by the cut-down Hungary of the nineteen-twenties and nearly trebled in the thirties, while Rumania and Bulgaria rapidly raised their tariff walls as soon as the war ended.[1]

It was necessary, in the view of the peace-makers, to prevent the access of strength which might have come to Germany by a union with the rest of Austria: Article 80 of the Treaty of Versailles prohibited this, and the creation of a customs union between the two countries was vetoed by France and Britain in 1931. Attempts to create a Danubian free trade zone or 'a customs union from Danzig to Sicily'[2] similarly failed. Every country, struggling to pay war debts or meet reparations claims, tried to deal with its own difficulties on a national basis in the absence of any concerted attempt at economic rehabilitation. The lead for this, if it had come from anywhere, could only have come from the USA in conjunction with Britain, since the USA ended the war with a massive credit balance in place of her former large debts. But the administration turned a deaf ear to Britain's proposal for an all-round cancellation of debts (Britain being a creditor to all the other Allies, while like them she was also a debtor to America). Though American relief assistance saved millions from starvation—food to the value of £291m. was provided, only 29 per cent against cash[3]—American pressure quickly led to the ending of inter-Allied bodies for the control and distribution of raw materials, while others which had marked an impressive step towards international co-operation, notably the Allied Maritime Transport Council (initiated by the young Jean Monnet), were dismantled.[4]

Among those present at the Peace Conference was another young official, J. M. Keynes, whose inquiring and perceptive mind led him to conclusions expressed in his best-selling *The Economic Consequences of the Peace*. This protest against the irrationality and inhumanity of the peace treaties was based on a realisation, shared by few others, that the international economic order, apparently so permanent and stable—almost as if it were part of the moral order of the universe—was in fact peculiar and transitory, 'an extraordinary episode ... which came to an end in August 1914'.[5]

The system whereby the world, and particularly Europe, had lived, had ended and could not be revived. The 'delicate organisation' had operated with remarkable equilibrium through the part played by Britain, later described by Keynes as 'the leader of the orchestra'. For a century London had been the commercial and financial centre of the world, a kind of heart (to vary the metaphor) drawing in raw materials from overseas and finished goods from Europe, sending out coal and manufactured products, and services of all kinds, in exchange, while as air to its lungs an annual tribute of interest payments on capital invested abroad was taken in, with an approximately equal sum of capital being exported. A part almost as important had been played by Germany, round which 'as a central support the rest of the European economic system grouped itself.'[6] Germany was the best customer of Britain after India, and exported more to Britain than any other country except the USA. She was Britain's main partner in the multi-lateral pattern whereby Britain's credit balance with the primary producing countries overseas was offset by an import surplus from the continental countries, who in turn financed their import surpluses, from the primary producers and the USA, by their export surplus to Britain.

This system had been underpinned by the gold standard, on which all currencies were based, and whereby they maintained a stable relation to one another, so immensely facilitating the easy flow of trade and making possible the transfer of interest and export of capital on the enormous scale which acted as an 'engine of growth' for the under-developed world. This and Britain's free trade policies, together with the expertise of the London money market, corrected trade imbalances before they became too severe and, while yet restricting the industrial development of the backward countries, enabled them to achieve a measure of prosperity as the suppliers of primary products.

With a prophetic eye Keynes saw and proclaimed the dangers which lay ahead. 'Economic frontiers', he wrote, 'were tolerable so long as an immense territory was included in a few great Empires; but they will not be tolerable when the Empires of Germany, Austria-Hungary, Russia and Turkey have been partitioned between some twenty independent authorities.'[7] He called for 'a Free Trade Union, comprising the whole of Central, Eastern and South-Eastern Europe, Siberia, Turkey, and (I should hope) the United Kingdom, Egypt and India'. He thought that Belgium, Holland, Scandinavia and Switzerland might be expected to adhere to such a union if it were formed, and perhaps also France and Italy.[8]

When the USA took Britain's place as the world's largest creditor country she played Britain's role, but less effectively. Her loans overseas were far less than Britain's had been (or actually continued to be),[9] and were mostly short-term loans which fell off when the boom of the late twenties made investment at home so much more attractive, and which dried up altogether (the loans being recalled) after the Wall Street crash of October 1929. Furthermore, her high tariffs, raised even higher by the Hawley-Smoot legislation of 1929–30, made it impossible for most other countries to maintain a fair balance of trade with her. Settlement of war debts and reparations were indeed mostly made out of short-term loans to Germany and other countries, but the settlement of trade debts in gold meant that a vast hoard accumulated in Fort Knox, depriving world markets of so much gold that it ceased to be an effective means of international liquidity.

The withdrawal of the American loans had put the banks and businesses of Central Europe in difficulties. Investment ceased, development plans were stopped, unemployment increased, demand fell off, and a vicious circle of falling trade and rising unemployment continued until the world settled down to a phase of virtual stagnation at a level 50 per cent lower than that of the better post-war years—which itself had scarcely reached the levels of the years before 1914. The one major attempt to deal with the crisis, the World Economic Conference at London in 1931, was sabotaged by America, who, without regard to anyone else, devalued the dollar by a massive 41 per cent. The trading advantage which she thereby gained was offset by retaliatory tariff-raising by other countries. Britain, who had remained largely faithful to her free trade tradition, now (1932) clapped on a general 10 per cent tariff except for the more important foodstuffs and Empire products, with further tariffs later raising the duties to between 20 per cent and 30 per cent *ad valorem* on a range of industrial goods.[10] Apart from the Empire preferences accorded at the Ottawa Conference in the same year, Britain was becoming a notoriously high-tariff country, a position which she maintained after the 1939–45 war. When Belgium, Holland and Luxembourg attempted to form their own low tariff zone—a predecessor of Benelux—by the Convention of Ouchy in 1932, it was Britain who blocked their attempts.[11]

In such ways—tariffs, devaluations, deflations and quotas—each country tried to protect itself against every other, to reserve for itself whatever of domestic activity could be maintained to prevent already catastrophic unemployment from becoming worse, a macabre game of beggar-my-neighbour which aggravated economic miseries and gave the Nazis and other authoritarian groups the chance of gaining power in various lands. Even in the face of the Nazi threat Hitler's potential victims failed to draw together, and before war broke out in September 1939 he had been able to begin, with Austria and Czechoslovakia, the process of subduing them one by one.

These were the years before Keynes' diagnosis was accepted, which condemned the policies pursued by almost every country, both internally and in external economic relations. It took time after the publication of *The General Theory of Employment, Interest and Money* in 1936 for this diagnosis and his proposals for remedies to penetrate. But his book succeeded in doing what he had predicted in 1935 to Bernard Shaw that it would do: 'largely revolutionize—not, I suppose, at once but in the course of the next ten years—the way the world thinks about economic problems'.[12]

Before the war ended, at the Bretton Woods Conference, Keynes made a start in working out plans for an international monetary system which, though it did not go as far as he thought necessary, at least opened the way to a new era of international economic co-operation. His doctrines had now become commonplace, the assumptions on which were built full-employment policies such as that of Britain, so markedly different from the deflationary unemployment-ridden approach of governments after 1918, and which determined the thinking of those Americans who eventually made possible Marshall Aid.

Along with this new approach in matters monetary and financial went ideas and also habits of international co-operation, with a measure of supranational control, which went further in the Second World War among the Allies than in the First World War. Many of these war-time experiences, like some of those in 1914–18, were due to Jean Monnet. These two men, Monnet and Keynes, must rank among the leading pioneers who made the era after the Second World War so dramatically different, especially in Western Europe, from that which followed 1918.

REFERENCES

[1] *New Cambridge Modern History*, XII (second edition), 55.

[2] Ibid., 223.

[3] Ibid., 56.

[4] Ibid., 52; J. M. Roberts: *Europe 1880–1945* (London, 1967), 271.

[5] J. M. Keynes: *The Economic Consequences of the Peace* (London, 1919), 7, 9.

[6] Ibid., 14.

[7] Ibid., 249.

[8] Ibid., 251.

[9] A. K. Cairncross: *Home and Foreign Investment 1870–1913* (Cambridge, 1953), 3; W. Ashworth: *An Economic History of England* (London, 1960), 300.

[10] W. N. Medlicott: *Contemporary England 1914–1964* (London, 1967), 271–5.

[11] Institut Royal des Relations Internationales (Brussels): *Chronique de Politique Etrangere*, X, no. 1/2, Jan.-March 1957, 417; *New Cambridge Modern History*, XII, 61.

[12] Michael Stewart: *Keynes and After* (London, 1967), 70.

3

Konrad Adenauer and the Rhineland as a Bridge to Unity

After Europe's disintegration in 1914 and the traumatic experience of the long years of mass-slaughter on a scale never known before, hopes of a new order blossomed again when Franco-German reconciliation seemed to be realised with the Locarno Agreements of 1925. The League of Nations (which, with the defection of the USA, was primarily a European organisation) provided the framework for the expression of the new spirit in the days soon after Germany's entry into the League when her Foreign Minister, Gustav Stresemann, hobnobbed at Geneva with his opposite numbers, Aristide Briand of France and Austen Chamberlain of Britain.

Expectations were premature. Briand sponsored a motion at the League of Nations for 'some kind of federal bond' between the European states (September 1929), and Edouard Herriot published *Les États-Unis de l'Europe*, which appeared in 1930.[1] By then however the international order, based on the unrealistic assumption of the continued weakness after defeat of Russia and Germany, was breaking down. The slide to war was aggravated—and largely occasioned—by the economic depression set off by the Wall Street crash of October 1929, which was instrumental in bringing Hitler to power.

Stresemann's success in gaining Germany's acceptance again as a great power had been spectacular, but it was shallow-rooted. He failed to move far towards a genuine settlement with Germany's Eastern neighbours, and even with France he rejected a policy which offered hopes for permanently defusing the ancient enmity between the two countries. This policy was proposed by German leaders, prominent among whom was Konrad Adenauer. The aim was to link together economically the Rhenish provinces of the two countries, in such a way as to render virtually impossible the occur-

14

rence of a future war between them. Although the policy was rejected by Stresemann, it reappeared after 1945 with Adenauer's backing, and provided basic elements of the settlement between the German Federal Republic and France as initiated by the Schuman Plan.

The borderlands of France and Germany had been a growing point of Western civilisation on the cessation of the anarchy and marauding of the Dark Ages. Economic facts as well as history had given them a unity transcending the political frontiers, since coal and iron ore lay in complementary neighbourliness on either side of the Rhine, and of its tributaries to east and west, the Ruhr and the Moselle. France, with the strength of a nation-state while Germany was weak and divided, had seized much of the land on the left bank of the Rhine from princes and cities of the Holy Roman—in fact German—Empire; and had gone on to proclaim the 'natural frontiers', and particularly the Rhine itself, as the aim of her expansion. Though France had effectively endowed the peoples she had conquered with her own culture, the claims on Alsace and part of Lorraine which Bismarck, in the name of the restored Reich, could make, were historically by no means groundless. Germany's forced annexation of Alsace and Lorraine in 1871 was in fact no solution to a question which, over the centuries, had moved into a new context; and though their retrocession in 1918 appeared to be definitive, their re-occupation by Germany in 1940 suggested that the provinces could continue almost indefinitely as a shuttlecock between the two powers.

Konrad Adenauer's father was a minor official of the municipality of Cologne, who instilled into his son an immense capacity for work, a deep love of home and family, and a devotion to his Catholic faith. During the inter-war years Adenauer was a leading member of the Centre Party, though far from being a clericalist in outlook. For him conscience had to be the guide, even if it meant taking an unpopular or dangerous line, as was the case when it came to dealing with the Nazis.

After reading for the Law at university and entering on a legal career, Adenauer married into one of the families which traditionally held the affairs of Cologne in their hands. He entered local government and became an outstanding member of the city administration from 1906 to 1917, when he became Oberbürgomeister.

Though this may be translated as Lord Mayor, there is no real comparison between an English mayor and a German burgomaster. The latter rules his city—at least Adenauer certainly did—with as much real (if not nominal) power as any Prince-Bishop of Cologne in the days of its medieval glory. He restored the city from a condition of decline to being one of the most progressive municipalities in Europe, aiming at making it a cultural bridge between Germany and her western neighbours. He became President of the Prussian State Council and was at one time asked to accept nomination as the Centre Party's candidate for becoming Chancellor of Germany. In the Rhineland, before the coming of the Nazis, much power was concentrated in his hands: he was Chairman of the Provincial Landtag and presided over the Council of Rhenish cities.

Having successfully overcome the problems of provisioning his city during the 1914–18 war, and those of the revolution of November 1918—when he maintained order with (or in spite of) the self-appointed revolutionary committee—he found himself faced with the separatist movement, whose leaders wished to set up an independent Rhine Republic, an aim which could only be secured with the backing of the French. It was, indeed, the French objective to detach from Germany the left bank of the Rhine, and control permanently the bridgeheads which they had occupied. As long as this seemed a possible danger, Adenauer was prepared to back the establishment of a West German state federated with other such states within a Reich which should possess a strong central government. In supporting this plan Adenauer wished to take the wind out of the separatists' sails—and this may well have been his main objective—but he evidently was not averse to ending the situation in which Prussia had inherited from earlier times a position far outweighing that of any other of Germany's component states (Länder), dominating the Rhineland which it had annexed. Before the Treaty of Versailles was signed he hoped that such proposals would go far to satisfy France's desire for security, which he maintained the Germans ought to take into consideration. Such proposals, he hoped, would enable the Saar to be kept within the Reich, and would help Germany's case over reparations and the occupation.

Adenauer was not disappointed when these proposals fell

through. He was mainly concerned with pushing them to the extent that they might have prevented worse solutions imposed by the Allies or by the activities of the separatists. But such proposals moved again into the realm of practical politics in 1923 with the occupation of the Ruhr by France and Belgium, as a pledge for securing the reparations payments on which Germany had defaulted.

Not only did the idea of the West German state federated with the rest of the Reich come to the fore again, but the grave economic situation gave attraction to a project of linking the adjacent French and German industrial areas on the Rhine and Moselle. In November 1923, with Hitler's putsch at Munich and with galloping inflation (the mark dropped to 12 billion to the dollar at Cologne), it seemed as if the country might disintegrate. The Government at Berlin launched a new currency, the rentenmark, but announced that, to maintain it, they would have to curtail public expenditure drastically and stop the subsidies to the Ruhr and Rhineland which had enabled the workers to carry out passive resistance against the occupying authorities. They were prepared to leave the Rhinelanders to their own devices, to negotiate with the French for the best terms they could get; failing that it seemed they might even sacrifice the Rhineland to France as the price of her calling off the occupation of the Ruhr and abandoning reparations.

Adenauer fought vehemently against this possibility, and though he also secured a continuation of the subsidies, he entered on negotiations with the French designed to open the question of a West German state within the Reich, which would be economically linked with the mining and industrial areas of Lorraine and Luxembourg. He had hopes, though they seemed to him slender, that France might be persuaded by the advantages of such a project to call off the occupation, and revise the reparations arrangements and the Treaty of Versailles itself. Again, although his move was tactical in respect of these immediate objectives, he saw long-range advantages in satisfying the French desire for security (for he was prepared to accept an international gendarmerie or some other form of demilitarisation of the West German state), while he was certain that, even if the French carried out their own policy of turning the Rhineland into one or more buffer-states, it would never serve the aim of peace. Germany would only strive for a war of revenge and in the next war, he pointed out, the Rhine and Ruhr would be the cockpit.

As for the economic aspects, he pressed the advantages strongly, backed as he was over this by Hugo Stinnes, the Ruhr steel magnate, and by French steel-masters in the Comité des Forges. The proposals put forward by Stinnes and Adenauer foreshadow in a remarkable way those which were eventually worked out in the Schuman Plan of 1950. In fact these proposals had a highly respectable ancestry, in that in previous centuries Huguenot immigrants had worked out close co-operation with their fellow-entrepreneurs across the frontiers in developing the early coal, iron-ore and steel industries.

Adenauer tried to bring his proposals to the attention of the French Prime Minister, Poincaré. 'The Rhenish-Westphalian, Lorraine and Luxembourg industry has been created and has grown as a united economic organism. If we succeed—and it is entirely possible—to form commmon economic interests between the peoples of the federal state and France through a reciprocal interweaving of these industries, this federal state would exercise its influence in Germany even more strongly in the sense of peaceful co-operation with France, and peace will be thereby that much more strengthened'.[2]

Stinnes was prepared to implement such a plan by exchanging a quarter of his shares against a quarter of those of the Lorraine undertakings. His vision was for a customs union including Germany, France, Holland, Belgium and Switzerland. But Stinnes died in April 1924, and shortly afterwards the whole situation changed. Stresemann as Chancellor, and now as Foreign Minister, was entirely against the plans of Adenauer and Stinnes. The French found themselves isolated, with the British strongly opposing their policy (they equally opposed the Adenauer-Stinnes policy, a point also not without relevance for the future). The French failure to get the Ruhr industry working under their control meant that financially they lost heavily on their adventure: the franc slipped steadily as the rentenmark strengthened, and they showed themselves ready to accept revised reparations schedules. With Poincaré's fall at the elections of May 1924 the Ruhr occupation was brought to an end.

Stresemann's fulfilment policy led up to Locarno, and it seemed as if the questions of Ruhr and Rhine, and their relation to the territories westwards, had ceased to be of practical importance, apart from the purely business arrangements, made largely under cartel schemes for limiting production and sharing markets, which the West European steel-masters made during the years of depression. But the depression also helped to bring Hitler to power, and with this event Adenauer's situation dramatically changed.

Adenauer was on the Nazis' black list even before he had the swastika flags removed from the Rhine Bridge on the occasion of Hitler's visit to Cologne in February 1933. He was soon hounded from office and had to seek refuge at the Maria Laach Abbey, which was presided over by an old friend from school-days, Ildefons Herwegen. He was briefly imprisoned at the time of the night of the long knives (30 June 1934) and for some time after was on the run from the Gestapo. Though he was left undisturbed for most of the war, after entering on a life of complete detachment from politics and from virtually all activity except gardening and looking after his children and grandchildren in the isolated village of Rhöndorf, he was again imprisoned following the July plot in 1944. He escaped, but was later recaptured (his wife also was imprisoned), and was lucky to be released just before the arrival of the Americans at Rhöndorf brought his part of the war to an end.

The Americans reinstalled him as Oberbürgomeister of Cologne. Adenauer had his schemes for restoring the shattered city to its former glory and of using the opportunity for replanning it in various ways, while coping with the almost impossible tasks of removing rubble and securing at least elementary amenities. When the British took over Cologne from the Americans he fell foul of the occupying authorities, notably by refusing to cut down for fuel the trees which lined the streets, demanding instead that coal requisitioned by the Military Government should be released for civilian consumption. The result was his dismissal—for inefficiency—in a manner which, with due allowance for the unusual circumstances, can only be described as grossly rude. He was obliged to sign a paper promising, among other things, that he would not 'indulge either directly or indirectly in any political activity whatever'.

In fact this uncomprehending action by a British brigadier projected Adenauer from local into national politics. He joined the Cologne branch of the newly-established Christian Democratic Union, and attended as its representative an inter-zonal conference. The chairman arriving late, he took the chair himself with the words 'as the oldest person here, I assume this chair is for me'[3] (he was already 70). With the Allied decision to establish a West German state in 1948, Adenauer was chosen as Chairman of the Parliamentary Committee for working out the constitution; and the constitution was duly worked out along those federal lines which he had thought desirable many years before. After it was eventually promulgated, and the Bundestag convened, Adenauer was elected—by one vote—as the first Chancellor of the German Federal Republic in September 1949.

'Times of political catastrophe are especially suitable for new creative ventures'[4]—this had been Adenauer's attitude (as he expressed it) in the months and years immediately after the First World War. Though Germany was shattered and broken to an extent which had not occurred before, the situation was in many ways remarkably parallel. The idea of a separate Rhine-Ruhr state was once again projected by the French, and Adenauer, through press interviews, countered it with similar arguments as before. He warned against the dangers of a policy which might throw East Germany permanently into Russian hands, but if it came to the point of Russia refusing to allow Germany to be reunited the next best thing would be a federal state covering the zones occupied by the Western Allies—the solution which they eventually applied. Further, Adenauer was again, in 1945, promoting the idea of satisfying the French desire for security by integrating the economy of what became the German Federal State with that of France and Belgium. 'Common economic interests', he said, 'are the best foundations for a rapprochement between the nations and the safeguarding of peace'.[5] This was the policy eventually applied.

REFERENCES

[1] See also the English translation, *The United States of Europe* (London, 1930).

[2] K. D. Erdmann: *Adenauer in Rheinlandpolitik nach dem ersten Weltkrieg* (Stuttgart, 1966), 154.

[3] Terence Prittie: *Germany Divided* (London, 1961), 198.

[4] P. Weymar: *Konrad Adenauer* (London, 1957), 68.

[5] Ibid., 180.

4

War-time Resistance Movements and European Federalism

The germ of the European Movement, as it developed after the Second World War, is to be found in the resistance movements against Nazi domination.

Altiero Spinelli, who eventually became a member of the EEC Commission at Brussels, traces its origins, on the Italian side, to a group—among them himself—incarcerated by Mussolini on the island of Ventotone in 1940–41. This group saw the future of Europe in federal terms, and looked to the setting up of a European authority to which the conduct of foreign policy, defence and the economic system would be transferred. Like many others in the resistance movement, they saw in federation a particular advantage in that it would facilitate dealing with the question of Germany when eventually she would be defeated.

After the fall of Mussolini, Spinelli and his friends founded the European Federal Movement at Milan (August 1943). He then went with one of them, Ernesto Rossi, to Switzerland, where he joined with resistants from seven other countries to issue, in July 1944, the 'draft declaration of the European resistance'. This document referred to the anarchy which the old Europe had represented, and stated that this 'could be solved only by the creation of a federal union among the European peoples'.

The meeting took place in the house of Dr. W. A. Visser't Hooft of Holland, Secretary of the World Council of Churches, who provided a link between the German resistance and that of other countries. It was to his house that Dietrich Bonhoeffer had come during his two visits to Switzerland in 1941, when he had attempted, through Visser't Hooft, to alert the British Government as to the existence of the resistance movement in Germany, in the hope that British policy would take account of this fact and encourage the anti-Nazis there. These hopes had been disappointed, despite the powerful advocacy of such a policy by Bishop Bell of Chichester, the friend of Bonhoeffer to whom Visser't Hooft had brought his messages, along with a memorandum from another resistance leader, Adam von Trott, in April 1942. Von Trott was to suffer with his life for his part in the plot against Hitler of July 1944; Bonhoeffer's execution did not take place till the eve of Hitler's defeat, in April 1945. Another victim of the Nazis who was a convinced European was Karl Goerdeler, formerly Lord Mayor of Leipzig and Price Commissioner in the German Government from 1934–35. He was able to attend secretly one of the meetings of resistance leaders at Geneva[1] before being imprisoned by the S.S. in August 1944. Designated for the post of Chancellor by the conspirators in the plot of July 1944 against Hitler, his execution in February 1945 was a foregone conclusion.

The German resistance movement sprang in large measure from the Christian convictions of men like Bonhoeffer, the most outspoken and radical leader of the German Confessing Church, and of the members of the 'Kreisau circle' of whom von Trott was one. Such convictions, which impelled these Germans and others to militant action and—in almost all cases—a martyr's death, existed also among countless others who saw no way to put them into effect during the war. There were few Germans who could pray, as Bonhoeffer did, for the defeat of Germany as 'the only possibility of paying for all the suffering that my country has caused in the world',[2] but there were many, who, once that defeat had occurred, were ready to put all their efforts into rebuilding Germany and Europe on foundations which accorded with their Christan faith. Of these Konrad Adenauer is an example.

Federalism for Europe was, when the war ended, part of the vision for a better world which inspired so many people of diverse political standpoints in the defeated as in the victorious countries: it had its origins, as Spinelli writes, 'in that crucible of passions and dreams which was the resistance'. The French contribution to the cause came through the underground paper *Combat* edited by Albert Camus. After a congress called by its staff at Algiers in March 1944, contact was made with the Italians and other leaders of the West European resistance, preparing the ground for a meeting in liberated France in July of that year. Delegates from the various resistance movements drew up a declaration to the effect that only federal union could safeguard European unity and make possible the peaceful participation of the German people. Such a union, it was underlined, could only be effective if it was a genuine federation, having common organs for government, justice and defence.[3]

A further meeting took place in March 1945, largely organised by the Italian federalists. Besides resistance leaders like Spinelli and Camus, there were some British participants, notably George Orwell and the Labour M.P. John Hynd. The lead given on this occasion by André Philip and other French Socialists was important in bringing that party to support a European federation. The hopes to which the presence of British Labour representatives gave rise were however to be disappointed.

Among French Socialists of his vintage Philip was somewhat exceptional. Born in 1902, he had made his mark before the war as an economist and university professor who had become a Socialist and gone into politics because of his Christian convictions. He was exceptional too as a Protestant, descended from Camisard ancestors who had fought to maintain their faith in the Cevennes against the dragonnades of Louis XIV.[4] He was much influenced by his study of the Belgian Henri de Man, who regarded the original impulse of socialism as a revolt against the capitalist social order on the part of the workers in pursuit of an ideal—a moral absolute. It was a revolt 'in the name of all those spiritual values—the ideal of equality, the sentiment of human dignity, the desire for justice and caring—which Christianity has brought to the world',[5] and he believed that, during the previous decades, socialism had been betrayed by the pursuit of material goals through putting the accent on the acquisitive instinct of the masses, thereby leading them away from the older revolutionary, cosmopolitan idea to a bourgeois and often nationalist reformism.

Philip followed closely in the tradition of the great nineteenth-century Socialist Jean Jaurès (1859–1914), and his disciple Léon Blum who resumed the leadership of the Socialist Party (Section Française de l'Internationale Ouvrière—S.F.I.O.) after returning from German prison camps in 1945. Jaurès had been a man of deep spirituality and wide humanity, a politician who had much of the philosopher and even the poet about him, and who, though a follower of Marx, saw socialism as preparing a revolution of

B

justice and harmony which would bring about 'a *new fact* in the universe . . . making possible vast renewals of the religious spirit'.[6] His colleague, and sometimes opponent, had been Jules Guesde, who stood for Marxism of a narrowly dogmatic type, and who had nurtured those tendencies in French socialism which led to the splitting-off in 1920 of the Communist Party from the S.F.I.O., taking with them a majority of the members together with the newspaper *Humanité* which Jaurès had founded.

Blum had fostered both the concern for democracy and the passionate internationalism bequeathed by Jaurès. The publication of his book *A l'Échelle Humaine* early in 1945 was 'like a voice from the dead'[7], since Blum was still in Germany—the book itself having been written in a prison in Vichy France and smuggled out early in 1942. It had an enormous influence, the more so because of the time and circumstances of its composition, calling as it did for a spirit of reconciliation and harmony—for a socialism whose achievement demanded a framework far larger than that of the national state, a 'federation of free and equal nations' on a European basis.[8] Further, in Blum's view, such a framework provided the only way 'to make Germany harmless in a peaceful and stable Europe', by incorporating her in an 'international community powerful enough to re-educate her, discipline her and, if necessary, master her'.[9]

The last consideration may have been the decisive one[10] which eventually brought the Socialist Party, under the influence of André Philip and Blum's successor in the party leadership, Guy Mollet, to support the cause of European integration—its support, with its 105 votes, at the time of the launching of the Coal and Steel Community in 1950–51, being essential for the success of the venture, as again was its support, under the premiership of Mollet, when the Treaty of Rome was being prepared and came up for ratification in 1956–57. Nonetheless, the powerful internationalist tradition of French socialism was 'the intellectual backcloth'[11] for these developments—'this strong idealistic, moral element in the revisionist case which fashioned internationalism in a revisionist mould—a concept based upon the idealistic and utopian belief in the nobility of man's reason and the perfectibility of human nature'.[12]

Philip agreed with Blum that distributing better the goods which capitalism produced would not in fact go far towards bringing about a world nearer to the ideal of socialism. What was needed were new structures, and the challenge to a Socialist government was whether these could be created. The experience of the Popular Front government of 1936 had indicated that the limits of distributive socialism had already been reached, partly because France was too small an economic unit to support the wage-increases and other advantages (such as paid holidays) accorded to the workers without provoking a rise in imports which could not be offset by exports, especially since these had correspondingly become dearer and more difficult to sell. This had prompted Philip and his friends to begin thinking of uniting Europe as a means of creating the wider market of which France and the other European countries so evidently stood in need.[13] At the same time to make possible a larger cake which could—correctly divided—increase the workers' living standards, socialism had to bring about technical development and greater efficiency. To this end a plan with its directing commissariat was envisaged, and was presented to the Socialist Congress in 1934; it was to be under the control of an economic and social council representing industrialists, workers, farmers and consumers on an extra-parliamentary basis.[14] After the war both these bodies were brought into existence, though the one to be really—and brilliantly—effective was the Commissariat of the Plan under Jean Monnet.

At the end of the war and in the first years of peace, the European movement passed through its most idealistic phase. This phase was marked by an increasing convergence of men inspired by the European idea; some veterans like the pioneer 'European' of Austrian birth, Count Coudenhove-Kalergi, founder of the Pan-European Movement, and others of a younger generation like the Swiss Denis de Rougemont or the Dutchman Henri Brugmans.

Leaders like Spinelli joined with others who had been in America or with their governments-in-exile in London, to plan meetings for launching a full-scale federal movement. 'In those days', de Rougemont writes, 'a strange driving passion, unknown to this generation, inspired the militants of Europeanism . . . a concerted concentration of psychic and psychological factors'. Among these men something of 1789 and 1848 lived again. Europe, they felt, could be taken by storm or—to change the metaphor—could be hustled into a new era before people fully realised what was happening. Meeting after meeting took place, bringing together a widening circle of people committed to the idea of uniting Europe. This preparing of the ground in public opinion was an essential phase preliminary to launching the communities.

Two tendencies were noticeable among those working for this cause: 1. The thorough-going federalism of men like Spinelli, de Rougemont and Henri Brugmans, who viewed the hoped-for development in political terms, with the calling of a European constituent assembly as the first step in their strategy; 2. The gradualism of those, mostly French, who, while no less in favour of federation as the aim, believed that economic and social developments should be promoted as an essential part of the process, with advances in various sectors or on certain levels, such as the customs union which had recently been achieved by Belgium, the Netherlands and Luxembourg (Benelux).[15]

A third tendency, however, one that temporarily became dominant, entered the situation in September 1946. Just as the representatives of continental federalism were moving towards a united front with a meeting at Hertenstein, in another part of Switzerland Sir Winston Churchill stepped on to the scene, at Zürich, with a speech which resounded throughout the continent, calling for the formation of 'a kind of United States of Europe'.

In two statements which he had made on the subject of European unity during the war (a memorandum for the War Cabinet of October 1942 and a broadcast six months later), Churchill had his eyes on the possibly 'measureless disaster' if 'Russian barbarism overlaid the culture and independence of the ancient states of Europe'. He had declared as the aim a United States of Europe under a Council 'of perhaps ten units including the former Great Powers', to be a 'really effective league, with all the strongest forces woven into its texture, with a High Court to adjust disputes, and with armed forces, national or international or both, held ready to enforce these decisions. . . .'[16]

In fact the 'union' which Churchill advocated turned out to be something quite other than a federation, and in this he was in line with most British people who gave any thought to the matter. He might support federation for continental countries, but was opposed to Britain taking part in such a system. As far back as

1930 Churchill had written favourably of Coudenhove-Kalergi's project of a European federation, with the proviso that whereas Britain could give encouragement to such a project, she could not participate in any organs which might be created owing to her centre of gravity being in the Empire and Commonwealth. 'We are linked, but not comprised', was his formula. 'We are with Europe but not of it. We are interested and associated, but not absorbed'.[17]

In his Zürich speech Churchill showed boldness and realism in calling for Franco-German reconciliation as the foundation of the new Europe: 'The first step in the recreation of the European family must be a partnership between France and Germany. In this way only can France recover the moral leadership of Europe. There can be no revival of Europe without a spiritually great France and a spiritually great Germany. . . . In all this urgent work, France and Germany must take the lead together. Great Britain, the British Commonwealth of Nations, mighty America, and I trust Soviet Russia—for then indeed all would be well—must be the friends and sponsors of the new Europe and must champion its right to live and shine'.

For those who wanted progress towards integration whatever form this progress might take, Churchill's intervention was eagerly welcomed. Meetings took place at The Hague and Luxembourg the same autumn (1946), at Amsterdam in April 1947, at the Albert Hall, London, in May, and—canalising 'most of the currents of European thinking previously unknown to each other'[18]—at Montreux in August 1947.

The Labour National Executive decided, against Churchill's appeals, to boycott the great meeting at The Hague in May 1948, called as a follow-up to his Zürich speech by a body now including representatives of virtually all those concerned with building some form of integrated Europe, the International Committee of Movements for European Unity. But, for the eight hundred participants drawn from all the notables of Europe, the Congress, in the resplendent hall of the Knights of the Netherlands (the Ridderzaal, meeting-place of the Dutch Parliament), was an impressive occasion. To many it seemed the realisation of the dream of the States-General of Europe, which would transform itself into a Constituent Assembly for creating the new federal régime.

The importance of these meetings lay in bringing together representatives of countries which had been on opposite sides in the recent war. At The Hague there were fifty-one Germans present, led by Adenauer, and fifty-seven Italians, with the much larger numbers of French, British and nationals of the smaller countries, so helping to promote the reconciliation of the ex-combatants which was the pre-condition for success in making any kind of European union. It also set up a permanent, though unofficial, organisation with Churchill, Blum, de Gasperi and the Belgian Foreign Minister, Paul-Henri Spaak, as Presidents of Honour, and an executive whose members were to play leading parts in European integration, notably Jean Monnet and Robert Schuman. This body presided over the negotiations which led to the setting up of the Council of Europe a year later.

The federalists cherished the greatest hopes that this Council would lead on to the kind of union they wished to establish, but in this they were disappointed. Britain's position at the time was so strong that the line which she took in regard to the Council was decisive. At the start of negotiations this was one of unconcealed antagonism to any kind of federal development—the weakest form of confederation was the only European body which Labour—all but a few dissidents—were prepared to support. 'I don't like it. I don't like it', Bevin was reported to have said. 'If you open that Pandora's box you will find it full of Trojan horses'.[19]

A way of going along with the 'Europeans' while keeping their movement strictly under control, was opened by the creation of Bevin's own brain-child, the Brussels Treaty Organisation. In October 1948 its Consultative Council appointed a five-power 'Committee for the Study of European Unity'. Meeting under the chairmanship of the veteran 'European' Edouard Herriot to consider a Franco-Belgian proposal for a European Assembly with the functions of a parliament, the continental delegates were stunned by the British counter-proposals for a purely consultative inter-governmental organ, from whose strictly defined terms of reference vital matters such as defence and the economy were to be excluded. At one point the discussions broke down, and there was talk of a European Assembly without Britain. But eventually the British government gave way so far as to agree to a Council of Europe composed of a consultative assembly meeting in public and a Committee of Ministers, whose decisions had to be unanimous, meeting in private. These were the terms of the Statute by which it was set up in May 1949.

The aims of the Council were however boldly stated, to 'create an economic and political union', for which purpose member-states 'must agree to merge certain of their sovereign rights'. This was in line with the thinking of 'Europeans' like André Siegfried, who pointed out the total change in conditions of world trade since Britain, as the greatest trading nation in the nineteenth century, had been able to operate a financial and monetary system based on sterling and the gold standard. Now in the new conditions Europe was realising that 'she must, at all costs, constitute herself economically, and that to do so it was indispensable that she should also constitute herself in a political form'.[20]

When the first meeting of the Council took place a few months later the federalists found the aim of creating an economic and political union restated in a form which was more watered down—'closer unity between all like-minded countries of Europe' to be attained by creating 'an organisation which will bring the European states into closer association'. Nonetheless they had scope, so they felt, to act as a constituent assembly for implementing the original resolution of The Hague. Since the Assembly was composed of members of the various national parliaments chosen from the parties in proportion to their strength, these spoke and voted according to party views, not those of their governments. This made it possible for the British participants to speak with divergent voices. A Labour federalist like R. W. G. Mackay could favour the formula 'the creation of a European political authority with limited functions but real powers' while the official Labour line was plugged by Herbert Morrison and Hugh Dalton, who fought successfully a rearguard action to maintain the Council as the weakest possible inter-governmental body.

Out of deference for the British Labour delegates, the French Socialist leader, Guy Mollet, as rapporteur of the Committee which considered these formulas, was not prepared to record in his report the support in the Assembly for the aim of a European political authority with limited functions but real powers. The federalists however obtained eighty signatures for an amendment supporting this aim. Although this was voted successfully in the Assembly, the work of the Council was to be paralysed by the caution of the Committee of Ministers, which—owing to the need for unanimity—could scarcely agree on anything worth while. By the next year, 1950, the recommendations brought before the Assembly had become less bold: most federalists saw the need of compromise in the face of the British attitude—which in fact remained the same even when, in the following year, the Conservatives under Churchill once again came into power. The Assembly was reduced to little more than a talking-shop, though by then an entirely new development, through the Schuman Plan, had broken through the obstacles which appeared to prevent further progress towards the integration of Western Europe.

REFERENCES

[1] Jean-Pierre Gouzy: *Les Pionniers de l'Europe Communautaire* (Lausanne, 1968), 23.

[2] W. A. Visser't Hooft: *Zeugnis eines Boten*, 7, quoted by Eberhard Bethge: *Dietrich Bonhoeffer* (London, 1970), 648.

[3] G. Bonnefous: *L'Europe en face de son Destin* (Paris, 1953), 92.

[4] Information from André Philip. See also *André Philip par Lui-Même* (Paris, 1971), 143 seq.

[5] A. Philip: *Socialisme et Rationalisation*, in *Henri de Man et la crise doctrinale du socialisme* (Paris, 1928), 53.

[6] Harvey Goldberg: *The Life of Jean Jaurés* (Wisconsin, 1968), 136; see also Philip, *op. cit.*, 122.

[7] Léon Blum: *For All Mankind* (London, 1946), from Preface by translator W. Pickles—*For All Mankind* being the English title of *À l'Echelle Humaine*.

[8] Ibid., 115.

[9] Ibid., 119.

[10] Byron Criddle: *Socialists and European Integration* (London, 1969), 100.

[11] *Idem.*

[12] Ibid., 7.

[13] A. Philip: *Les Socialistes* (Paris, 1969), 91 n.; Criddle, *op. cit.*, 25.

[14] Ibid., 72–3. For the similar scheme proposed by Jaurès, see Goldberg, *op. cit.*, 135.

[15] Benelux monetary agreement, October 1943, was followed by the customs union, 5 September 1944.

[16] A. H. Robertson: *The Council of Europe* (London, 1961), 1, 2.

[17] Arnold J. Zurcher: *The Struggle to Unite Europe 1940–58* (New York, 1958), 6.

[18] *Government and Opposition*, April-July, D. de Rougement: 'The Campaign of the European Congresses'.

[19] Lord Strang: *Home and Abroad* (London, 1956), 190; Robertson, *op. cit.*, 6.

[20] *L'Année Politique*, 1949, vii.

5

America's Part

While West Europeans were trying to work out a new political structure for their part of the Continent, there was a danger of a complete economic collapse from which Stalin might be the only beneficiary. Despite American occupying troops and the temporary American monopoly of nuclear weapons, it was clear that no real stability and therefore no secure defence could be expected before the economic situation markedly improved. The hope of the Americans and British had been that the arrangements made during the war for a new start on the global level for monetary and trade matters would swiftly bring the world, including Europe, back to economic health.

What the Anglo-Saxons had not reckoned with, however, during their war-time meetings, was the extent of the devastation and the amount of rebuilding of factories and of the general infrastructure that would be required at the war's end—the task which the United Nations Relief and Rehabilitation Administration (UNRRA) undertook. Further, the two institutions which sprang from the Bretton Woods conference (1944)—the International Monetary Fund and the World Bank—did not start functioning properly until 1947, and when they did so were restricted in the scale of their operations. This was partly because the arrangements were not on a scale, and had insufficient reserves, to make the difference between success and failure in the vital short-run period following the end of hostilities. It was only in the longer-run that the new institutions, emasculated as they were by comparison with the plans Keynes had proposed for them, began to play a major part in creating a new international monetary and commercial structure, enabling trade to flourish and the tide of prosperity to rise throughout the world.

The foresight and enlightenment—even if the enlightenment of self-interest—of the Americans had indeed been great, and their determination to learn the lessons of the post-1918 failures is to be praised. Cordell Hull, Secretary of State when the war ended, had as far back as the Reciprocal Trade Agreements Act (1934) reversed the protectionist trend and initiated liberalisation, eventually to the enormous benefit of the world as a whole. But in the cheerless aftermath of war this tide in affairs had not yet begun to flow to the advantage of those on the Continent who were among the hardest-hit of the war's victims.

The crisis of the winter of 1946–47 made it clear that Britain was no longer in a position to sustain the role of a Great Power *à trois*, along with Russia and the USA. So slender was her own margin for recovery after the exertions of the war that the exceptionally severe weather and the consequent demand for electricity overstrained the system to the point where half the industry of the Midlands was closed down, in addition to the most rigorous rationing of current to the private consumer. It was not surprising that other countries, who had suffered worse restrictions and a greater run-down of plant than Britain, were in even grimmer plight. Despite the $3,750 million line of credit from the USA, Britain had been unable to initiate recovery to the point of ceasing to be dependent on continued massive infusions of dollars. She was unable to feed properly the inhabitants of her occupied zone of Germany, many of whom starved or froze to death that winter, and she was obliged to inform the State Department on 21 February 1947 that within six weeks she would have to default on her economic commitments to Greece and Turkey with consequent withdrawal of military support in the face of intensive Communist activity.

This emergency was met by as remarkable a group of men as any who have directed the destinies of the United States. They were well fitted to be the upholders, from their side of the Atlantic, of those common values on which European civilisation and its American extensions are based. Of the leading members of this group—Truman, Marshall, Acheson—none made a parade of their beliefs, but all were men of character, drawn from a background where the Christian faith in its Protestant form was implicitly accepted.

Harry S. Truman, the man who became President 'by accident' as he was not beyond saying (the accident of Roosevelt's death while he was Vice-President, another office which he had not sought), was a remarkable example of the ordinary man doing extraordinary things, rising to the fulness of stature with which an office such as the Presidency of the United States could endow a man. Yet the relatively unknown Senator for Missouri who suddenly found himself thrust upward into his new position on 12 April 1945 was better prepared by destiny than his compatriots knew. A Baptist among people who had long been Baptists, of authentic middle-American stock hailing from Missouri and Kentucky, he was a simple practitioner of his faith who maintained his integrity during his slow rise to civic responsibility under a corrupt party boss running the local Democratic machine. No intellectual but a great reader especially of history, a sensitive man who had nearly essayed a career as a concert pianist, a respected presiding judge for eight years in the County Courts, he made his mark as a senator during the war by bringing about the creation of the Truman Committee (the Special Committee Investigating National Defence) for dealing with graft and inefficiency in the war programme.

The Committee in fact was a natural stepping-stone to the Presidency as it enabled Truman to make 'such a study of big government under pressure as had hardly ever been made before'.[1] so that he could move from the already large area of decision-making concerned with the embattled USA to the even larger one of the world embroiled in the cold war. Once in his new position he soon began to impress his associates with 'his extraordinary courage, common sense and decisiveness in dealing with foreign affairs'.[2]

Like Truman of partly Kentucky stock, George Catlett Marshall could claim a more distinguished ancestry—since the eighteenth-century Marshalls had been eminent in the army and the law. A man of great intelligence but modest intellectual accomplishments, he was an avid reader of history and biography, a pursuit which stood him in good stead during the long years of slow promotion in the army between the First and Second World Wars. Persistence, patience, hard work and self-discipline, a warm and sensitive nature which was rarely demonstrated, all these were among the qualities of character which made it difficult for Americans, in his later years, to compare him with any lesser man than George Washington. As Chief of Staff during the Second World War, he contributed more, it has been claimed, than any other person to his country's vast and successful military effort.[3]

He entered on his office as Secretary of State after a frustrating year as Special Envoy in China, vainly attempting to bring about agreement between Chiang Kai-shek's Nationalists and Mao Tse-tung's Communists. Appointed Secretary in January 1947, his focus moved over to Europe. Here he felt on firmer ground. As he said soon after taking office: 'One usually emerges from an intimate understanding of the past, with its lessons and its wisdom, with convictions which put fire into the soul. I doubt seriously whether a man can think with full wisdom and deep convictions regarding certain of the basic international issues today, who has not at least reviewed in his mind the period of the Peloponnesian War and the fall of Athens'.[4]

Dean Acheson's background was less typically American than either Marshall's or Truman's. His father was a clergyman of Scottish/Irish origins who came to the United States via Canada, and who maintained strongly British loyalties until he took American citizenship comparatively late in life (he became Bishop of Connecticut); his mother was a Canadian of English stock whose enthusiasm for King and Empire had been strengthened by schooling in England. Intellectually brilliant, as proficient with his pen as in the spoken word, a successful lawyer, he came into political life with a war-time appointment as Assistant Secretary of State for Economic Affairs and later as Under-Secretary. At the dawn of Senator McCarthy's witch-hunts a few years later, he made clear, at a press conference on the Alger Hiss case, the principles of his public and private life—those of the Sermon on the Mount. 'One must be true to the things by which one lives', he said to a Senate sub-committee in this connection. 'It is not merely a question of peace of mind, although that is vital; it is a matter of integrity of character'.[5]

An effective advocate of teamwork, Acheson was frustrated during his earlier years in the State Department by the lack of this quality among those concerned with conducting America's external affairs. Cordell Hull was constantly by-passed by Roosevelt, who acted as his own Foreign Minister, and (after the brief interregnum of Stettinius) James Byrnes, as Truman's first appointment to the office, followed Roosevelt's example of going for advice and briefing almost anywhere except to those who were in the State Department for the specific purpose. Furthermore his constant travels, for the most part in Europe—more than even the increasingly acute confrontation with the Russians really warranted—made it impossible for him to reorganise the Department in a way which could enable it to function effectively.

This however was what Acheson was able to do, from the day that Marshall succeeded Byrnes in January 1947. A fresh start was literally made by moving the Department to new buildings; much dead wood was pruned out, and a clear chain of command began functioning in a way that had not been known for years. The General's military experience helped markedly in this development —'line duties [were] separated from staff duties; supervision was made effective through the Central Secretariat; planning—looking around, ahead and behind—confided to a competent staff; research and intelligence centralized'.[6]

Acheson, regarded by Marshall as his Chief of Staff, was the essential link between him and the rest of the Department, and to all those in it he imparted a sense of participation, calling together his closest colleagues daily in a meeting (known as his 'prayer-meeting') at 9.30 a.m., and setting them to work in groups with other members on specific problems. In these four or five groups Acheson often took part himself, bringing logic and direction to the discussions, and giving himself a grasp not merely of the problems, but of the general situation in the Department. He knew the staff, it was said by one of his colleagues, 'as few men before or since have known it. A man with a profound philosophy and a highly logical mind, he had learned the hard way how the Department should be run if it were to be an effective instrument in the conduct of foreign relations. . . . It led . . . to an *esprit de corps* that has never been surpassed, encouraging the full creative contribution each officer had to offer'.[7]

Besides including in this comprehensive manner all who could profitably contribute to the creation and formulation of policy, Acheson ensured good relations and a free flow of ideas between himself, Marshall and Truman. Truman, always awed by Marshall's prestige and personality, and inhibited by his dry, unrelaxed presence, needed the ease and freedom which he found with Acheson for bringing out the best of which he was capable, while

Acheson swiftly found a basis of understanding with the General.

This was the group of men faced with making unprecedented decisions, as new responsibilities for Europe and the world fell on them during the first months of 1947. Already in September 1946 in a speech at Stuttgart, Byrnes had stated a major reversal of policy in pledging his government to begin rebuilding the economy of that part of Germany where its writ could run, and backed it with another: that America would not, as in 1919, bring all the boys back home, but would leave an army not so much for occupation but as a deterrent against a possible Russian advance, for as long as might be needed.

Truman, who had for some time been concerned about Russian pressure on Greece and Turkey, called a meeting for 27 February 1947 with Marshall, Acheson and the Congressional leaders, immediately on hearing that Britain could not longer undertake her commitments there.[8] This gave Acheson his first chance to strike out for a new policy which would gain wide national support. Among those present was Arthur Vandenberg, leader of the Republicans and Chairman of the Senate Foreign Relations Committee. Vandenberg, a notorious isolationist in the nineteen-thirties, had been converted to the opposite point of view in consequence of Pearl Harbor, and now, if properly approached and briefed, could be counted on for supporting the shift in United States policy which would bring the country to shouldering the world-wide responsibilities which Britain was perforce having to abandon.

Acheson made the point that 'for the USA to take steps to strengthen countries threatened with Soviet aggression or Communist subversion was not to pull British chestnuts out of the fire; it was to protect the security of the US—it was to protect freedom itself. For if the Soviet Union succeeded in extending its control over two-thirds of the world's surface and three-quarters of its population, there would be no security for the US, and freedom anywhere in the world would have a poor chance of survival'.[9] Vandenberg's response was instantly positive, requesting a Presidential Message to Congress with a statement of the grim facts. This was particularly important at a time when the elections for the Eightieth Congress in November 1946 had made the Republicans the majority party. Vandenberg's support for a bi-partisan foreign policy and his refusal to make party capital at the expense of the Administration over these issues, were a decisive factor in the success of American policy during this period.

At this point Marshall had to leave for the Foreign Ministers' Conference at Moscow. The speed and smoothness with which, in his absence, the new policy of American aid was formulated and proclaimed in what came to be known as the Truman Doctrine, was a tribute to the spirit and organisation which had just been created in the State Department. Marshall left instructions that policy was to be prepared and action taken without reference to his negotiating position vis-à-vis the Russians, thereby giving his subordinates a remarkably free hand.

Acheson's method of getting officials thinking in groups and contributing to the creation of policy was swiftly successful. A conference which he called with the Departmental Staff on 28 February 1947 was a land-mark. His presentation of the larger issues, done with 'an unusual gravity of manner' produced an atmosphere of 'controlled excitement . . . It seemed to those present that a new chapter in world history had opened and that they were the most privileged of men, participants in a drama such as rarely occurs even in the long life of a great nation'.[10]

The immediate outcome of all this activity was Truman's speech to Congress on 12 March 1947, in which he stated that 'it must be the policy of the USA to support free peoples who are resisting attempted subjugation by armed minorities, or by outside pressure' —a statement which the press recognised as comparable with the 'doctrine' enunciated by President Monroe over a hundred years before—and followed it with a request to Congress for $400 million as aid to Greece and Turkey, and the despatch to those countries of military and civilian missions.[11] Thanks to the briefing of the leaders and the nation-wide discussions which had been initiated, public opinion, somewhat bewildered at first, soon rallied behind the President's move. Congress duly authorised his request. It was the end of the *Pax Britannica,* and the establishment instead of the *Pax Americana* over what was coming to be known as the 'Free World'.

The next step was to survey the needs of other countries besides Turkey and Greece. Various committees started work in the State Department, undertaking tasks 'in which they found release from the professional frustrations of years'.[12] Two such groups were the Near East Affairs staff under Loy Henderson, and the Economic Aid Group under Will Clayton with Joseph Jones as its rapporteur. Later George Kennan was put in charge of a Policy Planning staff committee, while the State-War-Navy Co-ordinating Committee secretariat undertook the overall study of policy procedure and costs of assistance to foreign countries.

Clayton and Kennan both had a particularly formative influence on American policy at this time. Kennan, who had long experience on the staff of the Moscow Embassy, won distinction with an 8,000-word cable from there in February 1946, which laid the basis of the 'containment' policy shortly to be initiated,[13] and which he spelt out in a much-quoted article, 'The Sources of Soviet Conduct', in *Foreign Affairs* of July 1947, under the pseudonym 'X'. Clayton, formerly head of the world's largest firm of cotton brokers, and now Under Secretary of State for Economic Affairs, was a man of conscience and idealism who was appalled at the growing plight of post-war Europe. Like Kennan's cable, a memorandum which he wrote on the plane after travelling to most of the West European countries, in May 1947, had a decisive effect. Talking with the leaders and making his own observations he was convinced that recovery had stalled and Europe was sliding into chaos. Other reports and letters which he sent to officials at Washington underlined this view, which, he suggested, indicated the need for a far greater effort of overseas aid than anything which the USA had yet undertaken, if minimum living standards were not to collapse with resultant revolution and political disintegration. A highly important point in Clayton's proposals was that whatever was undertaken should be done on a *European* basis. He advised a three-year grant of $6 or $7 billion in goods, 'based on a European plan which the principal European nations headed by the UK, France and Italy, should work out'. He also suggested that a framework would be necessary if this approach was to be effective —an 'economic federation'[14]—of the order of the Belgium-Netherlands-Luxembourg Customs Union—a recommendation which was also a prophecy of the eventual European Economic Community. A more cautious paper from Kennan agreed on the importance of the European countries producing their own plan.[15]

Marshall arrived back from Moscow on 28 April after seven

weeks of frustration in the face of Russian stonewalling over Germany and Austria, determined to set on foot a policy which could enable the countries of Europe not in the Soviet grip to begin their effective recovery, whatever the Soviet reactions. Soviet strategy was evidently to keep the situation in a state of deadlock until economic collapse, hunger and desperation would enable them to clamp their hegemony over Western as well as Eastern Europe. In this case further talks such as those which had just been broken off at Moscow would be simply playing their game—'the patient is sinking while the doctors deliberate'. He asked Kennan and his improvised Policy Planning Staff to produce a paper within a fortnight as a basis for decisions.[16]

Truman at his Cabinet meeting of 7 March had asked for a programme of communication on the needs and the new lines of policy to be worked out, so that leaders, particularly in business, throughout the country, would appreciate the larger implications of the problem. The press took a leading part in alerting the people to the crisis and America's responsibility, particularly through Walter Lippmann's articles in the *New York Herald-Tribune* and elsewhere. He stated the need for 'political and economic measures on a scale which no responsible statesman has yet ventured to hint at ... The measures will have to be very large—in Europe no less than an economic union, and over here no less than the equivalent to a revival of Lend-Lease'.[17] He further proposed that 'after we have discussed the separate needs of Britain, France, Italy and the rest, we should suggest to them that they meet together, agree on a general European programme of production and exchange, of imports to the outer world, and that they arrive at an estimate of the consolidated deficit for as much of Europe as can agree to a common plan. Such a consolidated deficit will be smaller than the sum of the separate national deficits'.[18]

Acheson was able to alert the public directly about the new policies being formulated in a speech to the Delta Council at Cleveland, Mississippi, on 8 May 1947, based on the preliminary report of the State Department's Economic Aid Group—the report became the basis of the Marshall Plan. This was a trial balloon, for which he secured publicity in Europe by tipping off of a group of British journalists with whom he kept contact, Leonard Miall of the BBC, Stewart McCall of the *News Chronicle* and Malcolm Muggeridge of the *Daily Express*. The response was favourable: the countries of Western Europe, it was clear, could not be brought into an anti-Soviet crusade, but opinion could be fired by the idea of European unity.[19]

This was the theme of another influential paper produced by a group including Charles Kindleberger, an expert on the German situation. It suggested that the strategy should not be one of assuming the inevitability of conflict with the Soviets, but should rather leave an opening for their co-operation while making it clear that the USA intended 'to go ahead with a consistent and adequate recovery programme for non-Communist Europe with or without the USSR'; to work if possible through the United Nations Economic Commission for Europe in order to get rid of the tangle of exchange controls and bilateral agreements and so move towards the long-term objective of the European customs union. In any case, the move towards unifying the economy of non-Communist Europe would give the people a powerful aim which would help fill 'the ideological and moral vacuum', and could initiate 'a tremendous emotional drive in Western Europe behind the supra-national ideal of European unity'. It would have to be a European recovery plan—partly to avoid injuring sensitive national feelings—aimed at 'the raising of European production and consumption through the economic and functional unification of Europe'.[20]

Apart from using the ECE as the organ for administering aid, these principles formed the basis of the Marshall Plan as formulated in the Secretary of State's speech at Harvard on 5 June 1947. By this time there was a wide consensus among the leadership both on the Republican and Democratic side as to the need and the lines of a solution. Already for some weeks previously, 'the tide of public expectation was so high that it was no longer a question of whether the United States would aid Europe, but when and how the initiative should be taken'. Marshall's proposals at Harvard were the outcome of an extraordinary 'interplay of ideas between the nation's leaders and the public'.[21] The main concepts, intensively sifted and considered in the State Department committees, were drafted by Charles Bohlen mainly from the memoranda of Kennan and Clayton, Marshall himself sharpening the passage about European initiative.[22]

'Our policy', he said in part, 'is directed not against any country or doctrine but against hunger, poverty, desperation and chaos. Its purpose should be the revival of a working economy in the world so as to permit the emergence of political and social conditions in which free institutions can exist . . . It would be neither fitting nor efficacious for this government to undertake to draw up unilaterally a programme designed to place Europe on its feet economically . . . The role of this country should consist of friendly aid in the drafting of a European programme and of later support for such a programme so far as may be practicable for us to do so. The programme should be a joint one, agreed to by a number, if not all, of European nations'.[23]

The importance of Marshall's speech might have gone unrecognised, at least for some time—it was said that the British Embassy, harassed by requests from London to keep cable expenses down, was sending it by pouch—had not Acheson tipped off his three British journalist friends to make sure it was given swift and wide publicity in Britain, and brought to Bevin's attention. He at once saw the importance of the proposals, and 'grabbed them with both hands'.[24] But though the French Foreign Minister, Georges Bidault, and other Western statesmen quickly followed suit, Molotov made it clear that Russia would have none of it, on the grounds that there should be no preliminary planning among the European states nor arrangements for mutual aid. The satellites were obliged to toe the line. Czechoslovakia, not yet fully within the Russian camp, decided after a unanimous cabinet meeting to accept, but after Prime Minister Gottwald and other members had been summoned to Moscow, was obliged, equally unanimously, to refuse. The Russian action was a step towards securing Czechoslovakia completely within the Soviet bloc by the coup of 20–25 February 1948. This in its turn heightened the Cold War, speeding the creation of a joint defence system by Britain, France and the Benelux countries through the Brussels Treaty of 17 March 1948, which, with the accession of America, Canada and other countries through the Atlantic Pact (4 April 1949), laid the foundations of NATO.

Meanwhile the American initiative of Marshall Aid had led on to the setting up of the 16-nation Organisation for European Economic Co-operation (OEEC) on 5 June 1948, matched by the Economic Co-operation Administration[25] at the American end. This virtually took over the functions of the United Nations Economic Commission for Europe, whose role diminished as it became evident that the purpose for which it had been founded, the recovery and development of the Continent as a whole, was impossible of realisation.[26] Hopes were high among the European federalists that the degree of co-operation implied by membership of OEEC would be completed by further movements on the political level. The question was whether these would lead on to a genuine federation, or the weaker arrangements which were the most to which the British government could be brought to agree.

REFERENCES

[1] Jonathan Daniels: *The Man of Independence* (London, 1961), 221.

[2] Joseph M. Jones: *The Fifteen Weeks* (New York, 1955), 113.

[3] General of the Army Omar N. Bradley in Forrest C. Pogue: *George C. Marshall: Education of a General* (New York, 1963), ix.

[4] Speech at Princeton, 22.2.47.

[5] Dean Acheson: *Present at the Creation* (New York, 1969), 360–1. For Acheson's earlier life and background, see *Morning and Noon* (Boston, 1965).

[6] *Foreign Affairs*, July 1971, Dean Acheson: 'Eclipse of the State Department', 601.

[7] Jones, *op. cit.*, 110, 113.

[8] Harry S. Truman: *Years of Trial and Hope 1945–1953* (London, 1956), 109.

[9] Jones, *op. cit.*, 141.

[10] Jones, 140.

[11] Truman, *op. cit.*, 111–112.

[12] Jones, 147.

[13] See the long extracts in *The Forrestal Diaries* (ed. W. Millis, London, 1952), 142–6.

[14] Memo of May 1947, Acheson: *Present at the Creation* (*op. cit.*), 231; Max Beloff: *The United States and the Unity of Europe* (Washington D.C., 1963), 20; Jones, 247–8.

[15] *Idem*.

[16] His report of 23.5.47 was largely based on the State-War-Navy Coordinating Committee report together with an outline of the findings of the Foreign Aid Committee. *Political Science Quarterly*, Vol. 38, Dec. 1958, W. C. Mallalieu: 'The origin of the Marshall Plan', 487.

[17] Quoted in Jones, 229 (Article 'Cassandra Speaking' of 5.4.47).

[18] Quoted in Louis J. Halle: *The Cold War as History* (London, 1967), 127, (Article of 1.5.47).

[19] Beloff, *op. cit.*, 16.

[20] Beloff, 15–16.

[21] Jones, *op. cit.*, 226.

[22] Jones, 225.

[23] Beloff, 22; Truman, *op. cit.*, 120.

[24] 19.6.47, *Hansard*, Vol. 438, col. 2353–4.

[25] For the Economic Commission for Europe (ECE—not to be confused with ECA—Economic Co-operation Administration) see D. Wightman: *Economic Co-operation in Europe* (London, 1956).

6

Robert Schuman and the New Public Opinion

Despite all the frustrations which dogged the advocates of a united Europe, an important outcome of their activity was the change in public opinion which prepared the way for the real measure of integration initiated by the Schuman Plan.

The change in public opinion is not easy to define. Such a change however did take place among Frenchmen and Germans in the immediate post-war years. It was not enough that, after three wars within seventy years, many people in both countries were convinced that a new way must be found of settling their differences, and that the old methods of the victor attempting to control the vanquished, leading inevitably to counter-claims and *revanchisme* by the latter, were quite out of date. But, logical though it might be to seek a new approach, such an approach could not have been found, or would not have been applicable, without the liberation of at least an effective minority in both countries from the accumulated hatreds and fears of the past. For this to be attained, the challenge of new ideas was required.

Those who had stood up against the dictators, who had been pursued and persecuted, or who had risked everything in the Resistance, had taken their stand for the most part because of their principles. Whether Christian, Socialist or Communist, their convictions denied them the easy paths of compromise. Among the men who were to 'make Europe', Adenauer had been ousted from office and had seen the inside of Gestapo prisons, Schuman had been in solitary confinement, and had been hunted by the Nazis, while De Gasperi had only escaped the Fascists through the sanctuary he was given in the Vatican library.

It was while on the run from the Gestapo that Schuman first gave expression to his views about rebuilding Europe. Harboured by a family in the south of France in November 1942, he surprised his hosts by speaking—for two hours—about the need to include the Germans in this task. As M. André Fauvet, who was sheltering him, wrote later, he and his family felt 'somewhat doubtful ... about this optimism which it was really difficult to accept at that period: to realise Franco-German unity—"build Europe"—in 1942! One must have lived through those days of struggle and resistance, this daily secret combat and ceaseless threat of confiscation, of concentration camp, perhaps death, to understand how much this project could appear then as an illusion, a mirage, an impossible dream, almost a Utopia ... Schuman, in his place of concealment from the Gestpo, was already thinking big, of the necessary reconciliation, of this Europe "which we must all make together." '[1]

These convictions must be understood in the light of Schuman's background and upbringing. He was born on 29 June 1886 in Luxembourg. His father had fought for France in the war against Prussia in 1870. When his part of Lorraine was ceded to Germany in 1871 he moved from his village, Evrange, the last before the border, to Luxembourg, in order to avoid taking German citizenship. The family language remained French: Schuman always wrote in French to his mother and friends, but he was a brilliant scholar who was equally at home in the languages and culture of both France and Germany. His education took place at German universities, Berlin, Bonn, Munich and Strasbourg, and while qualifying in jurisprudence he embarked on a special study of the comparison between Roman and Germanic Law. At Strasbourg his French patriotism was awakened by friends whom he made— Alsatians who were passionately French, and who like him belonged to the Catholic association 'Unitas'. His residence at Metz from 1903 onwards in no way marked any compromise with this essential patriotism, but rather his affirmation of his primary loyalty to Lorraine.

Schuman knew little of his father who died when he was quite young, but he had a particularly deep and affectionate relationship with his mother. When she was killed in a carriage accident in 1911, he seriously thought of taking holy orders, but renounced the project while determining to consecrate the rest of his life as a kind of priesthood in the service of others. 'I chose to aid atheists to live rather than Christians to die', was his reflection on this act of commitment many years later.[2] It was his response to the counsels of his friend Henri Eschbach: 'In our society the apostolate of laymen is an urgent necessity, and in all sincerity I can't imagine a better apostle than you. . . . You will remain a layman because you will succeed better at doing good, which is your unique preoccupation . . . In my opinion the saints of tomorrow will be the saints in jackets'.[3] Schuman accepted the challenge, though he never thought of himself as a saint, only as 'a very imperfect instrument of a Providence which makes use of us in accomplishing great designs which go far beyond ourselves'. This conviction he said, 'demands of us the greatest humility, but also gives us a peace of heart, which our ordinary experience, regarded from a purely human point of view, could not justify'.[4]

His life was to be an apostolate, in the sense of service to his fellow-men. It was no ambition which pushed him on to the highest offices. As a lawyer in Metz his integrity and loyalty, together with much shrewdness and powers of exposition, won him a reputation as a man eminently qualified to defend not merely the personal interests of clients but the wider interests of the city and eventually of Lorraine itself. For this reason, still in Metz after it had again become French in 1918, he was asked to stand as Deputy in the National Assembly, and he continued to represent Metz or Thionville—a working-class stronghold—with increasing majorities until shortly before his death.

In his small property of Scy-Chazelles just outside Metz, overlooking the Moselle valley, he lived something of a monastic life in the increasingly rare leisure periods which he could take from his work at Paris. He never married, neither wanting nor expecting to find a relationship with anybody as deep as that which he had known with his mother. Celibacy, as he put it, 'was decided by life', with the rationalisation that 'to be up to the mark for fulfilling properly one's task as a political man one should not be loaded with the responsibilities of a family. . . . A statesman cannot have a private life: he belongs entirely to the country. . . . We exist with other people and for other people whose destiny is, to a certain extent, entrusted to us'.[5] For relaxation he had his books, a large and comprehensive library of historical, theological, legal and literary works: his one passion—apart from politics—was for autographs and rare manuscripts, of which he possessed a remarkable collection in his later years. He often wished that he had taken up teaching as his profession, as a means of employing that thirst for knowledge which he satisfied with reading. Reading, together with prayer and meditation, sometimes in the little chapel opposite his house, and regular attendance at the mass, were his activities during his days of leisure at Scy-Chazelles.

Stories are many of Schuman's humility, his scrupulous economy, and his refusal to trench on the time and goodwill of others for his mere personal convenience. As Minister of Finance he would go around turning out unnecessary lights in the building. He preferred to untie parcels himself, so that the string should not be cut, but kept ready for re-use in a drawer reserved for the purpose. He was indignant when he caught his first chef de cabinet, Jacques de Bourbon-Busset, cutting string off a parcel. 'You don't do that', he said, 'I haven't been brought up in that way!'[6] He would not accept the style of living of one of the great ones of the world, and—for the sake of economy as well as simplicity—refused special trains and the company on journeys of all but the most essential retinue. Even as Prime Minister he would travel 'in an overfull compartment, where squeezed in a corner he worked all the way to Paris without raising his head'.[7] He did not wish to separate himself from the lot of the common man. For ordinary formalities he would join the queue in the Prefecture at Metz, and would go around the town on foot or by bus. On one occasion, while Minister of Finance, he arrived late at night at his home at Scy-Chazelles, and not wishing to disturb his old nanny who acted as his housekeeper, he insisted on the chauffeur sitting down while he prepared supper for both of them.

His care for detail, the almost deferential attention given to every visitor or questioner, his down-to-earth realism—all these qualities, combined with a deep religious dedication and the most profound perspectives on the Christian heritage of the West and its importance for the world, made Schuman a unique personality in the politics of his day. As Vincent Auriol, Socialist leader and President of France, said of him, 'Robert Schuman, et alors! c'est un radical qui va à la messe'.[8] Gandhi was the one statesman with whom comparison seemed apt.[9]

During the first years in Parliament Schuman limited his activities to the work of re-integrating Alsace and Lorraine in France, and to questions of Franco-German relations. His growing interest in international affairs was evinced during these years by his journeys abroad, often with his friend Eschbach, in the course of which he studied closely the countries which he visited. He also concerned himself with economic problems, as a member of the Assembly's Finance Committee. These widening perspectives never caused him to sit loosely to his responsibilities to his own people of Metz and Lorraine, defending vigorously, among other matters, their rights in religious education.

Politically he moved in a liberal direction away from the right-wing group of Louis Marin, and found his place in the Parti Démocrate Populaire equivalent to Don Sturzo's Popular Party in Italy—the one being later transformed into the Mouvement Républicain Populaire (MRP), the other into De Gasperi's Christian Democratic Party. His first call to office came as Under-Secretary of State for Refugees in the Ministry of Paul Reynaud, in March 1940, shortly before the fall of France. Here his close knowledge of the affairs of the frontier provinces served him well in making arrangements for families displaced at the start of the war from the area of the Maginot Line, though the flood of refugees after the German invasion of May became uncontrollable by himself or any man.

In the conditions of near-chaos at Bordeaux, Schuman gave his vote to Marshal Pétain as head of the government to make the armistice, though, disliking the tendencies of the new government, he soon withdrew from its affairs and made his way to Metz in order to look after the interests of his people at that most critical time. He took this step at considerable personal risk, as a public figure critical of the Nazis—and, in fact, was shortly arrested, the first French Deputy to suffer this fate. His seven months in solitary confinement was not merely a matter of retribution: Gauleiter Bürckel was eager to bring Schuman, with his perfectly bi-lingual culture and his strong local following, to become a collaborationist. This was a prize worth working for, but Schuman's obduracy demonstrated that confinement was not affecting the desired end.

A conversation is reported between himself and Bürckel at this time:

'We would like to name you Gauleiter of Alsace-Lorraine.'

47

'That's very interesting, but it seems to me rather difficult for a French MP.'

'In that case, I shall deport you to Germany.'

'That is something which you can do at any time, but it isn't an argument.'[10]

Schuman was indeed deported to Germany, but the change was for the better. He was able to live as a guest in a hotel, though under surveillance, in the little Black Forest town of Neustadt. Bürckel had not given up his attempts to gain Schuman's collaboration: he simply set his sights lower: would Schuman do some writing for the press? Schuman's reply was typical of his ironic humour. He said that he could not take on such work, partly because he had missed everything as to what was going on during his seven months in prison, and the gaps were too big to fill, and partly because the press, particularly in war-time, had as its object the strengthening of national feeling. 'Above all in Germany even the smallest contribution to the press is inspired by the ideals of National-Socialist doctrine, otherwise it would be badly received. My conviction is that today less than ever would amateurism be tolerated in so important a work. One must be a good National-Socialist to take part in such a task: I do not feel up to the level of it'.[11]

Supervision of his movements become increasingly lax, and he did not find it difficult to escape in August 1942. But then came a lengthy period which he passed in hiding, or moving around under a false name, seeking shelter in monasteries or families as he made his way towards unoccupied France. Once arrived there he was still pursued by the Gestapo, but combined living in semi-anonymity with a work of visiting and encouraging the refugees from Lorraine, and of looking after their interests generally—not forgetting to do what could be done for those who were under direct German occupation. When the Germans took over the whole of France in November 1942, he returned again to the life of concealment in monasteries and homes—a life which enabled him to read, study, pray, and attend services even at two in the morning—one of the rare periods of his career, as he said later, when he was able to do what he liked. The rigours of such an existence by no means, for him, offset the blessings. Though at the appropriately-named Nôtre-Dame des Neiges he suffered chilblains from the cold during the winter of 1942–43, he was able, while there, to study Roman history and improve his English by reading Shakespeare.

With the liberation of France, Schuman was able to return to Metz, where, according to his biographer, he was 'littéralement plébiscité par la population'.[12] A year of humiliating delay however elapsed before he was able to re-enter national politics, since a slur was cast on his patriotism on the grounds that he had voted for Marshal Pétain in 1940. At that time no one foresaw a career of distinction for the old parliamentarian who now re-entered the Assembly. It was by chance that he came by his first appointment. There was no obvious candidate for the chairmanship of the Assembly's Finance Committee, but having taken part in it for many years before the war, Schuman was chosen for the place. There Mendès-France came to know him and appreciate his qualities. 'He found him a man to be respected, serious and very honest, acute and of a sound judgement'. He proposed Schuman to Bidault for the post of Minister of Finance, and the appointment was made in June 1946.[13]

For Robert Schuman the Christian origin of the values on which European civilisation was based, and of democracy which he regarded as their expression in politics, was of decisive significance. He wrote later:

> Democracy owes its existence to Christianity. It was born on the day when man was called to realise in his temporal life the dignity of the human being, in the freedom of each person, in respect for the rights of each and by the practice of fraternal love for all. Never before Christ had such ideas been formulated. Democracy ... has recognised the primacy of the inner values which ennoble man. The universal law of love and charity has made each man our neighbour, and on this law from then on have rested the social relations of the Christian world. All this teaching and the practical consequences which have flowed from it have turned the world upside down. This revolution has operated under the progressive inspiration of the Gospel which has formed the generations by a slow work, sometimes accompanied by agonising struggles ...
>
> In the long and dramatic development of this civilisation it has by no means always been the believers who have made the most decisive progress for democracy. Christian ideas live on and are active in the subconscious of men who have ceased to practise a dogmatic religion, but who continue to be inspired by its great principles ...

Christ's kingdom was not of this world. That means also that Christian civilisation should not be the product of a violent and sudden revolution, but of a progressive transformation, of a patient education, under the action of the great principles of caring, of sacrifice and of humility, which are the foundations of the new society. It is only in the course of long centuries of interior struggles and successive purifications that such a civilisation can evolve towards the great ideal which has been set before it, and disengage itself from the dross of pagan humanity, at the cost of repeated questing and grievous struggles.[14]

Schuman believed that democracy had to be continuously developing—it could have no truck with the totalitarian 'illusion of possessing truth which was not only complete but definitive and directly applicable ... Democracy takes account of the evolution of ideas and of the correctives which experience—that is to say the lesson of success and failure—brings us through the medium of free discussion and evaluation. The working out of this vast programme of an expanding democracy in the Christian sense of the word finds its flowering in the making of Europe'.[15] In thus relating politics so closely to religion, he went back to an old tradition, but he was moving against the current which had led to the divorce of religion from politics, and hence to the progressive spiritual and political fragmentation of Europe. By bringing the two together again Schuman helped to lay the basis for the reintegration of Europe at the deepest levels.

In France, Schuman with his 'European' ideas, was in advance of most members of his party, the Mouvement Républicain Populaire (M.R.P.) which he joined at the Liberation. The M.R.P. was the equivalent in France of the Christian Democratic parties which existed, or came into existence, at the war's end in several countries. Through the initiative of Robert Bichet, Secretary-General of the M.R.P., the Nouvelles Equipes Internationales were launched in 1945 as a means of bringing the Christian Democratic parties in the various countries together. Though the N.E.I. formed in no sense a kind of 'international' with authority over these parties— not all of which entered the association[16]—it provided conferences and other occasions for bringing together those who regarded political, and especially international questions from a similar point of view.

The war-time pioneer of the M.R.P., Gilbert Dru, who was shot by the Germans, was a convinced 'European', believing in the necessity of a federation in which the participating countries would renounce their absolute sovereignty.[17] Representatives of other Christian-Democratic parties whose governments were located in London during the war, particularly the Belgians and Dutch, began to find a basis of unity in their common ideas regarding the future of Europe. Even the ancient divisions between Catholics and Protestants were blurred, a tendency which was marked when the Christian Democratic Union, founded in Germany after the war, though predominantly Catholic, attracted many Protestant adherents.

Schuman belonged to the group in the M.R.P. which participated in the N.E.I. (the party itself not being affiliated). In Germany one of its strongest supporters was Konrad Adenauer, who owed to the N.E.I. his first post-war contact with public men abroad. He succeeded in obtaining an invitation to its conference at Luxembourg in January 1948. Officially he was invited only as an observer or 'guest', but in fact he scored a great success by a speech which he was allowed to make, particularly in his frank admission of Germany's guilt during the Nazi period, and his pledge that he and his party would work for a united Christian Europe. 'Today', he said, 'I regard myself primarily as a European, and only in the second place as a German'.[18] Though the outcome was a discussion in the conference as to whether the C.D.U. could be admitted as a member of the N.E.I., the question was only with difficulty resolved in the affirmative, due to the strongly anti-German orientation of the M.R.P. at the time. The French delegates insisted that if the German party was to be admitted it could only be on condition of restating the crimes for which not merely the Nazis but the Germans in general were responsible. Adenauer made the strongest possible protest about this, and won his point. At the next session the C.D.U. was admitted to the conference,[19] and during that year (in which Schuman took over as Foreign Minister), there was a significant shift in the attitude of the M.R.P. towards Germany.

Adenauer had further contacts with men of affairs outside Germany along with a number of his compatriots at the European Congress at The Hague in May 1948,[20] and at a meeting of burgomasters at Brussels in July. In 1948–49 there were informal meetings of other Germans with French, Dutch and Belgian representatives of the N.E.I. at Geneva.[21] Also in Switzerland, at the Moral Re-Armament Centre at Caux, Adenauer and many of his compatriots from the Western Zones who were to take a leading part in politics and trade unions met people from other countries during this period.

Though Schuman did not come to Caux until later, he welcomed its approach in preparing for what he regarded as nothing less than a revolutionary change, transforming social relations and making possible new political structures. While admitting that 'statesmen have been only moderately successful thus far in "remaking the world",' he gave it as his conviction that 'it is their duty, more than anyone else's, to apply themselves to this task'. He went on to say that Moral Re-Armament offered a 'philosophy of life applied in action' (*un état d'esprit mis en action*).

> What we need, and what is quite new, is a school where, by a process of mutual teaching, we can work out our practical behaviour towards others; a school where Christian principles are not only applied and proven in the relationships of man to man, but succeed in overcoming the prejudices and enmities which separate classes, races and nations. To begin by creating a moral climate in which true brotherly unity can flourish, over-arching all that today tears the world apart—that is the immediate goal. The acquisition of wisdom about men and their affairs by bringing people together in public assemblies and personal encounters —that is the means employed. To provide teams of trained men, ready for the service of the state, apostles of reconciliation and builders of a new world, that is the beginning of a far-reaching transformation of society in which, during fifteen war-ravaged years, the first steps have already been taken. It is not a question of a change of policy; it is a question of changing men. Democracy and her freedoms can be saved only by the quality of the men who speak in her name.[22]

The conferences at Caux and their outreach throughout the countries of Western Europe and beyond found a wide response among those, both Christian and non-Christian, who were challenged in the war and its aftermath to realise in a better social and political order the values which had been so nearly overwhelmed. Survivors of the German resistance were among the first to be permitted by the occupying authorities in the Western Zones to come to these conferences. Equally they found a response among Germans whose ideology had been shattered by defeat.

But in days when Germans could only with difficulty travel beyond their frontiers, or even within their own country, much of the work of creating a new spirit which could lead to reconciliation between the former enemies fell on those who were able to visit Germany.

Among the French who devoted themselves to this task was Madame Irène Laure, Member of Parliament for the Marseilles area and Secretary-General of the women's organisation of the Socialist Party. Having worked for Franco-German unity before the war, she had reacted strongly against the possibility of doing so again on account of the German invasion of 1940 and the sufferings which followed: she had become a leader of the French Resistance, members of her family and friends had been tortured and killed by the S.S., and she had wished for nothing better than the total erasing of German cities by the bombs of the Allies. A visit to Caux in 1947 marked a fundamental change in her outlook.

Finding some Germans there, she was on the point of leaving, when she was forced to recognise in them (one of whom was the widow of Adam von Trott, whose husband had been involved in the July 1944 plot against Hitler) people who had suffered more at the hands of the Nazis than she had. She realised the impossibility of building the future on hate, and apologised to the Germans present for her bitterness and desire for vengeance. The response was overwhelming: the Germans expressed, with the sincerity of a new realisation, their regrets and shame for the sufferings they had caused to her and her country. This prompted her to go to Germany where she met the men who were coming forward in the Western Zones into public life, and spoke to many thousands of people there and in Berlin, as well as to the Länder parliaments. The effect of her speeches was electric, bringing about a widespread change of heart. Others from France went with her, including two men who had lost most of their family, the one fifteen and the other twenty-two, in the gas-chambers of Himmler's death camps.[23] Such personal decisions and actions, costly and difficult as they were, played their part in preparing the ground for the political decisions which made it possible for the statesmen to carry through on another level the work of reconciliation, and open a new way towards the future of Western Europe.[24]

Without the response of Germans on a large scale, the action of people like Irène Laure would have done little to effect reconciliation between the two countries. It was this response, and the general change of attitude on the part of Germans, which made progress towards integration possible, and in this change the Churches, both Protestant and Catholic, played their part. Though the crushing of the resistance movement after the abortive plot of July 1944 had left few survivors to carry forward the aims for which men like Bonhoeffer had stood, the post-war religious revival reawakened interest in finding a new basis of Christian unity and in rejecting false doctrines of race and nation. Men like Martin Niemöller and Reinhold von Thadden undertook heroic tasks to foster this new spirit and to rebuild the links which the war had broken with those who were working for unity through the Protestant Churches in other countries. This movement further widened its scope as Catholics, following the Encyclicals of Pius XII, pursued their own way towards unity as an ecumenical aim with political implications.

On a more purely cultural level was the action stemming from a group of officials in the French Zone of Germany who realised the dangers of keeping people cut off from outside influences—at that time even French newspapers were not on sale there. Taking a courageous stand against bureaucratic bumbledom they made arrangements for parties of young French people, and later for older ones as well, to come into the zone to meet Germans of similar age-groups. 'A movement was launched which was to grow continuously and to be imitated in the other zones. The young people could be numbered by tens who met each other in Germany in the course of 1945. They were 1,000 in 1946, 1,200 in 1947, 2,000 in 1948, 5,000 in 1949, the year in which the French frontiers were at last opened to young Germans.... This movement was only possible because of the existence in France of a constructive tendency among a minority. Its true results only became visible some years later, when the young people whose outlook had been shaped in the Franco-German encounters began to take over responsible duties in trade unions, political parties, universities or embassies, forming in this way a kind of permanent infrastructure for a clear and rational policy between the two countries'.[25]

In these ways various influences began to change the outlook of Germans and to make them more ready to look on old questions in a new light. This they were disposed to do after so many barren victories followed by the catastrophe of collapse and occupation, and the long drawn-out agony of starvation and economic stagnation. Disillusionment with Nazism and the ending, for the time being at least, of all the old dreams of expansion and whatever else may be covered by the word 'nationalism', made many Germans ready for a settlement which would to some extent compensate Germany's loss of territory by giving her larger scope in a federal Europe.

REFERENCES

[1] Robert Rochefort: *Robert Schuman* (Paris, 1968), 127.

[2] Rochefort, 51.

[3] Rochefort, 44.

[4] Georgette Elgey: *La République des Illusions* (Paris, 1965), 304.

[5] Cited in Elgey, 305.

[6] Ibid., 304.

[7] Ibid., 144.

[8] Elgey, *op. cit.*, 304.

[9] Rochefort, 150.

[10] Elgey, 305.

[11] Rochefort, 101.

[12] Ibid., 137.

[13] Elgey, *op. cit.*, 143.

[14] Robert Schuman: *Pour l'Europe* (Paris, 1963), 56–70.

[15] Ibid., 77.

[16] A. Grosser: *La IVe République et sa Politique Etrangère* (Paris, 1961), 128.

[17] Ibid., 121.

[18] Weymar: *op. cit.*, 197.

[19] Though, according to Grosser (p. 128), participation of the C.D.U. in conferences of the N.E.I. only began in 1951.

[20] See p. 27.

[21] Much of this information was given by M. Auguste-Edmond de Schryver of Belgium, President of the N.E.I., 1949–59.

[22] Frank Buchman: *Refaire le Monde* (Paris, 1950), 1; reprinted in translation in Frank Buchman: *Remaking the World* (London, 1953), 239.

[23] Gabriel Marcel: *Un Changement d'Espérance* (Paris, 1958), 3–19.

[24] Article by Adenauer in *New York Journal-American*, 31.1.60.

[25] Grosser, 201.

7

Jean Monnet: International Administration and the Modernising of France

'L'Europe est née d'une rencontre: un jour, un homme qui a une idée l'écrit à un homme qui a le pouvoir, et qui l'exerce le lendemain pour proposer cette idée aux peuples d'Europe'.¹

Like all feats of great artistry, the inception of the Schuman Plan, which led on to the Treaty of Rome and the Common Market, appears to have been simplicity itself. One man, Jean Monnet, Commissaire-Général of the Plan for the Modernisation and Equipment of France, on 28 April 1950, gave the Foreign Minister, Robert Schuman, a memorandum advocating the setting up of a High Authority to administer jointly the coal and steel industries of France and Germany, and any other countries which would come into the arrangement. Schuman accepted it, and a few days later gained its acceptance by the Cabinet. The adherence of the Federal Republic of Germany had already been secured; Italy and Benelux also adhered; within a year these countries had worked out all the necessary arrangements, which were then ratified by the parliaments of the countries concerned, and in August 1952 the High Authority began its operations in Luxembourg for establishing a common market and agreed methods of investment and production for the coal and steel industries of 'the Six'.

The seizing of the psychological moment had much to do with the success of the initiative. But the fact which was decisive was the convergence of men, Schuman, Adenauer and Monnet, at this precise historical moment with ideas, positions and functions which were complementary; while a tiny group of other men formed with these statesmen a working team completely committed to the strategy which they jointly devised, and prepared to subordinate

56

everything in order to launch their proposals with all possible speed, efficiency and discretion. Others played an important part, notably Alcide de Gasperi, Prime Minister of Italy and leader of the Christian-Democratic Party, whose support was decisive for Italian agreement at the initial stage; André Philip, who did much to prepare the way for the launching of the Schuman Plan, and in devising its details after its inception; and the Belgian and French Socialist leaders, Paul-Henri Spaak and Guy Mollet, who as leaders of the European Movement ensured the acceptance of the Plan by the Socialist parties in their countries.

The germ of the Plan, which was incorporated in Monnet's memorandum of April 1950, had been in his mind for a long time previously, and was the outcome of his unique experience as an international administrator and as Commissaire-Général of the Plan for the Modernisation of France.

In his own way Monnet was, like Schuman, a man of the frontiers, though spiritually and not by birth. A native of Cognac, born in 1888, he travelled on behalf of the family brandy firm in Canada, where he gained the large perspectives and the realistic approach which marked all his essays in statesmanship. He found in Canada the stimulus for what became his special enthusiasms: for teamwork and the pooling of resources. Soon after his arrival there he asked a passer-by on horseback how to reach a certain place. 'Take my horse', said the stranger, 'and when you have finished with it, hitch it to this post'. Monnet was the first European, as distinct from the many American builders of economic empires, to realise that the new frontier was in the east—east of New York, that is to say—rather than in the west. He looked at France as a country ripe for development, as part of a newly developing Western Europe, which should be economically integrated and politically unified.

Returning to France through London at the outbreak of the First World War, he was appalled at the waste in the allocation of scarce materials on the part of France and England. By persistent effort the unknown young man obtained an interview with the Prime Minister, Viviani, and helped to set up, and served on, the joint supply commission[2] which eventually was the outcome of his initiative. Having made his name as a budding international administrator, he was asked to become Assistant Secretary-General of the

League of Nations. He was disillusioned before long with the League as a mere international 'switchboard', and moved to a variety of jobs—managing the family business, helping to stabilise the currencies of Poland and Rumania, spending two years in China as head of the China Finance Development Corporation, whose business was mainly financing railway-building. By the time the Second World War started he was again in the employment of the French Government, concerned with the procurement of military aircraft from the USA.

At the outbreak of war he immediately took steps to initiate the Anglo-French pool for co-ordinating the purchase and supply systems of the two countries, and became Chairman of the Franco-British Committee for Economic Co-ordination. Just before the fall of France he persuaded Churchill, with de Gaulle's backing, to make the astonishing offer of political union and joint citizenship with Britain which—if accepted—would have set going the process of European integration in a particularly dramatic way. This failed because of the disorganistion and defeatism in the French cabinet, as did Monnet's attempt to bring the French Government from Bordeaux to England in a Sunderland flying-boat.

After France's surrender he became a member of the British Supply Council in Washington, and a leading light in the joint Anglo-American war effort, doing much to create the 'Victory Programme' for aircraft production and being credited with inventing Lend-Lease.[3] His work, according to Lord Keynes, contributed to shortening the war by a year.[4] As a member of the French Committee of National Liberation at Algiers from 1943 onwards Monnet organised Lend-Lease and other supply arrangements between Free France and the USA. He was also involved in settling the rival claims for leadership of the Free French between Generals Giraud and de Gaulle—a conflict which he helped to resolve by means of a formula thought out by himself and André Philip, the Socialist leader.

In dealing with this matter, according to Philip, inspiration came to the two men while walking on the mountain behind Algiers.[5] For Monnet this was characteristic: his regular routine of morning rambles in the countryside wherever he was staying (Monnet has always arranged to live outside the towns where he worked) has often been fruitful of inspired hunches, and given him the advantage of coming fresh to the questions of the day, and with a clear line of action for dealing with them, however embroiled they might become.[6] He has carried into his approach much of the peasant shrewdness of his Charentais forebears. A man whose formal education ceased at the secondary school level, his contribution has been through bringing a massive commonsense to bear on every situation, rather than in theorising about it. For statements and formulations of policy he has been dependent on others, particularly his personal brains-trust—and he has had the capacity of gathering around him younger men of brilliance and talent. His method has been to get one of them to make an initial formulation or draft, and then to criticise it, substituting words and phrases, sometimes working in this way for hours relentlessly with his team on a single brief document. It has been said that there were thirty versions of the Declaration of 9 May 1950 before it received its final form, and that none of his speeches has gone through less than twelve.[7]

He believes in giving himself to one situation at a time, concentrating on it, arriving at a decision as to the next step which must be taken, taking it, and so moving on, stage by stage, to the ultimate objective. 'There is no problem', he says, 'which can be dealt with in bits. You have to try to put all the elements together. You must make up your mind as to what is in common in the interests of the people concerned, and bring them to the point of seeing it. The majority are men of goodwill, but they only see things from their own point of view. You must get them together round a table and get them talking of that same thing at the same time'.[8]

This *'même chose'*, the thing in common which people should be aiming at achieving is not, in Monnet's view, to be attained by a compromise. It is a new situation which comes about through the change of attitude in people. 'Work it in a way that makes everyone see the means and objectives as common, create a unity of facts, and then the ideas of class-war, of national rivalries and hereditary hatreds will disappear of themselves'.[9] It is a formula which may not always work, but the *positiveness* of Monnet's approach is infectious. Don't speak in terms of giving up sovereignty, he counsels. 'The truth is that we are creating a common sovereignty'.[10]

Sceptical of the possibility of people changing in their natures, he is convinced that they change in their behaviour when the context in which they operate is changed. If you can persuade someone to change the way in which he does things, things will have changed, and a new situation will have been created which in its turn will act on people. Eventually these changes must be incorporated in rules and institutions. Two sentences from Amiel serve him as a kind of motto: 'Experience begins over again with every man. Institutions alone become wiser; they accumulate the general experience and from this experience and this wisdom come the rules which, once men have accepted them, change gradually not their nature, but their behaviour'.[11]

His superb sense of timing has been responsible for much of his success. At the height of the war, in 1943, he almost alone among those in official positions on the Allied side realised the folly of recreating a Europe of frontier-posts and tariff barriers. At that point he drafted a memorandum for the French Committee of National Liberation to this effect, but at the war's end eighteen months later the situation was not ripe for this revolutionary idea to be entertained by the restored governments. He had to wait for several years before he could begin working towards the realisation of this project through the Coal and Steel Community—a demonstration of his long patient waiting periods broken by swift decisions.[12]

Although his memorandum of 5 August 1943 had no immediate consequences, it is worth quoting as an example of his foresight and the early maturity of his ideas. He stated that the post-liberation governments would try to find the satisfaction of their people's needs on a national basis, whereas 'in the actual conditions of the world solutions can only be accomplished on an international basis'. This applied particularly to a country like France. 'Whereas the USA, Russia and Britain have worlds of their own into which they can temporarily withdraw, France is bound to Europe. . . . On a European solution the whole life of France depends'. France, he said, would have to act with her allies in 'the economic and political organisation of a "European entity," ' in which all the democratic liberties would be maintained, essential as the foundation of Western civilisation.

He pointed out that there would be no real peace in Europe 'if the states were reconstituted on a basis of national sovereignty involving as it would policies of prestige and economic protection. ... The countries of Europe are too cramped to ensure for their people the prosperity which modern conditions make possible and consequently necessary. They must have larger markets ... their prosperity and the indispensable social developments are impossible, unless the states of Europe form themselves into a Federation or a "European entity," which will make of it a common economic unit'.[13]

His advice was not heeded that 'economic sovereignties' should not be allowed to reappear in liberated Europe, by a self-denying ordinance on the part of the French National Committee and the governments in exile against re-establishing their tariff systems. In fact it was within the national framework that Monnet found he had to begin his post-war work, persuading de Gaulle of the necessity of a national plan for the modernisation and equipment of France, for which he was given the responsibility. He was backed in this by André Philip, who took over the Ministry of Finance and National Economy in 1946, and who saw in the Plan the application of the principles of de Man which had inspired him in the thirties.[14]

In preparing this plan and in piloting it as Commissioner-General, Monnet had his own way of going to work. A great believer in teamwork, the kernel of his activity was a small group of three or four, whose action could spread out and include an ever-growing number of accomplices or co-operators, whether they were directors of national enterprises and private companies, or trade union leaders and administrators. He was an adept at creating an atmosphere in which everyone worked together with a sense of genuine equality, and with none of the inhibiting barriers of age, class or function. The same freedom and spirit of give-and-take which existed between himself and his younger associates in his 'brains-trust' was extended to the larger meetings of the Commissariat and its commissions, so that bosses and workers' leaders, who had never met before and had been used merely to hurling demands and objections at each other from entrenched positions, were now able to discuss questions of production on the level of the country's needs in a spirit of cordiality and mutual confidence. These meetings provided neutral ground where business leaders and civil servants, including those from the different departments of the same Ministry, could 'come together and air their differences, uninhibited by considerations of personal status'.[15]

Monnet was something of a gate-crasher into the upper reaches of the administration, since he was not educated at the Polytechnic or a 'Grande École', and did not belong to that élite formed of the alumni of these institutions. But he could find the way of communicating with this otherwise exclusive old-boy network and use the services and training, and esprit de corps, of those who were its products.

He was not really an economist; in a sense he was not much of an administrator. For statistics or analyses of given situations he depended heavily on one or another of his younger colleagues, Etienne Hirsch, Robert Marjolin or Pierre Uri. But he worked hard himself and had the faculty of getting prodigies of work—and the best—out of others. 'You must get people to do', he said, 'those things that they know better than anyone else how to do—you must get other people working, explain to them the point of their work and listen to them. You must get people to work together; everyone takes part; and there must be authority'.[16]

The 'brains-trust' of three or four grew to thirty[17] for administering the Plan—but this itself was a very small number, including as it did the secretaries and ancillary staff, for carrying out such an all-embracing task on the national level. In this way Monnet was able to apply his belief in the effectiveness of a team in which everyone knew and understood everybody else, a flexible body which could be expanded, as it were, to include anybody, no matter what their position, whose advice or help were needed. 'More than a thousand people spread among all sectors and at all levels of the nation's life work for the first time at a common task. They are chosen without any regard for hierarchy, on grounds of their competence ... those who are most ready to work together and who are most listened to by their own people'.[18]

All this was revolutionary at the time—it was a real battle to ensure that the most qualified person, in this sense, presided at working sessions, whether he was an industrialist or a trade union leader, instead of the official of the branch of the civil service concerned.[19] Monnet had to deal with bureaucrats, but bureaucratic was the last thing of which he could be accused of being himself: he went in for no empire-building, and was suspicious of the tendency to sclerosis of all official bodies—besides, he knew that the continued existence of the Commission in the form which he required necessitated keeping its budget so low that, despite the chronic stringency of the national finances, no government would think it worth while to cut it.

One of Monnet's greatest contributions was to bring economic questions and projects of development into a new perspective. 'Modernisation isn't a state of things', he said, 'it's a state of mind'. Another of his convictions was that the most difficult thing, and the most essential, was to have a view of the whole.[20] One feature of the Plan was that it brought together all the sectors of the national economy, mines, transport, electricity, etc., which had been regarded as virtually separate entities and for which at the liberation separate plans had been drawn up, but for which there did not exist the resources for accomplishing any single one independently. Monnet however was able himself, and could bring others also, to regard the interdependence of all these different sectors as being of the first importance. For practical purposes he selected six basic sectors—coal, electricity, cement, steel, internal communications and agricultural machinery—as those whose development would most speedily activate the others and have the maximum effect on the economy as a whole.

Then, by a process of persuasion and discussion rather than by any application of *force majeure*, the Plan was put into operation. The basic sectors chosen for development in the first instance covered some 30 per cent of the nation's economic activity, and three-quarters of investment under the Plan went to the nationalised industries. It was evident that the private sector in any case could only function adequately through accepting the objectives of the Plan, and it was to those enterprises which were in line with these purposes that the remainder of the investment went. In the public sector planning could take effect by imperatives; in the private sector, it could only be by the indicative method, backed by incentives in the form of grants, loans, tax reliefs and public contracts[21] In these ways the economy was able to move forward in a unified way, and although the tempo of the Plan as originally formulated could not be maintained, it had already been initiated by the time George Marshall came forward with his proposals for a massive investment of dollars in Europe to fulfil the needs, according to their own estimates, of the various countries whose economies had to be put on their feet. The Plan answered specifically the requirements from the American side as to what was needed by France, who obtained 20 per cent of the total aid given to Europe between 1948 and 1952, and which, through the agency of the Monnet Plan, made possible the spectacular expansion of the economy during the subsequent decade.

This progress towards prosperity was, however, in danger of being arrested by 1949 owing to the fact that economies of scale and questions of marketing and research could no longer be adequately dealt with on the merely national level. This was particularly clear in the case of the steel industry, where plans for development in France, Britain and other countries were threatening a crisis of overproduction. The point had been reached where the different national economies of Europe were getting into the same situation as the various sectors of the French economy had been at the liberation, and where a new kind of planning for Europe as a whole was necessary, based on a consideration first and foremost of the interdependence of the countries concerned.

REFERENCES

[1] François Fontaine: *La Nation Frein* (Paris, 1956), 99.

[2] For the Allied Maritime Commission see p. 10.

[3] Richard Mayne: *The Recovery of Europe* (London, 1970), 172; *Dictionnaire biographique français contemporain* (Paris, 1950).

[4] Henri Rieben: *Des Ententes de Maîtres de Forges au Plan Schuman* (Lausanne, 1954), 328.

[5] Information from M. Philip.

[6] *Realités* (Paris), Christmas 1962, François Fontaine: *L'homme qui change le monde sous notre yeux*, reprinted under the title *Jean Monnet* by the Centre de Recherches Européennes, University of Lausanne (1963), 13.

[7] Ibid., 11.

[8] Ibid., 14.

[9] *Idem.*

[10] *Idem.*

[11] Ibid., 16.

[12] Ibid., 11.

[13] Centre de Recherches Européenes, Lausanne; printed in part in Jean-Pierre Gouzy: *Les Pionniers de l'Europe Communautaire* (published by the same institution, 1968), 10.

[14] See p. 23.

[15] Pierre Bauchet: *Economic Planning, the French Experience* (London, 1964), 43.

[16] Elgey, 420.

[17] In 1956 the staff had increased by 100, including typists, chauffeurs and all other personnel; in 1959, after amalgamation with the productivity services, it rose to 150—Bauchet, 33.

[18] *Idem.*

[19] Elgey, 421.

[20] Elgey, 421–2.

[21] Bauchet, 25.

8

Schuman, Philip and the German Question

In the winter of 1948–49 the need of a rapprochement with Germany was beginning to be clamant not merely on account of the political questions which had to be answered, but because it was realised that the economic development of a new unified Western Germany would have to be linked with that of France. In this sphere, as in others, the two countries could no longer afford to be rivals. Instead arrangements were required, from the French point of view, which would enable Germany's recovery to assist, and not compete against, the upsurge of the French economy which was still to be achieved. The economic stress within France had diminished as the post-war agricultural revolution began to throw food surpluses on to the market, reducing their prices and stabilising the cost of living, but it was apparent to the experts that this boom was only temporary. French exports had increased, but largely to soft-currency countries, and the economy was as dependent on dollars—now coming by way of Marshall Aid—as it had been at any time since 1944. More elbow-room was needed if the heavy industry of France, whose reconstruction was well on the way, was to be competitive in a wider area than that of the political frontiers.

Economic reconstruction had proceeded despite the handicap of considerable political instability. At the end of the war the Communists, Socialists and M.R.P. divided between themselves the bulk of the votes cast at elections, and for a time they essayed to govern the country together—the system known as *tripartisme*. The situation was in fact more complex than that which a coalition of three homogeneous parties would have created, because the divisions within the M.R.P. and Socialist parties were as marked as those between the parties themselves. There was a considerable difference between the former conservatives who had joined the

M.R.P. in the hope that it would be a conservative or even reactionary body and those who, like Schuman, had genuinely radical aims which brought them close to the idealist element among the Socialists. The latter, again, typified by André Philip, thought in different terms from those whose doctrine, basically Marxist and materialist, swayed them towards the class war and a strategy similar to that of the Communists. At the same time these Marxist Socialists were divided from the Communists by their refusal to accept the principle of 'democratic centralism' and the direction of Moscow.

Quite apart from conflicts over ends and means, sheer weakness and mis-management, notably in the sphere of finance, had ruled out the possibility of any genuine social progress measured in terms of a fairer sharing of wealth or opportunity. Production was still struggling back to the pre-war level, while real wages were far lower. Those who had ended the war rich had managed, for the most part, to hang on to their wealth, and to devise means of maintaining a good standard of living, despite the steady, and often rapid, inflation. The failure to reform the currency during the years of de Gaulle's ascendancy left a vast mass of depreciated francs as a drag on his successors' attempts to re-energise the economy.

When Robert Schuman became Minister of Finance in June 1946, he was eager to improve the lot of the worse-off citizens, but realised that, in the existing circumstances, there was neither the will nor the apparatus for moving further towards a state-managed or *dirigiste* economy. Raising wages was at best a temporary palliative, and in no direction could real progress be made unless the stability of the franc was assured. He brought to managing the economy of France the same scrupulous control as he exercised over his personal affairs, and the same war against wastefulness and extravagance in every form. With minute investigation, he drew up a national balance sheet which could serve as a basis not only for his own budget but for that of many of his successors—*l'inventaire de la situation financière de la France*.

He refused to consider devaluing the franc, since it was a measure which would hit those with the lowest incomes worse than anyone else. For these, allowances were granted to offset the rise in the cost of living, but measures of extreme austerity for the nation as a whole were necessary if the ordinary budget was to be balanced. Discontent with the gap between wages and prices was aggravated by the poor harvest and withholding of supplies by the peasants. It proved impossible in some places to honour the bread-ration, which in the autumn of 1947 was reduced from 250 to 200 grammes, while at times meat altogether disappeared off the market. Earlier in the year a wave of strikes began, largely in the public services, which the Communists, though members of the government, supported, notably in the case of the nationalised Renault car factories. On opposing the Government on a vote of confidence, the Communist Ministers were dismissed by the Prime Minister, Paul Ramadier (4 May 1947). The full blast of the party was then directed towards supporting and fomenting the strikes, this time mainly in the coal and steel industries. While the Communists and de Gaulle's newly-founded Rassemblement du Peuple Français were violently attacking each other, they were both aiming at torpedoing the government and even over-throwing the régime.

These were the circumstances in which Ramadier resigned and Schuman took over the premiership (24 November 1947). Riots at Marseilles and strikes throughout the south had virtually paralysed large areas. Two million workers were out, and the hated C.R.S. (Compagnies Républicaines de Sécurité) were on the move from one trouble-spot to another quelling the incipient revolt by methods which, if often effective, were nonetheless harsh. Schuman turned over the task of defending the franc to the new Finance Minister, René Mayer, who by such methods as applying super-tax on incomes over 750,000 francs, and withdrawing the banknotes of 5,000 francs, followed the same course as his predecessor, though a cost of living bonus was instituted for all workers.

On top of the other troubles General Leclerc, on whom the Government was counting to handle the growing troubles in Indo-China, was killed in an air-crash. It needed no ordinary courage for Schuman to stand firm, but despite days and nights of Communist filibuster in the Chamber of Deputies, Mayer's austerity budget was passed.

An indication of the atmosphere in the Assembly (Parliament) is given by a few extracts from the *Journal Officiel* for 4 December 1947. On that day Schuman requested, under the urgency procedure, powers to alter the law in order more effectively to curb sabotage and protect the freedom of workers against those who were forcing them into strike action, and to reinforce the police by a measure of mobilisation. These requests provoked an outburst of fury from the Communists. Directed first against the Government as a whole ('You are the government of misery and brutality') the insults soon became personal. Jacques Duclos, the Communist leader, after accusing the Government of having the habit of lying, went on: 'The President of the Council is a former German officer. He's a Boche, the President of the Council. Down with the Boches!'[1] Continued vituperation along these lines marked the Communists' attempts to discredit Schuman by claiming him to have fought for the Germans during the First World War—a pure fabrication, since Schuman never had any wish to serve in the German Army and had in fact been excused on health grounds.[2]

In the country the insurgents blocked the lines and derailed the Paris-Lille express, and strewed nails or placed rocks along the roads. The telegraph lines were cut in various places, public services paralysed and arms seized. But the Government's firmness convinced the majority of strikers that nothing was to be gained by such tactics, and the drift back to work became more marked. On 9 December the national strike committee ordered the return to work, and a few days later the non-Communist members of the C.G.T. executive broke away under Léon Jouhaux to form the Force Ouvrière. The Government seized the moment to guarantee the full cost of living bonus to all who immediately returned to work, while inviting the trade unions to start conferring with them again. The strikes were over, apart from sporadic attempts by the C.G.T. to restart them in the following months.

Schuman's government fell on 19 July 1948, in consequence of a decision by the Socialist party to withdraw its support—its 'lay' susceptibilities had been affronted by the Poinso-Chapuis decree making possible grants to free, i.e. non-state, schools where religious instruction was permitted. The government of André Marie in fact marked a shift to the right; in it the position of the M.R.P. remained strong, and it was able to impose Schuman as its nominee for the Quai d'Orsay. After a short period Marie fell, and Schuman was again (28 August 1948) asked by President Auriol to form a government. He failed however to muster the requisite support, and continued as Foreign Minister.

This was a moment when France was fighting a losing battle over her policy towards Germany. One of de Gaulle's main achievements as head of the Provisional Government had been to regain Great Power status for France. Excluded from Yalta and Potsdam, de Gaulle's efforts were so far successful that France was accepted without cavil as one of the four Powers meeting regularly at the post-Potsdam conferences of Foreign Ministers, along with Russia, the USA and Britain. But her policy of keeping Germany divided and weak was ineffective. She was strong enough to veto the plan, accepted by Russia as well as Britain and America, for unifying the economic administration of the country, and thus contributed to its permanent division between East and West; but she was unable to stand long against the pressure of America and Britain for unifying the Western Zones, and rehabilitating Western Germany economically. After Britain and America had united their zones economically by an agreement of May 1947, and were preparing the currency reform of June 1948 which set going the upsurge of the economy—later known as 'the German miracle'—the French had little option but to follow suit.

The acceptance by Bidault at a conference in London (20 April–1 June 1948) of the principle that a unified German government be set up over the three Western Zones was an abandonment of all the positions taken up by France since the liberation. Schuman, on taking over, was faced with this new situation, with no apparent alternative to continuing to fight the same 'constant rearguard action'[3] as his predecessor. As he said, the new policy of rehabilitating Germany was being carried out by the old methods—'concessions bitterly haggled over, torn from unwilling and mistrustful victors by the humiliated vanquished, increasingly conscious of their reborn strength. Moral rehabilitation was failing to keep pace with the progressive restoration of political liberties'.[4] The official French objective for Germany remained that of a loose federation, which meant opposing all moves towards centralisation, while maintaining and enforcing such economic controls as she possessed.

Particularly galling was the continued tendency of America and Britain to take the essential decisions and leave France to haggle about them afterwards, or merely to accept them with or without demur. One such instance, which caused a bitter reaction in Paris, was the decision, published by Generals Clay and Robertson (who commanded the American and British forces in Germany) on 10 November 1948, that the industries of the Ruhr should be handed over to the new German government, who would in due course decide whether to nationalise them or return them to private ownership. This aroused French fears that whether the German government nationalised these industries, as the British wished, or returned them to private ownership, they could once again be used for the unrestrained production of armaments and become a potential threat, as so often before, to Germany's neighbours. 'We cannot agree that this arsenal, unique in the world, should ever belong to a centralised German government', said Schuman. 'This even Hitler never had'.[5]

As a sop to the French they were invited by the British and Americans to participate in the two bodies which controlled the administration of the Ruhr industry, without waiting for the French to fuse their zone with those of Britain and America, which had been part of the plan agreed in London in June. Though better than nothing, this was a long way from detaching the Ruhr from the rest of Germany, which had been one of France's original postwar aims, especially since the arrangement would be in doubt once the new German state had attained sovereignty. The International Authority for the Ruhr (a scheme which was also part of the package for creating the new German republic) did not go far enough for the French, since Anglo-American policy was to confine it to allocating the coal and steel produced in the Ruhr, with no control over the industry itself. The control bodies, into which France had just been admitted, would not, in the Anglo-American view, continue after the new German state gained its sovereignty, a position which was soon to be reached with the promulgation by the Western Allies, including France, of the Basic Law of May 1949. It was clear that the German Federal Republic's demands for the abandonment of all controls by the former occupying powers would soon be made. Not only would the future of the Ruhr Authority be in question, but also the dismantling programme and the Saar.

Under agreements made with America and Britain in 1947 and

71

1948 the integration of the Saar in the French economy had been effected, and its separate political development under the Statute of September 1947 seemed assured. Schuman showed no intention of changing this policy. When Germany's membership of the newly-founded Council of Europe was proposed, Schuman agreed—but only on condition that the Saar also was admitted as an independent member. Schuman shared the fears of his compatriots that a revived Germany might one day again turn on France, and he was as vehement as any other French statesman in opposing German re-armament. 'Germany has no army, and ought not to have one', he said.[6]

At the same time opinion was growing in France that if the existing controls over Germany had to be abandoned, an alternative method of preventing her from becoming once again a threat to peace might be found along the lines of a federal system for Europe as a whole. It was reported from Paris, at the end of 1948, that 'many people believe that without federal Europe no amount of guarantees as regards Germany will prove sufficient for keeping the peace'.[7]

Along with Robert Schuman, André Philip played an important part in preparing the way for the solution of this question. After the collapse of France in June 1940, Philip was among the Socialists who had voted against giving Pétain plenary powers. He had joined the Resistance,[8] and eventually escaped to London where he became Commissioner for the Interior in the Free French government in exile under de Gaulle.

On the liberation of France Philip re-entered Parliament, and chaired the committee working out the constitution of the Fourth Republic. He was among those who had hoped that, by standing for the principles of Jaurès and Blum, the Socialist Party would have attracted many with liberal or radical views who had come to the fore in the Resistance—including Catholics like Schuman —who instead went into the M.R.P. But in the absence of Blum, still in prison in Germany, the Congress at the Mutualité in 1944 was almost as decisive as had been those of Strasbourg and Tours in 1920. Whereas the latter split the Socialist movement by leading to the formation of the Communist Party, the former gave excessive status and scope to the old Socialist Party members who looked askance at the younger ones of the Resistance. Its outlook narrowed to something like the Marxism of Guesde—a trend which Blum on his return resisted, but too late to make possible the creation of a wide party embracing many varieties of doctrine, like the British Labour Party.[9]

Philip was one of those who regretted most this outcome of the war's upheaval; henceforward, though still ready to work with the liberals of the M.R.P., as he did with Schuman, he had to do it outside the framework of a uniting party. He was Minister of Finance and National Economy (January to June 1946, December 1946–January 1947), and when Schuman took over Finance in January 1947 he continued as Minister of National Economy, a situation where only the closest team-work could serve to bring about the smooth functioning of two departments whose concerns overlapped at so many points. In fact this was the only period when there were no conflicts, otherwise so frequent, between these Ministries. 'A situation impossible in itself became possible', said Philip later, 'thanks to the entire confidence which existed between us, and there were no collisions'.[10]

Philip was also given the job of heading the French delegation on the U.N. Economic Commission for Europe. Both there and in the Assembly at Paris his proposals commanded attention. While the three-Power conference was meeting in London for working out the Ruhr Statute, in November 1948[11], he suggested enlarging the Authority for apportioning the coal and steel products of the Ruhr by attaching to it organisations for sales, price-fixing, and programmes of production; and he also proposed that this enlarged body should be linked with those concerned with the management of the Ruhr industry, in which the French had recently been included. Schuman, who was attending the debate, interrupted to say that he was in entire agreement with these proposals.[12]

Philip went on to say that the new Authority, with its powers covering all aspects of the production and sale of coal and steel, should be extended to the whole of northern Europe: it should become 'a public inter-European service for coal and steel'.[13] In this way it could be demonstrated to America that the Ruhr was the first concrete experiment in uniting Europe, an aim which they were encouraging the Europeans to pursue.

The British, he admitted, were showing some reservations about this goal, as the Labour Party's *Feet on the Ground*[14] report indicated. But since they had agreed to the creation of economic institutions, and wished to start on the economic level before moving to the political 'we should say to (them) ... 'come with us to make this first experiment of a common management of the coal and steel industries of Western Europe." ' He thought they might be convinced if they understood that these economic agencies would be complemented by institutions on a representative basis, 'capable of controlling and animating them.'[15] As for France, she would cease being a strap-hanger, alongside the 'Big Three' first-class travellers in their comfortable seats, and would become 'the spokesman of all Europe—a Europe who has been waiting, and still waits for us to take this initiative'. France's problem of security, vis-à-vis Germany, he concluded, could only be solved in a European context, and the same could be said for peace as a whole.

Schuman was the first to agree that re-building the German economy was a necessary part of rehabilitating Western Europe, which the Americans had undertaken through the Marshall Plan. This policy was given urgency by the Cold War challenge of Russia in 1948, the year of the rape of Czechoslovakia and the Berlin blockade: its ideological and political implications were clear, since Germany and other western countries, if weighed down by chronic scarcity and even hunger, could hardly resist the onslaught of Communism. The question was how to rehabilitate Germany so that she could make her economic contribution to the recovery of Europe as a whole, and yet prevent her from regaining her strength so far that she could once again be capable of posing a military threat to her neighbours.

'The problem which has to be resolved is certainly delicate and difficult', Schuman said in the Assembly a few days after André Philip had put forward his proposals. 'It is a matter of reconciling these different considerations and of maintaining the necessary restoration of Germany within limits and according to a rhythm which will put aside any threat of hegemony dangerous to the peace of Europe.' A new framework was needed—'France and Europe cannot bring about a sufficient and lasting level of recovery unless all the interested countries put in common their resources and their efforts ...'[16] Once recovery has been effected 'this Europe will be the building in which we will make every effort to install peace once and for all. That will be a common task or it will be nothing . . . The future Germany will have to be inserted into this building, first on the economic level, then on the political. The Ruhr ought to be a first, a precious, an indispensable contribution to the European association which is emerging. To sum up: a European solution for the peace, a European solution for Germany, a European solution for the Ruhr, such is our vision of the future.'[17] As for the practical means to accomplish these ends, Schuman said that he shared the ideas put forward by André Philip.[18]

The response of Germany to these proposals was guarded, though it gave some encouragement to the proponents of integration. Adenauer declared that the Ruhr Statute would be acceptable if similar arrangements were made for French and Belgian industry, 'so that the whole of European industry can be organised as an entity'.[19] Karl Arnold, Minister-President of North Rhine-Westphalia in which the Ruhr is situated, proposed a co-operative association for bringing together the industry of the Ruhr and Lorraine, which could be extended to include the heavy industry of the Saar, Luxembourg, Belgium and France.[20]

Philip seized the opportunity of a conference of the European Movement at Westminster in April 1949 to bring his proposals on a stage further. In the report of the Movement's Heavy Industries Commission, which he put together and presented at the Conference, he spelt out his scheme. The heavy industries—coal, steel, electricity, transport—of the countries concerned should be placed under a European Public Institution, which would define the general policy of the industries (e.g. investment, volume of production, prices). This Institution should be co-ordinated with two others: a consultative body composed of representatives of the employers, wage-earners and public, and industrial associations ('ententes'), comprising the chiefs of the public and private enterprises responsible for carrying out the directives of the Institution.[21] He focused attention on the impending crisis in the steel industry which over-production, shortly to be anticipated, would bring on, and he initiated an investigation into this state of affairs by the Steel Division of the United Nations Economic Commission for Europe.

REFERENCES

[1] *Journal Officiel* (Débats—Assemblée Nationale) Vol. XX, 4.12.47, 5243.

[2] Rochefort, 60, 177.

[3] Grosser, *op. cit.*, 210.

[4] Schuman: *Pour l'Europe*, 154.

[5] *New York Times*, 22.11.48.

[6] Rochefort, 253.

[7] *Christian Science Monitor*, 1.12.48.

[8] See p. 24.

[9] For the failure of the Blum-Mayer proposals (1946) for something like a Labour Party composed of Socialists and M.R.P., see Criddle, *op. cit.*, 53.

[10] Rochefort, 158.

[11] The draft agreement on the Authority was published on 28 December 1948; it came into operation on 28 April 1949.

[12] JO XXI (Débats—Assemblée Nationale), 30.11.48, 7312–7314.

[13] Ibid., 7314.

[14] October 1948.

[15] JO XXI, 7315.

[16] Ibid., 7345.

[17] Ibid., 7347.

[18] Ibid., 7346.

[19] Rochefort, 245.

[20] 1.1.49. See R. Massip, *De Gaulle et l'Europe* (Paris, 1963), 18.

[21] André Philip: *L'Europe Unie et sa place dans l'économie internationale* (Paris, 1953), 200–201; *Revue française de science politique*, VI, 1956; P. Gerbet: 'La Genèse du Plan Schuman', 527. Philip's report was adopted by the conference, 25 April 1949.

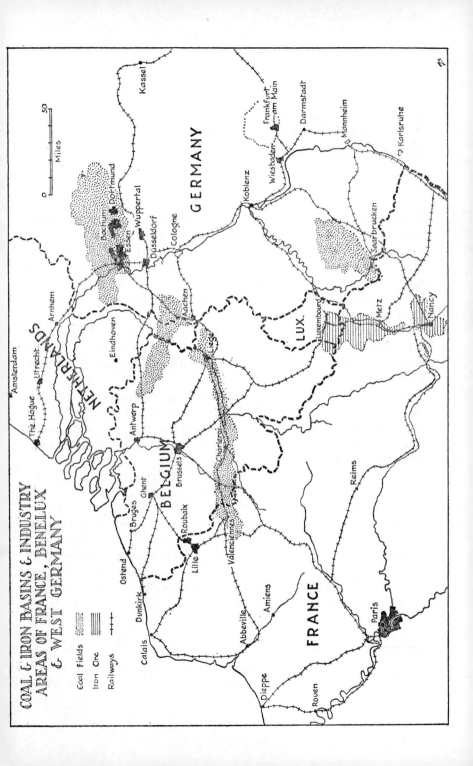

COAL & IRON BASINS & INDUSTRY
AREAS OF FRANCE, BENELUX
& WEST GERMANY

Coal Fields
Iron Ore
Railways

Miles
0   50

GERMANY

NETHERLANDS

BELGIUM

LUX.

FRANCE

Amsterdam

The Hague

Utrecht

Arnhem

Kassel

Dortmund

Bochum

Essen

Wuppertal

Düsseldorf

Cologne

Koblenz

Frankfurt
am Main

Wiesbaden

Darmstadt

Mannheim

Karlsruhe

Saarbrucken

Metz

Nancy

Luxembourg

Aachen

Liege

Eindhoven

Antwerp

Ghent

Bruges

Brussels

Charleroi

Roubaix

Lille

Valenciennes

Ostend

Dunkirk

Calais

Dieppe

Rouen

Abbeville

Amiens

Reims

Paris

9

The Dual Crisis and the Making of the Schuman Plan

These proposals came at a time when Monnet was working on an idea which he had launched during the war for a fusion of the coal and steel industries on both sides of the Rhine under a European authority.[1] He set Uri, Hirsch and others of his brains-trust on to preparing a blue-print for such a plan. He also drew in Professor Paul Reuter to make whatever adjustments were needed from the legal point of view.

Besides being an international lawyer of standing, Reuter had the advantage of personal experience of a kind of supranational body, since he was a member of the permanent Central Committee for Opium, composed of independent personalities who were not government representatives.[2] But the High Authority for administering the coal/steel pool which Monnet envisaged went far beyond any such body whose powers were advisory and whose decisions could only be effective when ratified by the governments concerned. The High Authority was to take over the sovereign powers, although in a limited sector only, of the participating states. Where the distribution of coal and steel was concerned, and in certain aspects of their production, the Authority was to enjoy sole powers in substitution for those of the states, where its writ would run in exactly the same way as the laws of the respective governments.

While this work was progressing, affairs were moving to a critical point in Franco-German relations, especially over the vexed question of dismantling German factories. This policy became obsolete as soon as it was decided that Germany was to be given a new start in her economy. 'Reactivation' of industry became the watchword. Instead of dismantling factories it was necessary to rebuild and modernise them. This reversal of policy was first put through by the Americans in their zone, but paradoxically dismantling continued and even reached a peak during 1948–49 in the zones of Britain and France.[3] This naturally produced great bitterness and discontent. The Social Democratic Party encouraged its members not to take part in dismantling, and fights were liable to break out when workers tried to prevent dismantling teams from proceeding with their business. From all over Western Germany resolutions from City Councils and other bodies poured into the offices of the Allied authorities, demanding or pleading for a cessation of dismantling.

In July 1949 Adenauer wrote to Schuman about the psychological damage which was being inflicted on the Germans by the continuation of dismantling, and the harm being done to the idea of European co-operation 'at its most sensitive spot. I entreat you, who have such an understanding for the reconciliation of France and Germany and for a joint European work together, to find means and a way to call a halt to these absolutely unintelligible measures'.[4] He followed this up by another letter a month later, putting forward a plan of Karl Arnold, the Minister-President of North Rhine-Westphalia, that, rather than dismantle the Thyssen steel works at Hamborn, it might pass, in settlement of reparations, under international ownership. Arnold's suggestion was that the production should be used for the benefit of needy people, and particularly the war orphans of Western Europe, and that it should be administered by an international committee of educators and statesmen of the democratic European states, who would ensure that its production should not be developed for war-like purposes. Adenauer strongly backed this line. Internationalisation, he pointed out, would help to improve Franco-German relations, while giving a boost to the new Christian-Democratic Government in Germany. 'Such international co-operation in the matter of the most important steel-works in Europe could form the seed of a very wide international co-operation in the realm of coal and steel, such as seems to me highly desirable for Franco-German understanding'.[5]

Arnold (1901–1958), was a tower of strength to Adenauer and a fervent supporter of the European idea, not merely as a solution of Germany's problems, but because for him a united Europe promised the sole security for civilisation based on Christian values. A man of profound faith, a Catholic from a peasant family in Swabia, Arnold had entered the Centre Party as the protégé of Matthias Erzberger, on whom had fallen the distasteful task of signing the armistice with the Allies in November 1918. Within the rather shaky framework of the Weimar structure, Arnold had made a name for himself as a leader of the Christian trade unions, and in 1929 became the chief spokesman for the Centre on the City Council of Düsseldorf.

He survived persecution and want during the Nazi régime, re-emerging in Düsseldorf as the most forceful leader among those who had refused to compromise with Hitler. The genuineness of his convictions, allied with great strength of character and an attractive personality, gave him the key part in building the Christian-Democratic party in the Ruhr, appealing to Protestants as much as Catholics. In January 1946 he became Lord Mayor of Düsseldorf, and Deputy Minister-President of North Rhine-Westphalia when this, the most populous of the states or Länder, of what was shortly to become the German Federal Republic, was set up. At the elections for this Land government in April 1947 the Christian-Democrats obtained the largest vote (somewhat to the surprise of the Occupying Power, since the Labour Government in London would have preferred, and expected, a Social-Democrat victory). Arnold became Minister-President, and until his resignation in 1956 was, along with Adenauer, one of the most powerful men in West Germany.

A new start, an ending of hate, and the acceptance of a European patriotism in place of self-centered national egoism—these were Arnold's themes in speeches which he made during this period, and he linked these objects with an internationalisation of the Ruhr by way of an association or partnership into which France would bring the ore-bearing region of Lorraine, and in which the Saar, Belgium and Luxembourg would be included.[6]

These suggestions were not immediately followed up by Schuman, and the dismantling continued. But while ideas of this kind were being aired, Schuman met Adenauer during a visit to the Rhineland[7] (August 1949) shortly before the latter was elected Chancellor, and had a long informal talk—being able to converse freely without an interpreter was an advantage—in which many points were covered. One suggestion particularly interested Schuman, that of creating a permanent economic link between France and Germany, for example by an electricity grid which would cover both the Saar and Lorraine. On his part, Adenauer was relieved to hear from Schuman that the eventual return of the Saar might be a possibility.[8] From a personal point of view the meeting was a great success. Schuman, with a quaint mixture of French and German, had said beforehand 'il faut l'approcher mit Vorsicht',[9] (he must be approached with caution), but so close were the two men in their background and ideas that not merely understanding but also friendship quickly developed.

Two months later, Ernest Bevin raised the question of the German government's participation in the Ruhr Authority. Although Schuman did not yet see how to make such a development coincide with a policy of 'Europeanising' heavy industry in general, he at least felt he was getting nearer to his two Western partners with a view to arriving at an understanding concerning Germany and her industry which would be acceptable to all. The fact that France had been admitted to the management of Ruhr industry was a step towards transforming the 'tête-à-tete anglo-saxon'[10] into a genuine colloquy of three, while the initiation of the Atlantic Pact in April 1949 brought France and her partners still closer together. This development was hastened by the exceptionally warm personal relations which grew between Schuman, Acheson and Bevin[11]—Acheson having returned to the State Department as Secretary in place of Marshall in January 1949, a year and a half after his resignation as Under-Secretary.

In that year and a half opinion in the State Department and Washington generally had continued to support the aim of European integration. On the morrow of Marshall's Harvard speech launching the new aid programme, Kennan's Policy Planning Committee had issued a staff paper (28 July 1947) looking to a European Customs Union as the long-term objective. It was hoped that the body to be set up in Europe to dispense Marshall Aid, eventually the Organisation for European Economic Co-operation (OEEC), would acquire some of the features of a supranational organisation, on the grounds that a partial delegation of sovereignty to it would be necessary.[12] The Select Committee concerned with appropriation pointed in the same direction. It looked to a political federation with Germany as a member, and assumed that an economic federation would be the first step in this direction.

This however had been blocked by the British. Though heavily dependent on American aid, first for an emergency grant after the loan replacing lend-lease had run out, and then on a steady flow of Marshall Aid which went on until December 1950, the British were able to preserve their autonomy in regard to tariffs and the sterling area, which the Labour Government believed necessary for its brand of economic planning. Acheson was sympathetic to the British approach, and only swung towards supporting integrationist moves with the coming of the Schuman Plan.[13]

Paul Hoffman, the administrator of the Economic Co-operation Administration (the agency for aid at the American end) was a convinced integrationist, who had been in touch with Monnet before taking up his appointment.[14] Another influential American who worked closely with Monnet was William Tomlinson, the Paris representative of the USA Treasury from 1948-55, while Monnet credited Clayton with stimulating some of the ideas on which the Schuman Plan was eventually based.[15]

At the same time the policy-makers in America were agreed that they could not force integration on Western Europe. The suggestion was turned down that grants should be made conditional on accepting measures of integration. However the need was clamant for 'a single pervasive and highly competitive domestic market in Western Europe of sufficient size and scope to support mass production for mass consumption'.[16] Now that the immediate objective of staving off collapse had been achieved, the strategy was to move towards economic unification. But attempts to get the member-states to work out a four-year overall master plan were frustrated because the governments could think only of their own needs and plans.[17] Early in 1949 this approach was abandoned, and $150 m. earmarked for encouraging trade liberalisation and setting up a payments union. The British were in the forefront of resistance to such developments, but the European Payments Union was nevertheless launched on 7 July 1950—a major step in freeing trade between the West European countries.

By this time the recovery of Western Europe had proceeded at a pace which scarcely anyone thought possible in the grim winter of 1946–47. Rationing and controls were being swept away, and a new problem, that of surpluses, was coming into view. In Germany mountains of rubble had already been removed from the shattered cities, and new blocks of flats, shops and public buildings were rising among the ruins. The currency reform of June 1948 had opened the way in the Western Zones to the economic miracle of those years—a reform which took effect with the same dramatic results in West Berlin after the Russian failure to hamper these plans or exclude the Western Allies altogether by the blockade of June 1948–May 1949.

These encouraging developments on the economic side had not however brought the political aspects of the German question any nearer solution. Though integrationists on both sides of the Atlantic still saw hope in some kind of federal development, there was frustration as the Council of Europe floundered and Britain, whose support and even leadership seemed essential for the schemes, continued to drag her feet. The break-through, when it came, was the outcome of the intense and growing concern about Germany, as Soviet threats made it increasingly necessary not only to re-establish her economic strength but her political sovereignty as a step towards bringing her into the Western defence system.

On this point much hard thinking was being undertaken in the State Department, where Acheson had initiated a thorough re-appraisal of the main lines of American foreign policy. The principles on which he was basing his policy were to confront the Soviet threat by creating 'situations of strength', and to transform Germany and Japan from ex-enemies into allies, attaching them 'by firm bonds of security and economic interest to the free nations of Europe and Asia'.[18] The achievement of this objective in Europe was in fact only indirectly the outcome of American action. It was through a French initiative that the *dénouement* over Germany eventually came, though American policy played a major part in moving the economic and political situation to the point where such an initiative could be both practicable and effective.

Bevin had shown himself ready to talk 'in the frankest possible manner' about all questions, such as those of Germany and Italy in relation to the Atlantic Pact,[19] and an opportunity for pursuing these points arose at the meeting of the NATO Council at Washington in September 1949. Up till then, as Bernard Clappier says, 'our English and American allies had tended to adopt their attitude in regard to Germany in the light of immediate interests rather than in accordance with a long-term plan'.[20] Now with a new confidence in French leadership, the Americans were ready to turn to France for the necessary initiative in tackling outstanding questions such as Germany, the Ruhr and the Saar, and the British followed suit. A meeting of Acheson, Bevin and Schuman took place in September 1949, at the time of the NATO Council.[21] When Germany was reached after a *tour d'horizon* of world problems, Acheson said, 'I think that we three will all be in agreement to confer on our French colleague the task of defining our common policy in regard to Germany'. Bevin gave a grunt, which Acheson took to be a sign of agreement, and Schuman felt, from then on, as if he had received an unwritten mandate or 'confirmation of his own strong purpose to find the best, that is the most durable solution', to the German problem.[22] As he wrote to Acheson some years later, 'I have always kept in mind the words you said to me one day, in the presence of our late colleague Bevin: "France must have the leadership of Europe". This was for me a programme and a personal responsibility'.[23]

Among the subjects which the three men discussed,[24] dismantling threatened to split them apart. Acheson pointed out that dismantling and Marshall Aid were incompatible. The matter was shelved, to be raised again by Bevin in a 'message' to Schuman, which he sent, with a copy to Acheson, at the end of October. Bevin proposed a meeting for discussing matters like dismantling and the participation of the Federal Government in the Ruhr Authority. He pointed out that the dismantling programme was anyway in jeopardy, since it aroused so much opposition that it was difficult to find Germans who would carry it out. He underlined the need of the three governments, French, British and American, to agree on a 'joint attitude' which could be 'translated into a general understanding with the German Federal Government, and so end the existing state of legal war'.[25]

Acheson went much further than Bevin in challenging Schuman to bring France forward with 'the initiative and leadership ... to integrate the German Federal Republic promptly and decisively into Western Europe' or (put rather the other way round) to consider 'what contribution we can make to the development of a Western European community in which the Germans can assume an appropriate position as a reasonable democracy and peaceful nation'. Schuman underlined Acheson's suggestion[25] that a stronger and more effective safeguard against the wrong sort of German resurgence than the judicial framework which had been constructed, would be 'the growth in Germany of a whole-hearted desire to participate in the political and economic development of Western Europe and the development in Germany of a truly democratic and peaceful society'. The means, he proposed, was that France should try 'to obtain rapidly the participation of the new German Government in all the international, political, economic and social agencies in which German association is possible ... ranging from such technical associations as the F. and A.O. to such political associations as the Council of Europe'. But in any case, he insisted, time was running out, and the moment should be seized—'we shall probably never have any more democratic or receptive atmosphere in Germany'—and if the opportunity was not taken it would deteriorate, as happened in similar circumstances in the 1920's, especially with Russia 'actively abetting the development of anti-democratic and aggressive tendencies in Germany, and ... prepared to exploit them to the full'. At the present, however, this Russian pressure was driving the Germans 'into the arms of Western Europe', so that they were 'psychologically and politically ripe to take measures for genuine integration with Western Europe'. He emphasised that 'we must give genuine and rapid support to these elements now in control of Germany if they are to be expected to retain control. Extremist views and weakening of the allegiance to democratic principles will come if these parties and their supports are not strengthened'.

To bring Germany into technical and political associations and to encourage 'a very much increased intercourse with the western world' was the way, in Acheson's view, to strengthen Germany's loyalty to international obligations and democratic procedures; equally, in domestic affairs the Germans must be given both

the substance of responsibility ... and the ability to make clear to the German people that their Government is acting on its own initiative in the interests of the people of Germany and of Europe ... We could, of course, take the attitude that, having given the Germans the Occupation Statute, we should wait for clear and definite evidence on the part of the Germans of behaviour in accordance with our expectations. Can we afford to do so, in view of the shortness of time still at our disposal? Might it not be wise to take the first step to advance to the Germans a political credit which they have not yet fully earned? ... I believe we would be wise to give an 'advance' of good will to the Germans in view of the strength of the safeguards which we have erected and our ability to call upon the powers we have reserved. Although we have powers we cannot reasonably hope to recreate a German will to co-operate if we once permit it to die for lack of nourishment.

I believe that our policy in Germany and the development of a German Government which can take its place in Western Europe, depends on the assumption by *your* country of leadership in Europe on these problems ...

We here in America, with all the will in the world to help and support, cannot give the lead. That, if we are to succeed in this joint endeavour, must come from France.[27]

Schuman accepted both Acheson's analysis and his conclusions. He was ready to take the leadership demanded of France. But the seven months which followed were a period of bafflement. He was sometimes tempted to feel that the time had come to retire to his books and start writing his memoirs, but his basic conviction remained that he should stay at his post to complete his task of reconciling France and Germany.[28] The hall-mark of his character was tenacity, and having put his hand to the plough he was not going to turn back. At the same time he was cautious, unwilling to embark on any action however promising in which he did not feel entire confidence. He was determined to wait for the right opening. The clue to his attitude was his 'confidence in Providence, confidence which, instead of encouraging him to run ahead of affairs, brought him to wait before taking action until the event invited him to do so; less to bring about the opportunity than to seize it when it presented itself, from which habit came a certain slowness before acting'. 'Often', writes André Philip, 'he has tacked about, delayed the decision, tried to dodge the call which was making itself heard in the depths of his conscience; then, when there was nothing more to do, when he was sure of what the inner voice was demanding, he took the boldest initiative and pushed it to its conclusion, equally heedless of attacks as of threats'.[29] As he later put it himself, 'the harsh lessons of history have taught me, as a man of the frontier, to mistrust hasty improvisations or over-ambitious projects, but they have also taught me that when an objective judgement, after mature reflection, based on the reality of facts and the superior interest of men, leads us to new and even revolutionary initiatives, we must—even if they

clash with established customs, age-old antagonisms and anti-
quated routines—hold fast to them firmly and persevere'.[30]

A solution to the questions raised by a renascent Germany and
her claim to complete sovereignty, and to related matters such as
the Ruhr and the Saar, could come, Schuman realised, through a
process of political integration whereby Churchill's vision of 'a
kind of United States of Europe' could be achieved. But he also
knew that it would be unrealistic to go straight for political integration. The Council of Europe had become stuck at the point
of providing a forum, but with no effective powers for its constituent bodies. To have attempted to endow such bodies with
powers and so achieve integration would have failed.

'In any case', as Schuman explained later, 'we could not start with
that. It would have been too ambitious and we would have failed
certainly in the face of the mountain of difficulties and obstacles which
would have risen in our way. The convergence of two categories of
problems, Franco-German on one side, European on the other, brought
us to envisage a concrete solution which was susceptible of answering
both the one and the other of our preoccupations.'[31]

A meeting between Acheson, Schuman and Bevin in November
1949 brought agreement on ending dismantling. As for other
questions, Schuman was feeling his way towards the solution which
ultimately came through the coal/steel pool, but his hints at this
possibility mystified Acheson, notably his contention that decisions
about Germany's steel-making capacity could only be reached by
looking at the question from the point of view of Europe as a
whole.[32]

The most acute problems in the 'European category' were
economic. How to apply such a solution in detail to both categories
Schuman did not yet see. André Philip was pressing for a step
to be taken, because of the economic crisis which he saw looming
if the unparalleled opportunities for development on a supranational basis were not seized.

'There is a great demand in the newly developed countries for high
quality mass production goods, the export of which could bring Europe
considerable prosperity', he wrote in an article published in November
1949. 'But this requires enormous capital and to be profitable the
industries concerned would have to spread the capital invested over a

D

great number of productions, in order to reduce the manufacturing costs of each. In other words, there can be no future for Europe unless a large standardised market is set up to ensure the development of the industries on which the resumption of our exports depends.

'Unless this is done, and done quickly, 1952 will see a crisis of exceptional severity, accompanied by social unrest which might bring the Communist parties into power and mean the Russian domination of our continent.

'Official bodies and national Governments cannot ensure this economic unification of Europe—it has been attempted on several occasions by the OEEC...European unity cannot be realised by negotiations between Sovereign States. It can come about solely through the creation of a political authority endowed with strictly limited functions but also with adequate power'.[33]

These considerations were the subject of a conversation which Philip had about this time with Tony Rollman, a Luxembourgeois who headed the Steel Division of the United Nations Economic Commission for Europe.[34] Rollman, a 'steel man' all his life, was convinced that steel and coal were the two commodities which should first be placed under an international authority, and he saw this as the first step towards an economic and political community along lines remarkably similar to those which Monnet was envisaging. With Philip as the intermediary he was drawn into the discussions which Monnet was carrying out with numbers of people in preparation for formulating what became the Schuman Plan.[35]

Philip was the French representative on the Economic Comission for Europe. In this capacity he had been able to implement the call which he had made at the European Movement's Westminster Conference of April 1949 for an investigation into the impending crisis in the steel industry due to over-production,[36] which he estimated would be 8 m. tons by 1952. The report, which was largely the work of Rollman, was now published (December 1949). It pointed out that the current building of excess steel capacity would involve the investment of two thousand million dollars of precious Marshall Aid which would produce no return at all in the foreseeable future. As for the plunging prices which would be the consequence of over-production, the danger would be of a reaction to the anarchy of laissez-faire or to the restrictive practice of pre-war cartels, with consequences of falling investment and production, and mounting unemployment and political unrest.

Rollman's report pointed also to the inefficiency and costliness of the existing system, where each country not merely worked out its own plans for production without any reference to its neighbours, but—in order to conserve dollars and maintain a favourable balance of payments—entered into a series of bilateral agreements while fiercely protecting its own economic domain by systems of import and export quotas, licences and tariffs. For this reason, the European market had 'become fragmented into a number of little markets' in which the cost of primary products was kept at levels well above world prices.[37]

The solution, suggested the report, was a close collaboration between the countries concerned, with a view to co-ordinating programmes of investment and production, and to maintaining the highest technical level. 'Since all the European countries are economically interdependent, the discussion of these problems and the conclusions of agreements aimed at solving them should take place within the framework of Europe as a whole'.[38] It proposed a supra-national 'public authority for steel' as the agency for harmonising production and investment on a European basis. The alarming consequences of failure to take adequate action in the imminent crisis were clear for all to see—for the Rollman report produced 'an immense sensation'[39]—and this brought the proposals for a European authority further into the realm of practical politics.

REFERENCES

[1] *Fortune*, Vol. 30, No. 2, (August 1944); John Davenport: 'M. Jean Monnet of Cognac'.

[2] Gerbet, 543n.

[3] Grosser, 209.

[4] Adenauer to Schuman, 26.7.49 (Private collection).

[5] Same to same, 25.8.49, Grosser, 209–210.

[6] Speech of 1.1.49, quoted in Rainer Barzel: *Karl Arnold* (Bonn, 1960), 31–32.

[7] At the residence of M. Hittier de Boislambert, the High Commissioner for the Rhine-Palatine Land, at Coblenz—Schuman: *Pour L'Europe*, 93–4; Adenauer speaks of a meeting in October 1948 (*Erinnerungen* (Stuttgart, 1965), 1, 296)), i.e. almost a year earlier, at Battenheim. Elgey also mentions that 'en 1949, lors de la rencontre de Nouvelles Equipes Internationales, ils vont passer ensemble une journée de receuillement à l'abbaye benedictine de Santa Maria Laach'—Elgey, 441. Schuman states that the Coblenz meeting was his first with Adenauer.

[8] Adenauer, *op. cit.*, 296.

[9] Elgey, 440.

[10] Rochefort, 254.

[11] Acheson: *Present at the Creation (op. cit.)*, 270–2.

[12] Beloff, 25.

[13] Ibid., 27–32.

[14] Ibid., 32.

[15] Ibid., 57. For Clayton, see p. 38

[16] E.C.A. staff paper, *The Problem of Western European Competitive Position in the World Economy and its Remedy*, July 1949, quoted in Beloff, 38.

[17] Gardner Pattison: *Survey of United States International Finance 1949* (Princeton, 1950), 136–7; Beloff, 36–7.

[18] Summary of document NSC-68, Acheson: *Present at the Creation*, 373–6.

[19] Bevin to Schuman, 29.12.48 (Private collection).

[20] *France-Forum*, Sept. 1967. The meeting of the three Foreign Ministers apparently took place on 15 Sept., just before the meeting of the NATO Council (17 Sept.).

[21] Acheson, *op. cit.*, 326.

[22] *France-Forum, op. cit.*

[23] 5.3.53, reprinted in Dean Acheson: *Sketches from Life* (London, 1961), 62.

[24] Acheson speaks of being able 'to unburden myself ... in our meeting of October'—but he may have mistaken the month. Acheson to Schuman 30.10.49 (Private collection).

[25] Same to same, undated, end of October 1949 (received by Schuman on 30th October), ibid.

[26] In a letter of Acheson to Schuman 30.10.49 (quotations in this and the following paragraphs are from this letter and another of the same date (Private collection)).

[27] *Idem.*

[28] Conversation between Schuman and Dr. Frank Buchman, October 1949. (Information from Mr. John Caulfeild).

[29] Rochefort, 231; quotation from Philip cited in *France-Forum*, November 1963.

[30] *Pour l'Europe*, 14.

[31] Quoted in Massip, 17.

[32] Acheson: *Present at the Creation*, 338–9.

[33] *European Affairs*, November 1949, A. Philip: 'A question of life and death'.

[34] See p. 75.

[35] Information from M. Rollman.

[36] See p. 75.

[37] *Rollman Report*, 72, quoted in Rieben, *op. cit.*, 315.

[38] Ibid., 84 (Rieben, 320).

[39] Rieben, 320. See also Philip's speech in the French Assembly of 25.9.50, JO July-August 1950, 5939–5943.

10

1950: Launching the Plan

In January 1950 Schuman made his first visit to the capital of the newly-founded Federal Republic. Bonn station was empty except for the Chancellor, who hurried him quickly to his waiting car. As he explained, he feared an attack on Schuman 'because you are on the way to absorbing the Saar'.[1] Closer understanding between the two men came through this visit, but no concrete plan emerged for dealing with the impasse into which affairs seemed to be running both on the political and economic levels.

The importance of the visit, in Schuman's view, lay in the opportunity for creating the climate for the future co-operation of France and Germany. This was the theme of a speech which he made while in the German capital. He harked back to the years 1923 and 1924 as an example of a time when the two countries had been closer together—a reference, apparently, to the Adenauer-Stinnes proposals for treating as a unit the mines and industry on both sides of the Rhine—this example he took as a justification of their hopes for proceeding towards a better future. He called for candour and much patience, for courage and pertinacity, and for understanding on both sides of the other's psychological difficulties. He stressed the peaceful contacts which had long existed between the two countries, in spite of all the wars and conflicts, and he referred to his days as a student in Bonn which 'created for him the basis of fresh spiritual and intellectual insight'.

Schuman expressed clearly his faith that the two peoples could work together, that their duties to their respective countries could best be fulfilled by undertaking a task together which would go far beyond the national frontiers for the benefit of all mankind, and he hailed the present as a time when the foundations were being laid on the Rhine for 'a future in community'.[2]

German forebodings about the Saar seemed however on the point of being realised. Much tension had developed between

France and the Federal Republic, due to the negotiations for defining more precisely the terms of the Statute which, confirmed by 95.5 per cent of the voters in the Saar elections of October 1947 (a figure which the Germans would never credit), had given the territory a high degree of autonomy—while the integration of the Saar in France, in economic but also in other spheres, continued apace. On 3 March 1950, less than two months after Schuman's visit to Bonn, conventions concerning these more tightly drawn political and economic arrangements were signed.

During the succeeding months the boldest proposal made by Adenauer was for a complete union between France and Germany, fusing their citizenship and parliaments along the lines of the plan prepared by Monnet for Anglo-French union which was put by Churchill to the French Government in June 1940. But the reaction in the French press was adverse, and the comparison with the British proposals of 1940 was not well taken—except by de Gaulle who said that 'one is almost dazzled by the perspective of what could be given by the qualities of Germany and France combined, the latter prolonged into Africa. There is a common field of development there which could transform Europe. It is a matter of taking up again on modern foundations, economic, social, strategic and cultural, the enterprise of Charlemagne'.[3]

Schuman had reservations about such a proposal. 'A union is a long haul and a laborious task to accomplish', he said. 'You can't improvise it. We don't reject the idea of an entente, but we want to gauge in advance the difficulties to be surmounted. Looked at from another angle we can't agree that we are evading the problem by talking in economic terms'.[4] In any case, though he felt urgently the need to bring about the reconciliation of the two countries, he wanted to effect this within a European framework. The Chancellor, on the other hand, preoccupied by questions such as the Ruhr and the Saar, and the danger of mounting bitterness on the German side on their account, wished to bring about their solution by means of some kind of Franco-German agreement. Such an agreement, in Schuman's view, should be the first step towards European unity, indeed this should be constituted around it; but unlike the Council of Europe, from which he thought not much could be expected, the new arrangements should be such as 'to engage not only our words but our interests'.[5]

Schuman was aware that the moment had arrived to effect this reconciliation. On 26 March 1950, he told the Central Committee of the M.R.P. that his two main aims were the realisation of a European community and the settlement of Franco-German relations, and that a detailed study should be made of economic unification, especially in view of the disparity of productive costs.[6] With Germany recovering there would be a danger of her returning to her old disastrous habits. An initiative was needed and 'it is our duty to act without delay'.[7] He was agonisingly aware of the dangers inherent in the Anglo-American policy of looking at Germany primarily in terms of the balance of power against Russia—a position which was already bringing them to support Germany against France, and so commit all over again the mistakes of the years between the wars. The question of German rearmament had already been raised, particularly in America, as well as that of the Federal Republic's adhesion to the Atlantic Pact. In April 1950 Acheson sent Schuman a forceful letter—France, he said, must determine once and for all her attitude in regard to the integration of the Federal Republic in Europe.[8] On the 11th May a meeting of the three Foreign Ministers was due to take place in London, when these matters would come up for discussion, and when the British and Americans were going to confront France with new demands for turning over the control of the Ruhr to the Germans.

Schuman had to watch warily the balance of forces at home, since this would tilt against him if he made any one-sided concessions to Germany. As he said later, 'We were in an impasse in almost whatever direction we turned ... we were surrounded by walls. In order to advance we had to open a breach. First of all we had to get rid of that terrible mortgage to fate—fear. We felt the need of some psychological leap forward ...'[9]

This *élan* or leap into the future was provided by Jean Monnet. The plan for a coal/steel pool had now been completed. He saw this as the way to establish a new context within which all the problems threatening to become endlessly bones of contention between France and Germany—the Ruhr, the Saar, German rearmament— would take on an entirely different aspect, thereby making their solution relatively easy. The strategy was to begin with the coal and steel of the two countries, by setting up a common directing authority, leaving other countries to accede to the arrangement; then extend the principle to other sectors, developing its political as well as economic implications, and so move towards the goal of an integrated economic community under a European federal authority.

If the goal was ambitious, the strategy was well conceived. How to get it started? It was partly a question of timing, more of finding the men in the right positions to undertake it. Monnet was turning over these questions when, in the spring of 1950, he was taking his usual holiday in the mountains. Mountain walks can be productive of inspiration, and Monnet was a great walker, whether in the mountains or on his morning rambles around his country home outside Paris. On this occasion the moment when 'the idea' came to him was precise—'le lundi de Quasimodo' (the Monday week after Easter, 17 April).[10]

From then on events moved with speed. Returning to Paris Monnet summoned his brains-trust to work out a memorandum for submission to the Government. By the Thursday of the same week (20 April) it was ready, and Monnet gave it to Pierre-Louis Falaize, the Prime Minister's directeur de cabinet. But Bidault, whose pre-occupation was with some kind of Atlantic union, put the memorandum in a drawer and gave it no further thought.[11]

Monnet had prepared a copy for Schuman, to be passed on to him by Bernard Clappier, Schuman's chef de cabinet. Clappier took a personal interest in launching Monnet's plan, since he was a friend of Monnet's and had already discussed the details of it with him. By some mischance Monnet was unable to give the document to Clappier for several days. When he eventually did so, and Clappier passed it on to his chief, it was already Friday, 28 April, and time was running short before the crucial Foreign Ministers' meeting on 11th May. Schuman was just leaving for a weekend at Scy-Chazelles.

He asked me to think about it and to find out discreetly the opportunities for the French steel industry in such an enterprise, and also the risks which it would run, while reserving for himself the task of weighing the pros and cons of the purely political aspects of the affair. The following Monday I was waiting for him at the Gare de l'Est with an impatience which it is easy to guess. I had gone there alone, for since absolute secrecy was imperative, no one else knew anything about the matter. Returning to the Quai d'Orsay, and in reply to the question which was burning my lips, he answered simply: It's yes. Then we exchanged the thoughts which we had had about it during the preceding days.[12]

The document which Monnet had submitted to Schuman was essentially the same as that which Schuman read a few days later, on the 9 May, to the Cabinet. It was written in the form of a draft for publication by the French Government. It began by pointing out the need for 'creative efforts on the level of the dangers which menace the peace of the world', and that in maintaining peace the contribution of Europe was essential. Immediately after this came a statement of the main political objective—'to this end Europe must be organised on a federal basis'. (This statement Schuman underlined as he did the two later references to the federal objective.) But before the step could be taken 'the age-old opposition of France and Germany has to be eliminated'. There followed a statement about the policy towards Germany, which was omitted from the final declaration, to the effect that her re-unification by peaceful means was a necessity, that the Government would use every endeavour to promote it, and that she ought immediately to be accepted on a basis of equality in the Council of Europe and the OEEC.

Obstacles which have mounted up prevent the immediate realisation of this close association of the peoples of Europe which the French Government takes on as its objective (a phrase which Schuman underlined). The way to overcome them is to direct action immediately on a limited but decisive point: putting in common the products of coal and steel would assure at once the establishment of common bases for economic growth, the first stage of the European Federation, and would change the destiny of those regions which have been for a long time devoted to the manufacture of the weapons of war, of which they have been the most frequent victims.

The French Government proposes to place the totality of the Franco-German production of coal and steel under a common High Authority, in an organisation open to the participation of the other countries of Europe.

The unity of production, which will thus be tied together, will demonstrate that any war between France and Germany will become not only unthinkable but materially impossible.

The establishment of this powerful unit of production, open to all those countries who will wish to take part in it, with the object of providing [them] ... with the basic elements of production on the same conditions, will lay the foundations of their economic unification ...In this way there can be realised simply and rapidly the fusion of interests essential for establishing an economic community, and for bringing to bear the leavening influence of a larger and deeper community on countries which have been divided one from another by centuries of bloodshed and strife.

The document goes on to list the immediate fields of action of the High Authority: 'the modernisation of production and the improvement of its quality; providing coal and steel on exactly the same conditions to buyers in France and Germany and in the other signatory countries; equalising living-standards and working conditions in the industries concerned'. Various proposals were presented for bringing this about in view of the very different circumstances in these countries, such as arrangements for equalising prices and a plan for investment and for the rationalisation of production. There followed a sentence which Schuman marked: 'As opposed to an international cartel for dividing up and exploiting national markets in order to maintain high profits by means of restrictive practices, the projected organisation will ensure the fusion of markets and the expansion of production'.

The memorandum ended by stating that a treaty should be signed by the states accepting these essential principles and commitments, and the method of drawing it up was proposed. The High Authority should be composed of representatives on a basis of parity, presided over by someone agreed upon by the participants, and its decisions should be mandatory in the countries concerned. A method of revision by appeal to the International Court, and a few other points, were briefly touched upon before 'the essential political issue' was once again brought forward in the concluding sentence: 'by putting basic products in common and by setting up a new High Authority whose decisions will be accepted by France, Germany and the other signatory countries, the first concrete conditions will be achieved for a European federation which is essential for the preservation of peace'.[13]

On the day of Schuman's return to Paris (Monday 1 May), Monnet had another memorandum ready for him, indicating some of the implications and the strategy of the plan which he had proposed. In the perspective of the cold war and the attendant dangers, 'the course of events must be changed, and to that end the mentality of men must be changed'. ('Il faut *changer l'esprit des hommes*'—Schuman underlined these words.) The kind of action needed should go to the deepest levels, and should be speedy and dramatic—something which would bring about an immediate change and make possible the realisation of hopes which people were on the point of abandoning. It should give the Germans new hope for the future and bring them into co-operation with the free peoples ('*collaboration*'—again Schuman underlined the word).

If the German situation was not dealt with in this way it would swiftly become a cancer for peace, but it could not be so dealt with unless the conditions in which action had to be taken were changed—'a dynamic action must be undertaken which transforms the German situation and the mentality of the Germans, instead of looking for a static settlement on the basis of the existing conditions'.[14]

At a lunch with Monnet which took place during this first week of May, Schuman agreed that the new plan had to be launched in a sudden and dramatic way. Monnet placed all his confidence in Schuman, whom he had got to know as Minister of Finance, though since those days their paths had not crossed much. He had a high regard for him, and knew him to be sound, honest and persistent—a good man, with moral fibre, who was also shrewd.[15] It was a warm day, and almost as if to underline the unconventional approach which the two men were plotting, Monnet removed his jacket and invited Schuman to do the same—which Schuman did, after protesting that it was not the done thing for the Foreign Minister to be seen in public in his shirt-sleeves, especially as he was wearing braces.

Monnet assured Schuman that he, as a man of known integrity, was in a unique position to pull off a great act of statesmanship, and give the lie to the *malentendus* and accusations of machiavellianism which might have been current in the case of other sponsors of such a plan.[16] But since the element of surprise was essential, both to give a salutary shock to public opinion and to escape those criticisms which might have nipped the plan in the bud before it even came before the cabinet, it was agreed that practically no one was to be told about it before the cabinet meeting the following Tuesday, 9 May. Two Ministers only were informed, René Pleven and René Mayer, who took part in preparing the declaration for the Plan—the one being Minister of Finance and the other of Justice (Garde des Sceaux), while the Prime Minister was told in general terms what was in the wind. Bidault dismissed the project as 'a soap bubble—just one more international body'.[17]

By chance it became possible to broach the plan personally to Dean Acheson shortly before the declaration was made, since he happened to be spending Sunday, 7 May, in Paris on his way to the London Conference. Acheson's immediate reaction was that the Plan might make possible the creation of a gigantic cartel, controlling all the basic sectors of industrial society, which went right against Allied policy, since one of its objects in Germany had been to demolish cartels. Schuman, however, brushed these objections aside, insisting that the main point of the proposals was political, to build the unity of Western Europe, and that as this unity was achieved national rivalries would be brought to an end, and Europe would enter a new and immensely productive era. 'As he talked, we caught his enthusiasm, and the breadth of his thought, the rebirth of Europe which, as an entity, had been in eclipse since the Reformation'.[18] A further session which Acheson had with Monnet and J. J. McCloy, the American High Commissioner to the Federal Republic ('whom Monnet had brought into the cabal', according to Acheson, 'to put some of Monnet's vagueness into political institutions of a sort'), was convincing. Acheson's warm and sustained backing of the scheme was to bring the support of the American Government, which was essential if the plan was to succeed, notably in respect of the ways in which it affected Germany.

Schuman was glad of this opportunity to alert his American colleague on a top-secret level (no word was to be dropped, no telegram sent), and prepare the ground with him for discussing the proposals formally in the forthcoming London meeting. But the government whose support it was absolutely essential to obtain beforehand was that of the Federal Republic. This meant, in effect, the support of Adenauer, and to him Schuman despatched one of his staff, M. Mislich, on the night before the cabinet meeting in Paris was due.

This was to take place on the 9th. Monnet and his team, now

including Jacques Gascuel, Editor of *Perspectives*,[19] worked out the final version of the Declaration. Three sentences and part of another were excised, of which the first, coming near the beginning of the original document, had made the point very bluntly that 'Europe must be organised on a federal basis'. The last of the omitted sentences had repeated this in a slightly different way in referring to the realisation 'of this close association of the peoples of Europe which the French Government takes as its objective'.

This omission had the effect of switching the emphasis away from the political objective of federation and directing attention rather more to the economic aims and methods which were proposed. The two later references to federation were left as they stood in the original document, but were couched in terms which—in comparison with the first omitted sentence—were tentative. The other sentence omitted concerned the peaceful realisation of German unity and the way in which it should be pursued. The new sentences read: 'In taking on the role during the last twenty years of the champion of European unity, France has always had peace as the essential aim to be pursued. But Europe has not been made, and we have had war. Europe will not make herself all at once, nor by an overall arrangement (*ni dans une construction d'ensemble*); she will make herself by concrete achievements, creating first of all a real unity (*une solidité de fait*)'.

Apart from these changes, practically the only other alteration was the transposition of some of the paragraphs. The document however had to be typed all over again at the last moment, when Monnet decided that another sentence was needed concerning the way in which an economically unified Europe could 'fulfil one of its essential tasks, the development of the African continent'.[20] Some sentences were added at the end,[21] to indicate to doubters that what was left of France's position vis-à-vis Germany would not be jettisoned before the new arrangements took effect: 'The institution of the High Authority in no respect prejudices the rights of property of the enterprises concerned. In the exercise of its mission, the common High Authority will take into account the powers conferred on the International Authority for the Ruhr and of the obligations of all kinds imposed on Germany, insofar as they subsist'.

On the morning of Tuesday 9 May the fateful meeting of the

Council of Ministers took place. Monnet and his colleagues were wondering whether Schuman would manage to insert the project into a crowded agenda, and there was a moment of suspense when the sitting was adjourned at 11 o'clock. The pause was apparently requested so that Schuman could have by telephone Adenauer's response to the proposals. This was not in doubt. It answered entirely, as Adenauer later said, to the ideas which he had held for a long time in regard to the key industries of Western Europe— the Plan was 'a magnanimous step . . . of extraordinary importance for the peace of Europe and of the entire world'.[22] The only condition he wished to make was that German approval of the Plan did not imply recognition of the autonomy of the Saar.[23]

After the break, Schuman read the proposal for the Plan to the Cabinet. His voice, always flat and unemotional, gave the impression that he was handling a matter of routine, rather than something of unique importance. Most ministers apparently failed to grasp its significance, not realising its scope. Bidault did not like the scheme, but the forceful backing of René Mayer won the day. 'You were like a torrent', President Vincent Auriol said to him afterwards.[24] It was with the utmost relief that Monnet and his associates, who had all the morning been glued to the telephone, heard the news.

REFERENCES

[1] Elgey, 422.

[2] Adenauer: *Erinnerungen*, I, 297–299.

[3] Rochefort, 260; Gerbet, 537.

[4] Rochefort, 262.

[5] Ibid., 265.

[6] Gerbet, 545.

[7] Rochefort, 261.

[8] Elgey, 442.

[9] Rochefort, 264.

[10] Elgey, 444.

[11] Statement of M. Falaize and note by 'R.M.' in *Figaro*, 20.6.68.

[12] *France-Forum*, September 1967.

[13] Memorandum marked 'Confidentiel et personnel, J.M.', 28.4.50. (Private collection.)

[14] Memorandum of Monnet, 1.5.50 (ibid.).

[15] Monnet to author.

[16] Merry and Serge Bromberger: *Les Coulisses de l'Europe* (Paris 1968), 122–3.

[17] Ibid., 124.

[18] Dean Acheson: *Sketches from Life* (London 1961), 43.

[19] He drew up an introductory 'chapeau', according to Gerbet, 548.

[20] René Mayer had pointed out to Monnet the need for such a reference (Gerbet, 545).

[21] They appear in the version given to the press, as reprinted in Gerbet, 548, though not in the Declaration as printed in Schuman: *Pour l'Europe*, 201–9.

[22] *News Chronicle*, 10.5.50.

[23] Bromberger, 125.

[24] Rochefort, 275.

11

The British Reaction

Meanwhile Dean Acheson had come to London for talks with Bevin preliminary to the meeting of the NATO Council on 11 May 1950. He had an uncomfortable time waiting, bound to the secrecy he had promised Schuman, after a message came on the 9th from the French Ambassador, Massigli, to Bevin, asking for an interview about an important matter. This interview took place shortly before Schuman's press conference announcing the Plan. When Acheson saw Bevin, 'he was in a towering rage, and at once charged that I had known Schuman's plan and kept it from him.... He rushed on to accuse me of having conspired with Schuman to create a European combination against British trade with the Continent.... He bristled with hostility to Schuman's whole idea'.[1]

These initial difficulties were smoothed over. Bevin was, physically, in bad shape. His heart had been troubling him, he had recently had an operation and was dependent on pain-killing drugs which made concentration difficult and frequently sent him off into a doze. He was in no state to grasp generously at another opportunity and exploit its creative possibilities. Other times, other circumstances, he might have done so, as he was an internationalist by conviction, a strong supporter of the federal idea in the days of his trade union leadership, and a man who normally took his decisions with much circumspection, and with insight derived from long acquaintance with trade union leaders and their movements in other lands. But now, as Acheson said, 'anger was added to bad judgment to ensure the triumph of the latter'.[2]

Acheson's view was that with a different strategy the result might have been otherwise. If he had persuaded Schuman, on the previous Sunday in Paris, to let Bevin into the secret before the declaration of the Plan on the 9th, all might have been well. He might have persuaded Bevin—and Attlee would have followed suit

102

—to consider the Plan in a more generous spirit, so that the follow-up by Monnet and Hirsch, who came over to London on the 14th, would have had a good chance of completing the conversion. As it was, the attitudes which already existed only hardened.

In this view Acheson was postulating circumstances which did not exist. Schuman was bound to adopt a conspiratorial attitude in launching the Plan, since little confidence existed between the various groups composing the coalition cabinet in France. Shock tactics were, in his view, of cardinal importance. Only so could the Plan be passed through the cabinet with general approval, or at least with lack of opposition, before potentially hostile colleagues both there and at the Quai d'Orsay had time to take up a negative position. Secrecy was therefore essential, and fear of a possible leak impelled Schuman to impose silence on Acheson.

Secondly, in Schuman's view, the essence of the Plan lay in France securing a new relationship with Germany. For this reason he could send a special emissary to Bonn on the eve of the Declaration, whereas he could not trust Acheson to be, as it were, his emissary to Bevin. Once the crucial element of German adhesion had been secured, other countries, notably Britain, could come in. But this was something of a bonus, which could not in any case be obtained if the agreement with Adenauer was jeopardised.

On this issue Schuman's attitude was, in effect, more strictly continental than that of Monnet. Monnet's strong Anglo-American connections gave him a wider vision, embracing an area much larger than that of Charlemagne's empire.

On the British side it was precisely this lack of vision that was to blame. Britain's leaders had spoken—sometimes they were still capable of speaking—the language of a Western Europe where the barriers of tariffs and other forms of discrimination were abandoned, and a new co-operative structure substituted for the old. Attlee himself had said in 1939: 'There must be recognition of an international authority superior to the individual states and endowed not only with rights over them but with power to make them effective, operating not only in the political but the economic sphere. Europe must federate or perish'.[3] Bevin too, in meeting after meeting of the pre-war T.U.C., had obtained majority votes for resolutions 'to further, through the international organisations, a policy having for its object the creation of a European public opinion in favour of Europe becoming an economic entity'—and so transform the Europe of the states into a United States of Europe.[4]

But for these leaders the main preoccupations, since their assumption of power in 1945, had been to keep Britain's economy moving despite traumatic shocks such as the cutting-off of lend-lease in 1945 and the crippling winter which followed, and at the same time to translate into reality at least some of the socialist doctrine which had been their stock-in-trade for so long. This, they felt, was their real achievement—using the war-time machinery of controls to strengthen the economy while maintaining and developing the war's legacy of 'fair shares' and planning. Further, they had initiated a system of West European co-operation organised through the OEEC and the Brussels Treaty. A third major element in Labour thinking was the economic importance of the Commonwealth, with the countries of which a network of trading agreements and preferential tariff arrangements (growing out of the Ottawa Conference of 1932)[5] were set within the great regulating mechanism of the Sterling Area.

Britain as the leader in an inter-governmental system, symbolised by her chairmanship of the executive committee of the OEEC, could see little advantage in a seemingly more restricted role in a supranational body. The official view was that the habit of co-operation among the West European states, secured by the pressure of circumstances and the encouragement of the USA, would lead on to an ever closer form of 'Western Union', of which both the concept and practice, in Labour's view, were largely their own achievement, and particularly that of Ernest Bevin.

This view could certainly be justified, and if 'European' institutions with a supranational element were later to function as well as they did, it was in large measure because of the habit of co-operation established in OEEC and the other inter-governmental agencies. The Brussels Treaty did in fact mark a new departure as a possible 'political nucleus', as Labour's 'Feet on the Ground' policy statement pointed out, with its 'functional organs' through which policy in many fields was integrated,[6] these fields extending into economic, and (it was hoped) social and cultural areas, as well as those concerned with foreign policy and defence. But as regards supranational institutions, there was the fear of losing control in shaping policies which could build socialism in Britain. Inter-governmental planning should go further—'the rapid extension of economic planning under Western Union offers the best, perhaps the only chance of solving the German problem'[7]—but, in the Labour view, there could be no question of 'a group of international civil servants without executive responsibility' deciding on the allocation of resources or the regulation of industries within state boundaries. For the same reason projects such as a customs union were chimerical. Apart from removing fiscal control from governments, which was needed by socialists in order to 'organise socialism in countries where they were a majority',[8] it would merely open the way for uncontrolled capitalism to flood 'the more provident planned economies' with 'luxury goods from scents to china-dogs'.[9]

The sense of being different in so many ways from her continental neighbours had been accentuated by Britain's war-time experience. As André Siegfried wrote at the time: 'The Island, having not known the occupation, did not react like the continent; it was scarcely as if she considered herself as fully having a part in the European system'.[10] Britain could still regard herself as a great power, in distinction to her former continental rivals, and her leaders could still claim to conduct affairs (at least when the Commonwealth was involved) on a basis of parity with the USA.

Labour's follow-up to 'Feet on the Ground' was 'European Unity' written immediately after the Schuman Declaration by Hugh Dalton, a Minister of State and former Chancellor of the Exchequer. Many of the same points were made more crudely: 'The Labour Party could never accept any commitments which limited its own or others' freedom to pursue democratic socialism, and to apply the economic controls necessary to achieve it'. Dalton arrogated to himself the right to speak for *all* Socialists in this vein, despite the fact that many on the continent came swiftly to support the Schuman Plan. 'No Socialist Party', he asserted, 'with the prospect of forming a government, could accept a system by which important fields of national policy were surrendered to a supranational European representative authority, since such an authority would have a permanent anti-Socialist majority and would rouse the hostility of European workers'.

The ineffable ignorance shown by this former economist and

Chancellor of the Exchequer of the convictions of continental Socialists and the welfare approach of governmental parties such as the M.R.P. in France ('more left-wing than the Labour Party')[12] was enough to make colleagues across the Channel gasp. Insular conceit was never shown to worse advantage than when, in this pamphlet and at the Council of Europe's Assembly later in the year, Dalton lectured the continentals on Britain's success in maintaining full employment. 'We in Britain', he said, 'had kept our unemployment percentage below 2 per cent since 1946, but some members of the Council of Europe had more than 10 per cent unemployed'[13]—forgetting, as *The Economist* shrewdly pointed out, that this happy achievement was not due to 'the successful application of socialist principles in Britain, but the successful working of capitalism in America'.[14]

Dalton was one of those characterised as 'the gentle and easygoing British Labour leaders', who 'would have been shocked to be called "national socialists;" but they were in truth incapable of imagining the two adjectives apart'.[15] On the European issue, Dalton could claim to speak for the Government front bench. 'Bevin, Cripps and I were all definitely anti-Federal', he wrote later. 'We were determined not to allow interference by a European Committee with our full employment policy, our social services, our nationalised industries or our national planning'.[16] As for the continentals, let them 'take the Federal road to Europe ... and good luck to them!' Britain would work with them only by the inter-governmental methods of the OEEC and the European Payments Union—organisations in which the supranational element had been entirely emasculated thanks to Britain's attitude—since possessing the veto she felt free to effect 'compromises' in her own interest.[17]

The effect of these so-called compromises was plain. The Council of Europe had been altered into a feeble caricature of the federal body desired by the 'Europeans'; Britain had rigidly and successfully opposed the American-backed efforts of the OEEC to operate as a supranational authority capable of planning for all the member countries as an economic entity; Britain had deadlocked for five months the creation of the European Payments Union until her sole control of sterling as a reserve currency was placed beyond dispute; the ECE Commission for reducing tariffs and eventually creating a customs union was perverted into a body for defining tariff nomenclature. Britain only agreed to projects involving the creation of 'community-type' authorities with limited but real powers on conditions which masked proposals based on different premises; as for instance when the OEEC proposal for a transport pool was changed into a European conference of the Ministers of Transport.[18]

The tactics applied by Schuman and Monnet were astutely designed to prevent this type of manoeuvre on Britain's part when it came to launching their Plan. All countries which wished to participate in the coal and steel pool were required to agree in advance to the principle of setting up a supranational authority for its administration. In the face of polite but determined requests by the French Government for a definite yes-or-no answer on this point, the British hesitated, prevaricated, and tried to avoid being pinned down.

The feeling in Government circles was that the French were trying one more desperate manoeuvre to escape from the awkward situation in which they found themselves vis-à-vis the Germans, and that the Plan which they proposed had only a marginal chance of success. It was also felt that the French were not trying really seriously to get the British in—that they had 'consciously adopted a procedure . . . which they knew would be unacceptable in London.'[19] This explains 'the curiously offhand way' in which the proposals were handled in London, and their relegation to a group of officials who were more concerned with their economic than political implications. Of these officials, Sir Edwin (later Lord) Plowden, the Chief Planning Officer, had already shown himself doubtful of the value for Britain of closer co-operation with the continental countries, and in fact a good case could be made that it was only the continental countries who had much to gain from it. Yet the decision was made on political grounds, hinging on Britain's position as a world-power which could not afford to involve itself—certainly not to the point of abandoning any sovereignty—with a group of continental neighbours.

The fact that both Bevin and Cripps were ailing and Attlee had shrunk into 'a sphinx without a secret', meant that a large measure of responsibility for the negotiations fell on the officials concerned and on the junior Minister, Kenneth Younger, deputising for Bevin. This made no difference to the outcome. Younger pressed for British participation in the Schuman Plan Conference while remaining sceptical as to its relevance to Britain's needs. 'Europe could offer Britain little economically; politically what mattered were NATO and OEEC and US participation in European affairs, on which the French outlook already diverged from Britain's ... The expressed aim of a European federation obviously raised fundamental questions about Britain's relations with the Commonwealth, which was just entering upon a major transformation following the independence of India only a couple of years earlier.'[20] He believed that if Britain declined the conference, and if the latter then failed, Britain might have incurred responsibility for missing an opportunity for ending Franco-German hostility. He repelled the cynical view that Britain should enter in order to sabotage the supranational aspects of the Plan.

In the event it was not only the Government, but British opinion generally which concluded that Britain could not enter negotiations on the terms proposed by France. The exchanges between the French and British Governments ran a predictable course. By 27 May the British Government was obliged to state that 'if the French Government intend to insist on a commitment to pool resources and set up an authority with certain sovereign powers as a prior condition to joining in the talks, His Majesty's Government would reluctantly be unable to accept such a condition'.[21] The Government held out for a meeting at ministerial level first, to discuss the principle of the Plan, but since such discussions were unacceptable to the French an air of unreality hung over the subsequent exchanges.

Equally unacceptable was the British view to the effect that, as the proposed pool was primarily a Franco-German affair, they might attend the conference as observers. Following what was virtually an ultimatum demanding a straight answer from the British, the French Government cut further exchanges short on 3 June, still hoping (as they said) that 'the British Government ... may find it possible to join or associate themselves with the common effort at the time when they judge it to be possible'.[22] *The Times* welcomed the outcome as inevitable. 'The British Government were entirely right in declining to undertake this prior commitment', it wrote. '... Few international conferences could open on the basis of prior commitment, and certainly no British Government could accept in advance a plan requiring the yielding of sovereignty to the extent of placing the country's coal and steel resources—its very sinews—at the discretion of an international authority'.[23] *The Economist*, while characterising Britain's refusal as 'the upshot of as sorry a piece of diplomatic muddling as the world has ever seen', agreed that the terms for her participation were too steep. 'They were invited to surrender a portion of their national sovereignty to a body whose composition was undecided and whose purposes were unelucidated, and they were invited to do so from one day to the next. Not unnaturally they objected'.[24]

In fact, *The Economist* professed to see an *arrière-pensée* inspiring the French Government's 'bouncing tactics': the French passionately wanted Britain to take part in the scheme, but not in the negotiations. 'They have had plenty of experience in recent years of Britain's skill in deferring and emasculating projects that have been accepted in principle'. The fact of the Labour Party issuing Dalton's 'European Unity' the day before the White Paper refusing participation was regarded as evidence to support the view generally held on the Continent, as well as in the USA, 'that the British Government's desire is to sabotage any moves towards European economic unity under cover of accepting them in principle . . . World opinion believes that Labour Ministers approach all these matters . . . like inverted Micawbers waiting for something to turn down'.[25]

Dalton's paper in fact did not affect the negotiations, as it came out after the exchanges had been completed, but it indicated a state of mind common to many members of the Government and the Labour Party. The view expressed by John Strachey, Minister of War, when he said that the Schuman Plan was a plot, which 'under the guise of internationalism' was designed 'to prevent the people really controlling their economic system',[26] echoed that of Bevin on his first reaction to the Schuman Plan. A lurking feeling persisted among certain elements of the Labour Party that the Plan and the communities which it foreshadowed were the product of capitalist-clerical circles on the continent whose conspiratorial activities would make the realisation of socialism impossible.

That the tactics adopted by Schuman and Monnet were designed not merely to force Britain to clarify her position from the beginning on the main point at issue in the proposed Plan, but actually to exclude her from the negotiations is unlikely. Opinion in France gauged accurately, from the beginning, the probable British response, that it would be a refusal of the French negotiating terms.[27] Whatever may have been the unspoken (or unpublished) thoughts of Monnet and his brains-trust, it is unlikely that Schuman himself, preoccupied as he was with the effect of the proposals on Germany, would have given too much thought to their probable impact on Britain. On the matter of the failure of the Anglo-French negotiations Bevin wrote Schuman a letter whose sentiments he certainly reciprocated. 'I am sorry that we could not get together over the basis of approach to the French coal and steel plan', he said. 'I know that you appreciate the reason which led us to take the view we did and I am sure that neither of us will allow the difference of approach on this issue to affect our mutual understanding and friendship'.[28] Bevin was right: Schuman's esteem for him remained undimmed, despite their disagreement over the Plan. Schuman realised that whereas European integration might receive Britain's blessing, 'only the constraint of events seems capable of forcing her adhesion'.[29]

Commenting on these events some years after, Schuman attributed Britain's refusal to psychological rather than political or economic factors.

'I have always in my mind's eye the face of my friend Ernest Bevin', he said later, 'who at that time spoke in the name of the British Government. It seemed to him impossible, unthinkable, that for an Englishman, for an English government, there could exist an authority superior to the English Parliament. No argument could shake this position, and not in consequence of a kind of obstinacy—the Englishman is capable of a great deal of empirical subtlety—but of logical reasoning: an English government could not grant to a European body more authority than the institutions of the Commonwealth, it could not be imagined that one could endow the European organs with supranational authority. For the Englishman primacy belongs to the Commonwealth, not only historically but as a matter of sentiment. That must be understood. At the start we didn't grasp that, and for that reason we were under the illusion that England could join in fully ... England knows how to keep her distance in everything. Without isolating herself, she observes. There is no country in the world more touchy when it comes to maintaining the inviolability of the home. Every violation of domicile, every interference, every indiscretion, is regarded with horror. A plan of integration seems to the Englishman like a violation of domicile, a very grave indiscretion'.[30]

At the time, and during the later debate in Parliament, Churchill and the Conservatives showed themselves zealous champions for participating in the conference of the six states which accepted the principles of the Schuman Plan, with a reservation similar to that made by the Dutch: 'in view of the fact that this text involves the acceptance of certain principles underlying the French Government's memorandum, the Netherlands Government feels obliged to reserve its right to go back on the acceptance of these principles in the course of the negotiations in the event of their proving impossible to translate into practice'. Nevertheless it is doubtful whether they, any more than the bulk of the Labour Party, were eager to bind an important area of the British economy to that of the continental states in the way the French proposed. As for the larger objective of European federation, most Conservatives agreed with Churchill that Britain could not 'be an ordinary member of a federal union limited to Europe in any period which at present can be foreseen ... Although a hard-and-fast concrete federal constitution for Europe is not within the scope of practical affairs, we should help, sponsor and aid in every possible way the movement towards European unity. We should seek steadfastly for means to become intimately associated with it'.[31] Britain's world role precluded, in his view, membership of a continental federation which might be exclusive in character. Western Europe was but one of the three 'circles' which Britain had to bring into closer mutual relations, the other two being the Commonwealth and the Atlantic community.

Churchill's vision was lofty, but the practice of the Conservatives, once they were again in office (October 1951), was not strikingly different from that of their Labour colleagues. Churchill might refer to the European Unity pamphlet as 'Dalton's Brown Paper', but (apart from its tone of doctrinaire socialism) there was little in its conclusions with which the Conservatives disagreed. Nor could they disagree fundamentally with Cripps, who, in the debate of 26 June 1950, quoted the French government's statement[32] that the proposals would 'build the first concrete foundation

111

of the European federation', and commented: 'this approach involves the other partners in the scheme not only in commitments in regard to the future political framework for Europe. In our view, participation in a political federation, limited to Western Europe, is not compatible either with our Commonwealth ties, our obligations as a member of the wider Atlantic community, or as a world Power'.[33]

It is a question whether this was the main consideration, or whether it was the more parochial one summed up by the backbencher who demanded that 'no supranational authority will be allowed to interfere with the Socialist Government's planning for full employment'.[34] Harold Macmillan later expressed much the same view: 'One thing is certain, and we may as well face it. Our people will not hand over to any supranational Authority the right to close down our pits or our steel-works'.[35]

In the welter of thinking on the subject there was one point which might be held to have more validity than others, that European integration might prove a weapon in the hands of those who wished to build a 'third force' standing between the USA and Russia. This conception to most British statesmen was unrealistic and fraught with danger, particularly that of driving America back to her hemisphere, so leaving Europe—and inevitably Britain also —a prey to possible Communist aggression.[36]

REFERENCES

[1] Dean Acheson: *Sketches from Life*, 42–3.
[2] Acheson: *Present at the Creation* (*op. cit.*), 385.
[3] R. W. G. Mackay: *Heads in the Sand* (Oxford, 1950), v.
[4] Nora Beloff *The General says No* (London, 1963), 52.
[5] See above, p. 12.
[6] 'Feet on the Ground' (see above, p. 104), 17. For the Brussels Treaty, see p. 104.
[7] Ibid., 19.
[8] Ibid., 20.
[9] Ibid., 13.
[10] *Année Politique*, 1950, xiii.
[11] 'European Unity, a statement by the National Executive Committee of the British Labour Party' (May, 1950), 8.
[12] R. W. G. Mackay: *op. cit.*, 19.
[13] Hugh Dalton: *High Tide and After—Memoirs 1945–1960* (London, 1962), 327.
[14] *The Economist*, 17 June 1950, p. 1314.
[15] Nora Beloff, *op. cit.*, 92.

[16] Hugh Dalton, *op, cit.*, 334.

[17] 'European Unity', 10.

[18] A. Albonetti: *Préhistoire des Etats-Unis de l'Europe* (Paris, 1963), 86.

[19] *International Affairs*, January 1967, 25 (Kenneth Younger).

[20] Ibid., 27.

[21] Cmd. 7970 (1950), Doc. 8.

[22] Cmd. 7970, (3.6.50), Doc. 17.

[23] 5.6.50.

[24] 10.6.50.

[25] *The Economist*, 10.6.50.

[26] *The Times*, 6.7.50.

[27] *New York Herald Tribune*, 10.5.50.

[28] 6.6.50 (Private collection).

[29] *Pour l'Europe*, 115.

[30] Ibid., 115–118.

[31] 27.6.50. *Hansard*, Vol. 476, col. 2157.

[32] Cmd. 7970 (1950), Doc. 2.

[33] *Hansard*, vol. 476, col. 1947–8.

[34] Harold Davies, *Hansard*, vol. 476, col. 38, 13.5.50.

[35] *Reports of Council of Europe Consultative Assembly* (Strasbourg, 1950), 7–28 August 1950, 434. Quoted in U. W. Kitzinger: *The Challenge of the Common Market* (Blackwell, 1962), 10.

[36] 'European Unity', 9. See also *Foreign Affairs,* January 1951; D. H. McLachlan: *Rearmament and European Integration,* 284. The last five paragraphs of this chapter and the first one of the next are re-printed from R. C. Mowat: *Ruin and Resurgence* (London, 1965), 227–8.

12

The Negotiations of the Six

British production of coal in 1950 was half that of Europe as a whole, and of steel about one-third. Britain's refusal to participate in the European Coal and Steel Community was therefore a serious blow to its creators, but they wasted no time before pressing on towards their goal, necessarily restricted though it now appeared. On 3 June 1950 the 'Six' (France, Germany, Italy, Belgium, the Netherlands, Luxembourg) announced their decision to work towards the pooling of their coal and steel industries under a High Authority whose decisions would be binding. On the 20th conferences began between delegations from the Six, in which the participants decided to work as experts without committing their governments, and by March of the following year (1951) a draft agreement was initialled by the delegations, ready to be presented to the governments for ratification.

This stage was not reached without much intensive discussion and give-and-take among the delegations. A French draft somewhat elaborating the orginal proposals was all they had to work on. Monnet, who presided over the negotiations, worked by the same methods which had proved so successful in the Commission of the Plan for Modernisation in France. Bargaining and horse-trading were reduced to a minimum; instead of these traditional methods of diplomatic negotiations the debates assumed the character of 'construction in common'.[1] It was a striking application of the new style of leadership which Monnet shared with men like Schuman and Acheson. As Schuman said, 'peace is not solely the absence of war, but the achievement of common objectives, of peaceful tasks undertaken together ... For the first time there was no discrimination between Germany and her former enemies and victims, neither in the negotiations nor in the execution. France alone was able to make this gesture ...'[2] Monnet led the negotiations, not as a Frenchman upholding the interests of France and haggling over advantages for her; his aim all the time was 'to define the general interest of the community the negotiators were establishing together'.[3] In fact they were not negotiations in the traditional sense at all. Monnet created a new climate in which 'the delegations, seated around the same table, worked together with the intention of building together a supranational edifice, in which national interests could meet and merge. In the place of particularistic narrowness there was a real spirit of a team—a spirit of co-operation and mutual understanding. This change of climate in itself marked a great step forward'.[4]

Monnet contrived, during the nine months of negotiations which turned the Declaration of 9 May into a treaty of a hundred articles and a number of annexes, to keep in view all the time the central objective of a European Community, and the proposed method of delegating power to common institutions. He saw to it that these aims were not lost 'in the mass of details about coal, steel, scrap, transport, wages, cartels, distortions and discriminations'.[5] In dealing with such details he was assisted by a drafting team which, in addition to his own brains-trust, at one time was reinforced by André Philip and the steel experts, Tony Rollman and Philippe de Sellières. In deciding on the general outlines of the new community the views of the governments concerned had to be considered, though it was understood that those participating in the conference would regard themselves as producing a draft which would not commit the governments. Where influence at the highest governmental level counted was in decisions such as that which set up the Council of Ministers, resulting from the demand of the Belgian and Dutch governments for an inter-governmental body with powers to review the proposals of the High Authority.[6]

Monnet himself wanted a body to play a parliamentary role. In the event the body that was set up might be regarded as analogous to a shareholders' meeting rather than to a parliament, since the only sanction available to the Common Assembly (as this body was called) was to dismiss the entire membership of the High Authority in cases where it might reject the Authority's policy.

An important decision was that against regional groupings, since it was realised that these might emphasise national divisions rather than diminish them. Regional groupings could also have given play to powerful vested interests, such as those of the French steel-masters or the Ruhr coal magnates. Schuman, who had so long represented the interests of Lorraine in government circles, spent much time dealing with the employers' organisation, La Chambre Syndicale de la Sidérurgie Française, which sent him a memorandum warning of dangers feared to be inherent in the Plan.

Modernisation of the industry was not sufficiently advanced, it said, while at the same time the programme of modernisation had put such heavy charges on the industry that it had been unable to build up any financial reserves as a cushion against too much competition. It was doubtful, in fact, whether the industry could stand up to the competition which the common market in coal and steel would create. There were grave doubts about the schemes for pricing and harmonisation, but above all about the High Authority itself.

'It is impossible to know in advance', stated the memorandum gloomily, 'what ideological or national orientation would show itself under this designation, what would be the doctrine of this body, or what would be its approach in undertaking its mission. All that one can discover from the texts or the commentaries indicates only that the High Authority is conceived as a 'super-governmental' body, whose designation is a political matter, and in which it does not seem as if competence of an industrial kind will find a place—which leaves one to doubt whether purely industrial needs will have with it all the weight they require'.

Profound and complex studies were necessary before going further, and there should be guarantees that none of the projects coming up for discussion should be damaging to French firms or their employés.

'Therefore', it concluded, 'at a moment when it is a matter of life or death for the French steel concerns, one cannot be surprised that it is impossible to conceive of handing them over, lock, stock and barrel, to an Authority which is for all practical reasons without responsibility, ill-defined, of unknown outlook, administrative and political in character, and which would interfere, with no appeal against its decisions, in order to bring about changes which would be almost always irreversible, in the exercise of a mission necessarily imprecise, and without any legal guarantees for those whose interests could be most gravely harmed'.[7]

Schuman gave the most serious attention to such objections. Much of his time during the ensuing months was spent in

patiently listening to the criticisms and difficulties of the steel industrialists and other interested parties. In his final reply to
M. Aubrun, president of the employers' association of the steel
industry, he said that between 29 December 1950 and 8 February
1951 he had attended eighteen sessions of the ad hoc government
committee dealing with the impact of the proposed arrangements
for coal and steel on French industry, and had listened to the
presidents of all the employers' associations concerned as well as
to the industrialists representing ten groups or companies whose
production totalled 80 per cent of French industry. His last word
on steel 'after these most intensive studies and discussions' was
that under the new scheme it would not be unfavourably placed.[8]

As for the employers' doubts about the powers and potentialities
of the High Authority, these were taken into consideration in the
detailed discussions on the extent of the Authority's powers and
the need to define them, for instance over governments and private
companies. Since such definitions could not cover all cases, the
French proposed a Court of Justice to deal with those which might
be in question.

The question of the German coal interests involved high level
negotiations. Clappier wrote to Schuman in September 1950,
while the latter was in America, that the conversations were proceeding 'in an excellent atmosphere'. At the same time he noted
how the German industrialists were defending their interests with
increasing toughness, as a consequence of the evident economic
and political rehabilitation of their country, though two conversations with Hallstein, the leading German delegate, had convinced
him that Adenauer's intention was unchanged, to bring matters
to a conclusion and to do so speedily.[9]

Nevertheless the difficulties with Germany could not be wished
away and they were brought into relief as a by-product of the
Korean War, which broke out on 25 June 1950. The increasing
urgency of the need which the Americans felt to integrate Germany
into a defensive bloc against the East gave the Germans a further
incentive to be tough. In September 1950 the Americans proposed
that in view of the new threat to the free world, the Germans be
permitted to raise ten divisions as their contribution to the
Atlantic Alliance. If this was accepted, the status which the Federal
Republic could claim as a member of the Alliance would speedily

involve the discarding of almost all the remaining checks on its sovereignty, and it appeared as though the Germans might gain all the freedom from post-war shackles which they wanted without incurring the obligations involved in entry to the Coal and Steel Community.

To allay French doubts that they were linking themselves with a potentially far too powerful Germany, the Americans were obliged to step in. If dismantling was to be stopped, at least the big cartels and industrial concentrations had to be broken up. Particularly the French were afraid that if Germany came in with its great coal-marketing agency intact (the Deutscher Kohlen-Verkauf), the Germans would have too much bargaining power and would not permit them access to Ruhr coke on the terms they wanted.[10] It needed all the efforts of the American High Commissioner in Germany, John J. McCloy, to bring about the necessary changes, but in the end they were accomplished. After several months of intense diplomatic activity, with the unfaltering backing of Chancellor Adenauer, McCloy succeeded in making arrangements which the French could accept, and these were incorporated into the treaty. This was initialled by the delegates on 19 March 1951, and a month later signed by the Foreign Ministers of the Six.

Ratification could have been a lengthy process. In France the opposition was divided: it was anyway difficult to answer Schuman's case, which was so obviously sensible and presented with such clarity and logic. The Socialists had been disappointed and somewhat bewildered by the attitude of British Labour, but André Philip and others of the 'idealist' wing were able to play on the international traditions of the party. The party leader, Guy Mollet, was won to the cause, and the Socialists gave their full backing to the treaty. It was eventually ratified by both Assembly and Council with quite unusual speed, the process being completed by April 1951.

In Germany the Socialist Party, under the leadership of Karl Schumacher, was intractable. He bitterly hated Adenauer and his policies, and mistrusted his strategy for German reunification. But the trade unionists, and particularly Hans Boeckler, their leader in the British Zone, favoured the Plan. These leaders were cultivated by Monnet, who pressed for trade union representation on the national delegations. He had formed excellent relations with the French non-Communist union leaders, and now extended his contacts to those of Germany and other countries. This particularly bore good fruit in the case of Germany, when, with Schumacher's death, the S.D.P came round to accepting the policy of European integration.[11] In the immediate context the decisive fact was the majority of the Christian-Democrats and their allies whom Adenauer could count on for ratification.

With similar speed ratification took place in Italy and the Benelux countries, and all the participants signed the Treaty of Paris on 18 April 1951. It entered into force on 25 September 1952, by which time the High Authority was beginning its work at its Luxembourg headquarters. Six months later, on 10 February 1953 the common market for coal, iron ore and scrap came into operation, and the common market for steel opened on 1 May.

REFERENCES

[1] *Rapport de la Délégation Française* [quoted in W. Diebold: *The Schuman Plan* (New York, 1951), 62].

[2] Extracts from speech, typescript in private collection.

[3] *Daedalus* (Journal of the American Institute of Arts and Sciences), 1964; Max Kohnstamm: *The European Tide*, 88.

[4] *Pour l'Europe*, 169.

[5] Kohnstamm, *op. cit.*, 88.

[6] Diebold, *op. cit.*, 62.

[7] Memorandum of 12.7.50 (Private collection).

[8] Schuman to Aubrun, 31.5.51 (Private collection).

[9] Clappier to Schuman, 25.9.50 (Private collection).

[10] Diebold, *op. cit.*, 73.

[11] Kohnstamm, *op. cit.*, 92.

13

The European Defence Community

While the negotiations following the Declaration of 9 May were just beginning, the opportunity arose for another leap forward.

The Declaration did not dispel the crisis which had arisen over the question of German rearmament. It simply changed its context. The need for swift action on the matter seemed the more urgent with the outbreak of the Korean War on 25 June 1950. If non-Communist Asia was threatened, what about the rest of Europe? Two years before, the rape of Czechoslovakia and the Berlin blockade had sparked off the first moves towards an integrated command and defence structure, to which the USA, Canada and various West European countries adhered by the Atlantic Pact (4 April 1949), thus laying the foundation of NATO.

Even before the outbreak of the Korean War American demands for a German contribution to West European defence were beginning to be heard. As American commitments in Korea increased, and fears arose lest Stalin would start another war in Europe these demands became impossible for the British and French to refuse.

So successful initially had been the Monnet-Schuman move to launch the Coal and Steel Community that the question of European defence seemed to offer the federalists an opportunity that had to be taken. When, with Monnet's aid, a plan for a European Army was devised, in which German units of only battalion strength would be included, its initial reception in the French Parliament in October 1950, when it was accepted in principle, seemed to augur well. The scheme was designed to allay fears—particularly French fears—that another Reichswehr would be created, since there would be no German general staff, only one for the army as a whole. It drew on the wave of idealism for a federal solution which the successful reception of the Schuman Plan had strengthened, since a European Ministry of Defence was envisaged responsible to a European Parliament.

120

In the end the scheme fell through: after being signed by the French Government in May 1952, followed by the governments of Italy, Western Germany, Belgium, Holland and Luxembourg, and ratified by the parliaments of the last four (Italy would have ratified too), it failed to achieve ratification in the French Parliament in a vote on 30 August 1954.

Had the motion been passed the Six would have taken a long step towards a full-scale federation. The set-back for the federalists was great. Yet it prepared the way for the strengthening of Europe by the alternative means of bringing Germany into NATO, and for relaunching the drive towards a six-nation federation by the more modestly functional approach of the Economic Community. This made Britain's eventual adherence possible, since she could not have entered a federation as fully developed as that of the European Defence Community.

Failure was virtually built in from the start, due to the fact that the scheme was not matured so long and carefully as that of the ECSC. The plan which Monnet passed on to the then Prime Minister, René Pleven, in October 1950, was a hastily improvised affair, a sickly infant which had not enjoyed the favourable gestation of the first-born. During those hectic weeks when the early stages of the Coal and Steel Community had to be negotiated Monnet and his brains-trust had little time or energy to think another exacting project through. Having to spend so much time at Luxembourg later on, as Chairman of the High Authority, meant that he could not be in Paris as much as he would have liked to help the new project through its more critical stages.

Nor did the project pass the Cabinet with the surprising speed of the Schuman Plan. The Socialists in the Cabinet were divided. One of their strongest Ministers, Jules Moch, was opposed to it, though he was persuaded to let it go forward at the time. Later he became one of its most implacable opponents.

This division at the highest level reflected the divisions in the country. Like all such issues in French politics, this had a polarising effect, with Gaullists on the right combining with Communists on the left in a relentless opposition. The main obstacle was reluctance on the part of ordinary Frenchmen to allow a German army to be recreated in any form, even in that of fairly small units scattered among a multi-national force (ultimately too it had to be recognised that no unit smaller than a division was practicable).

To many Frenchmen, and particularly to the followers of de Gaulle, the merging of the army in a European force seemed too great a derogation of sovereignty for a country which had in previous eras dominated Europe so long as a military power. Whereas the Germans, disillusioned with the power-game and chastened by defeat, did not, for the most part want a national army, the French, though defeated in the war, had come out among the victors with a claim to great-power status precariously based on the restoration of the country's military might. The reactions to the project by the French, divided as they were, resembled markedly those of Britain later to the possibility of joining the EEC.

The Communists naturally wanted to keep Western Europe weak, and prepare for the assimilation of France and the other Western countries with the 'peoples' democracies' of the Russian-dominated East. The ideological cross-currents and the propaganda churned out incessantly by the rival camps both favouring the same objective, i.e. the rejection of the European Defence Community——confused the ordinary Frenchman. Something like a paralysis of the will, another phase of *immobilisme,* began to afflict the country. A crisis was arising over Morocco; Tunisia and Algeria were restless; above all the war in Indo-China was dragging on with no clear end in view.

Materially the French were better off, and the rearmament resulting from the Korean War gave a fillip to the economy. This both helped and hindered the negotiations for the ECSC, since the French steelmasters and others were freed from the bogey of becoming uncompetitive under the new dispensation; on the other hand the fear of excess capacity for steel-making also disappeared. The hope of Monnet and the federalists was that the two projects, EDC and ECSC, would help each other—that the sense of a rapid movement towards the federal goal which the EDC promised would lift the ECSC off any shoals on which it might become stuck.

Such calculations were however awry. The ECSC was acceptable because it dealt with only a part, albeit a vital one, of the economy: the sacrifice of sovereignty did not seem too great, and the very use of the word 'pool' in the earlier stages indicated that it was not so much a loss of sovereignty as a pooling of it which was involved. But abandoning control of the national army was another matter.

In any case, despite some hitches and moments of despondency, negotiations for the ECSC went ahead on the basis of a positive search for agreement on ways and means, under the direction of Monnet backed by his personal advisers: to some extent the whole negotiating body drawn from the six countries became Monnet's team. This could not be said of the negotiations for the EDC. Here it was back to the old diplomatic bargaining, not so much the Six among themselves, but France striving to involve Britain, and the USA putting on pressure from behind the scenes.

The protagonists of EDC could make out a case for its failure being due to Britain. If there was something in this it was an argument based on a half-truth, because the initiators of EDC knew that Britain could never come into it. Her attitude had been clear from the beginning: it was consistent with that which she had shown towards all the attempts at integration from the Council of Europe to the OEEC and the Schuman Plan. What misled some continental observers was Churchill's rhetoric, just as it had misled most people at the time of the Zürich speech in 1946. Churchill called for a European federation and for a European army—he only explained later that Britain was *for* these things but could not be *of* them. The fact that he had made such a speech at the Assembly of the Council of Europe on 11 August 1950 fooled many: 'We should make a gesture of practical and constructive guidance by declaring ourselves in favour of the immediate creation of a European army under a unified command, and in which we should bear a worthy and honourable part'. Churchill had been out of office then. On returning to power the following year, October 1951, he needed no persuasion by his younger and more energetic lieutenant, Anthony Eden, who, as Foreign Secretary, decided to carry on the same policy as his Labour predecessors: support for the European projects, but no full participation. This was phrased as the 'closest possible association', but as for joining 'an army forming part of a European federation . . . we could not'.[1]

Britain's refusal of full membership of the Defence Community strengthened the qualms of those Frenchmen who had their doubts about going in themselves. After the initial support for the project in the Assembly, the Government was able to proceed, in 1952, with the five ECSC partners, towards signing a treaty setting up the Community, but from then on no French government had confidence that a majority existed in the Chamber for effecting its ratification.

This faltering by the French was alarming to the Americans. They were eager to strengthen Europe, but only on terms which included a greater effort towards self-defence on the part of the Europeans themselves. When Acheson took up the matter with the Pentagon, the latter refused to commit further forces or equipment to Europe except as part of a new package for 'beefing up' West European defence which would include a German contribution.[2] The EDC, as the 'package' produced by the French, was at first not much to the Americans' liking, but being backed by McCloy, the American High Commissioner in Germany, and by General Eisenhower as NATO Commander-in-Chief designate, American opinion veered towards it. The scheme seemed viable enough for the Americans to plan the development of NATO with a European Army attached to it, including a German element equivalent to ten divisions.

Though the launchers of the project were sincere and were not merely trying to buy time and American support while shilly-shallying about their own arrangements, the EDC project did have precisely this effect. Nothing was actually settled until August 1954 (and then only negatively), but at least the Americans were given sufficient confidence meanwhile to continue supplying the sinews of Western defence. At the same time they became increasingly restless as the negotiations dragged on: they began to over-pressurise the French, especially after Foster Dulles took over from Acheson in September 1951, culminating in Dulles' threat two years later of 'an agonising reappraisal', implying abandoning Europe to her fate while concentrating on attempts to 'roll back' Communist power elsewhere. These pressure tactics produced diminishing returns.

False hopes were raised by Spaak's campaign at the Council of Europe. Convinced by the experience of Belgium's impotence in face of the Nazi threat, Spaak had become a dedicated champion of the federal cause. When the Americans wished to introduce an element of supranationalism into OEEC, they urged him to take on the presidency of it. British obstruction was such, however, that he stayed in that office only briefly, and continued his political career in Belgium (where he had first been a Cabinet Minister in 1935 at the age of 36), until he became President of the Council of Europe in August 1949. In the Council, as Spaak relates, it was a period of intense enthusiasm and great activity when hopes were high that the new Europe could be created by the will of the delegates at Strasbourg. A year later, in 1950, a resolution in the Consultative Assembly of the Council favouring the creation of a European Army was passed by 89 votes to 5 (with 29 abstentions —still a substantial majority)—an army under a European Ministry of Defence which should be subject to proper European democratic control, and acting in co-operation with the USA and Canada.

This preceded by two months the introduction of the Pleven Plan for a European Army by the French Government, and could be taken as strengthening its hand. Then came the delays and hesitations, Britain's habitually negative attitude, and growing frustration at Strasbourg. 'Britain's participation in building Europe was ... derisory' was the sour comment Spaak later made.[3] At one point, in December 1951, he brought together at Strasbourg four of the leaders most closely associated with the European cause, Schuman, Adenauer, De Gasperi, and Van Zeeland of Belgium, so that from the Council's platform public opinion favouring the EDC would be aroused and momentum for achieving it be restored. But the response in the Assembly was modest, and Spaak resigned next day. 'If a quarter of the energy spent here in saying No', he fulminated, 'was used to say Yes to something positive, we should not be in the state we are today'.[4] Back in Brussels as Foreign Minister he thought up a plan for transforming the Common Assembly of the Coal and Steel Community into an *Ad Hoc* Assembly' for drafting the treaty for a European Political Community. Through this the Authority would be created to control the European Army. The other five Foreign Ministers of the Six agreed on this scheme in their capacity, along with Spaak, as members of the ECSC Council of Ministers. In six months (March 1953), the draft treaty was ready, projecting a European Executive Council, a Council of national Ministers, a Court of Justice, and an elected Parliament. All to no avail. With the failure of the EDC Treaty before the French Parliament the whole elaborate project collapsed like a house of cards. Once again the Council of Europe had shown its impotence in undertaking, or even in speeding up, the real work of integration.

When Pierre Mendès-France took over the French premiership in June 1954, he was convinced that there was no majority in the Assembly for ratifying the EDC Treaty as it stood. He was not a committed 'European' of the style of Monnet or Schuman, but he felt it worth trying for additional safeguards as a last chance of getting the treaty through. France's partners were dismayed at the prospect of renegotiating parts of the treaty which they had already ratified, while Britain had already gone as far as she possibly could in guaranteeing a military contribution alongside, if not strictly part, of the European Army. To relieve the French of the bugbear of a possible British desertion such as had occurred (along with the Americans) in 1919, Britain undertook not to withdraw from the continent as long as there was a threat to the security of Western Europe or the EDC, and she pledged herself to incorporate a British armoured division with the EDC forces and arrange for RAF units to participate fully with those of the EDC in NATO. On the political level Britain promised that a Minister would attend meetings of the EDC Council.

Nothing sufficed to stave off the *débacle*. At a final meeting with the representatives of the Six at Brussels on 21 August 1954, Mendès-France told Spaak that the treaty's failure was a foregone conclusion if it were put to a free vote in the Assembly—which would be the case if he did not make it a matter of confidence. This latter he would not do. He had decided to fly straight from Brussels to London and negotiate with Churchill and Eden. Since France had become the odd man out with her partners of the Six, the only alternative was to join forces with Britain in a new approach to the questions of Western defence based on an arrangement with NATO. This became clear in talks which he had with his English hosts at Chartwell on 22–23 August.

Mendès-France accordingly put no pressure on the members of his ill-assorted coalition to support EDC in the crucial vote. Had he done so the result might have simply precipitated the crumbling of his government—and Mendès was intent on solving other problems besides those of European defence. The affair in the Chamber was stage-managed to favour the anti-EDC forces, with the aged ex-Premier Edouard Herriot, formerly a supporter of a 'United

States of Europe', being accorded the major role in giving the project its *coup-de-grâce*. 'Speaking hunched-up on a back bench, too old and heavy to climb the steps to the Speaker's tribune, he seemed the perfect incarnation of the old, immobile forces that have prevented France from adapting itself to the twentieth-century world'.[5] Even so, it was only the 99 Communist votes which secured the project's defeat (the votes of the 'anti-national' party as its opponents called it). On a count of the votes of the 'democratic' parties only, EDC would have got through with a majority of 44.[6]

Before the rejection of EDC Eden had made plans to deal with the situation. He proposed enlarging the Brussels Treaty of 1948[7] by bringing Italy and Germany into it, and turning it into a mutual defence pact. The Americans were backing a NATO solution, and with this preliminary accomplished it would be possible, he thought, to overcome French opposition to bringing Germany into NATO. He at once took off for Brussels, Bonn, Rome and Paris, where he successfully sold the idea. At Paris the discussions were difficult, but eventually Mendès-France agreed that the arguments for Germany's entrance into NATO were decisive.

To help him gain a majority in the Chamber for the new policy Eden pledged Britain to an unprecedented commitment, to maintain on the Continent indefinitely the forces which had been assigned to NATO. A Council of Western European Union was set up to co-ordinate the defence arrangements of the Brussels powers; the occupation of Germany was to end; and a new Statute for 'Europeanising' the Saar was to be negotiated between France and Germany. After another cliff-hanging vote the French Chamber finally ratified the new arrangements (the Paris Agreements), and Germany entered NATO. Though the Atlantic Alliance was saved, the cause of European integration had suffered what seemed at the time a possibly irremediable blow.

REFERENCES

[1] *The Memoirs of Sir Anthony Eden: Full Circle* (London, 1960), 32.
[2] Dean Acheson: *Present at the Creation*, 437.
[3] P.-H. Spaak: *Combats Inachevés* (Paris, 1969), II, 48.
[4] Ibid., 50; Mayne: *The Recovery of Europe*, 169.
[5] *The Scotsman*, 1.9.54 (Nora Beloff).
[6] The voting was 319–264, with 43 abstentions.
[7] See above, p. 28.

14

The Re-launch and the Treaty of Rome

Long before the failure of EDC, steps had been taken which led to the 're-launching' of the European idea, whose vitality was seen in the successful meeting of the Foreign Ministers of the Six at Messina in June 1955. Though the Messina Conference caught the headlines, it would have lacked promise without the careful preparatory work of the Benelux ministers, and particularly of J. W. Beyen, who was joint Foreign Minister of Holland since 1952 along with Joseph Luns, another doughty protagonist of the European idea.

In the division of duties Beyen's sphere was European policy in general. He was well placed to watch over the developments towards economic integration since, even before the war, he had gained much experience in the field of international institutions—he had been on the staff of the Bank of International Settlements, and at the end of the war he had been at the Bretton Woods monetary conference. During the war, in London, he had a share in the negotiations which led to Benelux.

Benelux he regarded as an experiment, something in the nature of a gesture made during a dark period of war when Holland was occupied, and which in practice, first as a monetary union, then as a customs union, had not worked very well. At least it was possible to learn from all the mistakes and difficulties which had arisen from the attempt at economic integration of the 20 m. inhabitants of three small countries, a pilot-scheme which helped to show how things could be done more effectively when the larger enterprise of the European Community was launched.

Although the struggle to pass and ratify the EDC treaty had evoked immense enthusiasm, especially after the Treaty of Paris starting the Coal and Steel Community in 1952, Beyen was among those who doubted whether there was enough of a sentiment of unity in Europe to make such a step towards political integration possible. He believed that the best approach lay through economic integration. Up to 1952 this seemed to be going ahead satisfactorily through OEEC, but from that time the effectiveness of OEEC declined, at the same time as the impotence of the Council of Europe was revealed, indicating that it could not play a corresponding role as the body for political integration. With the EDC project running into difficulties from the side of France, it seemed that some further initiative was needed, to prepare the way and build up public opinion for supporting eventual political integration —an objective towards which it was useless to hasten quickly before the sentiment favouring supranational co-operation had been created.[1] To this end Beyen believed that small sectoral moves would not suffice: action to be effective as a means of leading ultimately to the integration of Europe would have to be on a large enough scale. A common market, if it could be brought into being, would be a big achievement of the kind required.

With these considerations in mind Beyen made a move at the inaugural meeting of the Foreign Ministers of the Six held in connection with the first functioning of the Coal and Steel Community in 1952. He brought in an amendment to an Italian proposal for setting up a committee to consider steps towards political integration, his object being to open the way for a parallel move towards a common market. At the following Foreign Ministers' conference in Rome in February 1953 the 'Beyen Plan' found a favourable reception, and came up as an amendment to the Statute of Europe for political union which the Council of Ministers was proposing for the consideration of Spaak's 'Ad hoc' Assembly.[2]

The plans for political union, being linked with EDC, came to grief when the latter failed to be ratified by the French Assembly— but the project of a common market lived on. Beyen re-wrote his Rome memorandum in the spring of 1955, and sent it to Spaak with the proposal that it should provide the agenda for a conference of the Foreign Ministers of the Six. In it he pointed out that a continuation of the attempt to integrate Europe sector by sector 'does not help to strengthen the feeling of Europe's solidarity and unity in the same degree as general economic integration'. It should be up to the Benelux governments to take a well-prepared inititiative for 'establishing a supranational community whose task it would be to achieve the economic integration of Europe in the general sense, proceeding by means of a customs union to the establishment of an economic union'.[3]

The moment was propitious, since the Mendès-France government had just fallen (6 February 1955), and had been replaced by one containing several well-known 'Europeans', among them Robert Schuman, now at the Ministry of Justice. Since Spaak's return to the Foreign Ministry, he, Beyen and Bech of Luxembourg, had regularly been dining together at meetings of the Six. Beyen did not share his countrymen's often antipathetic feeling to their Belgian neighbours, and he and his two Benelux colleagues formed the core of the group which made the re-launch successful. Something too was contributed to the favourable atmosphere and the preparation of public opinion by the high-level lobbying of Jean Monnet, though he was not at the time in favour of launching the Common Market. He believed in a sectoral approach covering transport and energy (of which nuclear energy was in his view the most important), as an extension of the Coal and Steel Community.[4]

Eventually the Foreign Ministers of the Six, along with Monnet's ECSC successor, René Mayer, met at Messina, 1–3 June 1955, this out-of-the-way spot being chosen since it lay in the constituency of Italy's Foreign Minister, Gaetano Martino, who was busy with an electoral campaign. Baron Snoy of the Belgian Foreign Office presented two drafts comprising alternative sets of the Benelux proposals, the one concerning sectoral moves for electricity, transport, etc., the other for the big project of the Common Market. The big project was accepted, to the surprise of its sponsors, though it was not the dominant theme at the conference, a fact which was reflected in the subsequent resolution, characterised by Spaak as 'un méli-mélo' of several proposals.[5] At least it stated certain definite aims: 'the establishment of a united Europe by the development of common institutions, the progressive fusion of national economies, the creation of a common market and the progressive harmonisation of ... social policies'.[6] Federation was not mentioned. Though it remained the hope of the sponsors as the ultimate goal, it was impolitic to mention it after the failure of EDC.

By itself the resolution might have led nowhere had it not been for the Benelux proposal to set up a committee of experts under a political personality for working out the draft treaties which could give effect to its stated aims. Here again the Benelux strategy succeeded, since the other Foreign Ministers had no plan and none of them had thought of procedure.[7] In proposing a political personality Spaak was thinking of his predecessor as Foreign Minister, Paul van Zeeland;[8] in the event the personality was himself. His work was destined to bring about, in his own words, 'the most important revolution our continent has known for a long time ... one of the greatest events of European history, of no less importance than the revolution of 1789'.[9]

Spaak's origins lay in one of the great political families of Belgium, liberal and socialist: a man bred in a tradition of public service—belonging to 'that cultivated *bourgeoisie* who consider it a supreme honour to devote themselves to the public cause'. His maternal grandfather spent his life campaigning, in the end victoriously, in the cause of universal suffrage; his uncle, Paul-Émile Janson, became Prime Minister; his mother, a Socialist, was Belgium's first woman M.P. Spaak himself, born in 1899, was just old enough (seventeen), as the First World War dragged on, to attempt escape from occupied Belgium to join with his countrymen on the Yser in the fight against the Germans—only to spend some months as a prisoner-of-war, letting off his high spirits in amateur plays and clowning. This frustrated desire to fight for his country co-existed with an attitude—like that of many Belgians—which can only be described as non-national: in fact from early years he was a 'European'. He was also a Socialist *sui generis,* which as Belgium's first Socialist Premier he defined as seeking 'a world with more justice, where merit is better rewarded'—this, he said, was his way of being a Christian.[10] In fact, as in the case of André Philip, his socialism gained deeply in content through the influence of another remarkable Belgian, Henri de Man.[11]

Frustrated as President of OEEC and again as President of the Council of Europe, he transferred all his natural aggressiveness into the fight for uniting Europe once the question of the Belgian monarchy was settled (a question in which he had been closely involved), and he did so in his capacity as Foreign Minister after re-entering Belgian politics in 1954.

Speed was of the essence, since the favourable political conjunction had occurred which might not be repeated. While the government of Edgar Faure in France supported developments towards integration, in Germany Adenauer's position was still strong, despite his advancing years and the challenge from colleagues like his Minister of Finance, Erhard, who preferred the OEEC approach to economic matters, though, as the author of Germany's 'economic miracle' Erhard could scarcely denounce a scheme which would open new markets to German industrial goods, particularly since the main opponents of the government, the Socialists, had now come round to favour the community approach. For these reasons he had sent a convinced 'European', Walter Hallstein, who had represented Germany at the conference setting up the ECSC, as a Secretary of State to Messina.

The Germans in general liked the idea of a Common Market, but were not so enamoured of a 'pool' for developing nuclear energy for civilian use. France, however, favoured this project, christened Euratom by the brilliant French engineer Louis Armand who had been drawn in by Monnet to advise on these matters. For the French a nuclear authority backed by all the Six might enable France to begin catching up with Britain, since its achievements could be adopted for military use and so help France become a nuclear power—and this was laid down by Faure as a national policy objective. It was the more important since Britain's special relationship with the USA in sharing nuclear 'know-how', which had existed during the war, had just been renewed through Churchill's efforts—and the French needed some alternative way to avoid the vast expense of advancing unilaterally towards nuclear power status.

It was sound strategy to launch these two projects jointly, since the one would help bring in the Germans and the other the French —and for the sake of the one they liked, each country might accept the other which it favoured less. Messina at any rate marked the partial reconciliation of these diverse interests, and Spaak could proceed with an intensive programme of securing agreement on all the multifarious points which had to be settled before the twin communities could be launched. He decided to operate in the same way as that which had proved successful in starting the ECSC— through governmental delegates assisted by experts, his own task being that of co-ordinating the different fields of work.[12]

Spaak in fact during the two years of negotiations played much the same role as that of Monnet in the earlier negotiations at

Paris setting up the ECSC. This time however the issues were vastly more complex, and Spaak needed all the help he could get from men like Pierre Uri of Monnet's brains-trust in carrying out his task. Monnet himself had now—after some hesitation—freed himself from his job as President of the High Authority at Luxembourg. His resignation took effect in June 1955, and he was able to devote himself to supporting the governments of the Six in their negotiations, partly through building up a pressure-group, the Action Committee for the United States of Europe, partly through his own tireless activity in keeping in touch with the leading personalities by visits and telephone calls, and encouraging his henchmen in every way he could.

At this committee a solitary British representative made a dismal impression. Britain, as a member of Western European Union, had been invited to participate, but the Government (under Eden's premiership since April 1955), would only send an Under-Secretary at the Board of Trade, R. F. Bretherton. The fact that an official of no higher standing was sent was designed to underline Britain's reservations towards the project, since Government policy viewed the community approach askance as much as in the days of EDC —and somewhat more so since EDC had failed. Such schemes were considered at Whitehall as projects dreamed up by the continentals which could only serve as diversions from the main stream for co-ordinating economic activity which, in the British view, should flow through OEEC. Hence the restrictive and negative brief imposed on the unfortunate Bretherton, whose attitude was characterised by Spaak as 'discret et sceptique'.[13] Part of the time Bretherton was joined by Frank Figgures representing the Treasury, both smoking pipes and saying nothing. Though at another time John Coulson from the Foreign Office was also present,[14] the appointment of a Board of Trade man as the British representative indicated the Government's determination to refuse entanglement with the political aspects of such schemes—or equally perhaps a blindness, largely self-willed, to the fact that there were any political aspects at all.

The experience of Benelux gave a good start in working out the practical implications of a customs union, since this was what Belgium, the Netherlands and Luxembourg had pioneered in 1944, and they had for some time been planning the next stage in their

133

evolution, an economic union, which was to take effect in 1958. The establishment of a customs union for industrial goods was the basis of the arrangements for the Common Market on which Spaak and his committee were working. In fact it was a question of working with several committees dealing with different aspects of the problems, but progress was not swift enough for Spaak. There was danger of the negotiations becoming bogged down in detail before the general outlines had become clear.

The turning-point came when he began dealing personally with the heads of delegations, to pin-point the essential ideas which would form the basis of the whole development,[15] and got away from trying to deal with a roomful of experts. He regarded it as his strength that he made no pretensions to expert knowledge—he was completely objective, especially on economic matters, about which it would have been fatal to have points of view, and he refused to inform himself about the agenda before going to meetings.[16] As it was he needed all his skill as a negotiator and all the resources of his powerful personality to keep his collaborators moving in the right direction. 'Pounding the table, imposing deadlines, threatening and cajoling, he forced the technicians to stick to the point'.[17]

Meanwhile he sent off to a quiet retreat in the south of France three experts, the Frenchman Uri, the German von der Groeben, and the Belgian Huppert, to draft a final report. This was done, largely by the hand of Uri,[18] and the report was presented to the six Foreign Ministers meeting at Venice, 29–31 May 1956.

By this stage it was already clear what the structure of the new Community should be. Patterned on that of the ECSC it was to have a Commission, fulfilling similar functions to that of the High Authority, able to take decisions in certain fields and endowed with powers of initiative, and a Council of Ministers to which the Commission would have to submit its proposals, and which would retain the ultimate responsibility. The setting up of a common market for industrial goods also implied more than a free trade area surrounded by a common tariff—it implied the creation of an economic unit out of the countries concerned, not least because of the intention to ensure genuinely free competition by unmasking and forbidding discriminatory protective devices, as well as by 'harmonisation' of social services, hours of work and other factors which affected costs of production. The accent in the Report was on positive action to create optimum economic activity. To establish normal conditions of competition and the harmonious development of the economies concerned, it was necessary to have rules for eliminating monopoly situations and those protective devices with which governments intervened in the market. It meant bringing into production new and under-developed regions and unused labour forces, re-directing declining industries, and stimulating the 'free circulation of the new productive factors themselves, capital and men'. Besides bringing together existing resources in the most productive way, the aim was to lead towards a convergence in monetary policies.[19]

The six Foreign Ministers got through their business at Venice with remarkable speed, accepting within two hours the Spaak Report as the basis of further negotiations, despite the fact that a knotty problem had been raised, the question of associating the colonial or ex-colonial territories of the participants (and notably of France) with the Common Market. France had got on to a good thing here—a way of maintaining an economic link with her dependent territories by some other method than preferential duties (one of the difficulties which kept the British Government from considering membership herself), since France proposed not merely access for her dependent territories to the Market but a development loan, the lion's share of which would be contributed by Germany (though she possessed no colonies) to be passed on—to the tune of 80 per cent of the total—to France for investing in her colonies.[20]

All the details about these and many other arrangements were left over for Spaak's committee to thrash out in the meetings which continued to be held, as intensively as before, at the Val Duchesse château near Brussels. Though there were stormy moments, the work generally proceeded in an atmosphere reminiscent of that which had obtained during the negotiations for ECSC.

In a letter to Schuman[21] Monnet signalised the progress that was being made at Brussels in the autumn of 1956. Whereas the French had been obstructive over all the issues and the Germans had been laying down conditions in regard to Euratom which would make its realisation impossible, great progress was now being made. The French Government had taken up a positive position.

It has passed from the stage of general obstruction to that of discussion on concrete issues which are difficult but which can be resolved. The French delegation—Maurice Faure and Marjolin—is very good and very convinced, and besides has the ear of the Government and in particular of the Prime Minister. We are in difficulties, but no longer in the desert. With the determination which there is now at Paris and with understanding for our partners we should reach a conclusion.

Regarding the German view about Euratom, there is no chance of reaching a conclusion in the present situation. But this situation can be changed if the Chancellor intervenes in the discussion which goes on endlessly among the German ministers themselves, and which has created this situation. The Chancellor, with whom I spent a lot of time at Bonn a fortnight ago, has assured me that he was going to intervene in order to bring Euratom to a conclusion and move the Common Market along. He insists on the necessity of giving all these questions a *political aspect*. I found him more positive and determined than ever. It is the moment for him to intervene with his Ministers. He said that he would do so. He said the same to Etzel[22] and the parliamentary group of the CDU. As you know, he will be meeting Guy Mollet at the end of this week at Brussels. They ought to "finish" the Saar,[23] but also speak about Europe and deal with essential questions'.

Mollet had taken over the French premiership in February 1956. As a long-time supporter of the European movement he could be expected to play his part in bringing the negotiations to a successful conclusion. Curiously, however, it was as much his non-European policies regarding Algeria and Egypt—failures though they were—which contributed to the final launching of the two communities, by sharpening the sense of urgency that something needed doing to strengthen Western Europe. On being greeted with rotten tomatoes and jeering from the French inhabitants of Algeria during his visit shortly after becoming Prime Minister, Mollet switched to a tough line aiming at ending the Algerian rebellion at all costs. With this in view he decided on a policy towards Nasser which could prevent Egypt continuing as a supply-base for the Algerians: he agreed with the Israelis to intervene against Egypt in a war which they would start, and brought the Eden government in Britain clandestinely into the plot. Hence the Suez War of 29 October to 6 November 1956. Its failure to topple Nasser, after intervention by the USA backed by the rest of the United Nations, showed the impotence of the one-time 'great' powers of Europe—and the humiliating experience of Suez was emphasised by the harrowing events of the same days in Eastern Europe, when Russian tanks moved into Budapest to crush the liberal régime of Imre Nagy. All this pointed to the necessity for the Western European powers to move towards a deeper unity if they were to have anything more than the shadow of autonomy in international affairs. Only a pooling of sovereignty, it seemed to many, could make sovereignty in any sense a reality again; and Western Europe, suffering from an oil shortage on the blocking of the Suez Canal, looked the more favourably on Euratom as a co-operative way of jointly safeguarding against energy deficiencies.

Further, with events in Algeria running beyond the competence of any likely coalition of the Fourth Republic to control, the shadow of its demise began to loom. The last elections had shown up the precariousness of the régime, with the Communists gaining 50 seats at the expense of the moderate centre (particularly the M.R.P.), to bring their strength to 150, and 37 Poujadists on the right showing themselves potentially far more dangerous than a mere political lunatic fringe.[24] General de Gaulle was waiting in the wings at Colombey-les-deux-Eglises, making it known to all the world that he was ready to take over power from its increasingly nerveless grasp. And de Gaulle had made it plain that he had little love for the Europe of the Six or the community idea.

Hence if the work was to be finished it had to be done quickly. France's partners had to be prepared to sacrifice if the still favourable conjunction of affairs was to be taken in time—in other words because French goodwill towards the project was an asset which might suddenly disappear, and because the other countries were entirely dependent on France to complete the project, she was in a strong position to demand specially favourable treatment. Adenauer in particular was ready to accommodate her, since he looked to the new communities for crowning his life work of Franco-German reconciliation.

It was not surprising that as the negotiations drew to a close France made a number of demands over which her partners had to yield. Not only was she obtaining large sums for development aid for her colonies: by associating them with the Common Market it seemed that she would gain 'a common market for her partners and a French market for herself'.[25] She now also gained a whole range of escape clauses and exceptions. Whereas her partners had to start abolishing import duties and subsidies at once, France could go on as before until a year after she had achieved a balance of payments with them—and this might not be until several years had elapsed. French farmers were to get the higher German prices for their wheat, and 'harmonisation' meant that her partners would in effect adopt her wage-rates and other systems (e.g. equal pay for men and women), so that their costs should be raised to be on a par with those of France.

The last stages of the negotiations were difficult, as the Prime Ministers of the Six and their Foreign Secretaries, meeting at Paris, made the final decisions about the associated territories. The 'miracle' of reaching agreement to accommodate France was accomplished. 'Fortunately', as Spaak observed, 'the chiefs of delegations did not consider themselves as adversaries. They had the conviction that they were working for the same cause. The difficulties of one were the difficulties of all'.[26] The work was completed at dawn on 20 February 1957, and the Treaty of Rome, setting up the European Economic Community and Euratom, was signed on 27 March.

Misgivings in the different countries, over various points, made it uncertain whether the treaty would be ratified. The Dutch were disappointed: their businessmen and farmers feared that satisfying French demands over harmonisation and minimum prices would increase their costs considerably and undermine their competitive position, while the federalists among them lamented the sacrifice of the supranational principle. In the Bundestag Erhard's antipathy to the Treaty was so evident that his speech supposedly supporting his party's line in favour of it was singularly unconvincing. At Paris it was uncertain whether a majority could be found to ratify it, since a majority which was neither Communist nor Poujadist could only take shape in a negative sense.[28] But despite these doubts and hazards the parliaments of the Six duly ratified the Treaty by the year's end.

The aim of the Treaty of Rome was implicitly political—to establish 'an ever closer union between the European peoples'.[29] Besides a common market and common external tariff, which were to be arrived at by stages covering twelve or fifteen years, common policies were to be devised 'for agriculture, for transport, for labour mobility, and for important sections of the economy'.

The constitutional arrangements for the EEC were on lines similar to those of the ECSC, which in turn owed something to the original Monnet model, that of the Commission for the Plan. Monnet had hoped that the High Authority for running the Coal and Steel Community would, like the Commission for the Plan in France, be an autonomous body whose powers for mandatory action would be extended by the indicative methods which had been used for controlling the private sector.[30] He had, however, accepted the Council of Ministers as a body which would deal with questions outside the range of the Authority's prescriptive powers. Although Monnet developed a system of 'dialogue' with the Council, even on points which were not necessarily within the Council's competence, and although the agreement of the Council on measures decided by the Authority was not usually difficult to obtain, in view of the highly technical nature of most of the decisions which had to be made, its existence was a portent for the future.

This was proved when the EEC was set up. The Commission was something like the High Authority in the ECSC: it had similar functions for initiating measures and policy, and for supervising administration, though it did not have the same supranational powers of decision. The other organs reappeared also—the Assembly or European Parliament (the former ECSC Assembly, which was enlarged and functioned also for the EEC and Euratom), the Economic and Social Committee (also advisory), and the Court of Justice. The Council of Ministers had, in the EEC, greater effective powers than had been envisaged for the ECSC: in fact the arrangements followed the system which had developed in practice, whereby the High Authority obtained agreement for a range of less important issues by majority voting, while for the more important issues it had to be unanimous, with the backing of the Council of Ministers. The supranational element as represented by the Commission was reduced relatively to the inter-governmental element represented by the Council. It was with the Council, as the decision-making body, that the locus of power lay.[31]

This cautious approach to supranationalism is understandable after the failure of the EDC on which the federalists had built their hopes. The supranational element was kept relatively slight because at the time it was as much—so it seemed—as the governments, and particularly that of France were likely to accept and the national parliaments to ratify. In the French Assembly's debates the Government spokesmen, together with well-known 'Europeans' like Schuman (who was no longer a member of the Government) decried any doctrinaire attachment to supranationalism or to a special European mystique.[32] The Government's view was that there should be no more supranationalism than was necessary to make the Communities function efficiently.

Maurice Faure, the chief Government negotiator, asserted that the choice for France lay between either going on as she had been, accepting that she would always be the feeblest, behind the others, producing at higher prices than anyone else, which was decadence, or accepting economic rehabilitation by Community procedures. The treaties, he admitted, were a compromise 'like all treaties anyway', but 'the very atmosphere of the negotiations, the freedom with which, at the end of some weeks, we exchanged our impressions, our views, our difficulties, to confront them finally in order to bring them to a common conclusion, is for me a good augury of the march into the future of our Community'.[33] He maintained that 'a Community spirit' had presided at the elaboration of the treaties.

The Foreign Minister, Christian Pineau, summed up what he saw as the main advantages accruing from the treaties:
1. Keeping open the opportunities in world economic competition
2. Reinforcing the position of the Western democracies
3. Establishing Franco-German reconciliation on a permanent basis
4. Promoting united action in favour of developing countries, particularly of Africa
5. Marking a first step towards a vaster construction.

'We are at the start of our action. We won't ever regard it as ended as long as there remains one free city of Europe outside our Community'.[34]

REFERENCES

[1] J. W. Beyen: *Het Speel en de Knikkers* (The Game of Marbles—Rotterdam, 1968), 223. Much of the information in these paragraphs came personally from M. Beyen.

[2] Ibid., 228.

[3] Mayne: *Recovery of Europe*, 231.

[4] Information from M. Beyen; Mayne, *op. cit.*, 232.

[5] Information from M. Spaak, M. Jean Rey, Baron Snoy et d'Oppuers and M. van der Meulen (Ambassador of Belgium to the European Communities); see also Baron Snoy et d'Oppuers: 'Les Projets de Marché Commun, d'Euratom

et d'Association des Territoires d'Outre-mer', conférence donnée le 12 mars 1957 (Royaume de Belgique, Ministère des Affaires Economiques); and Mayne, *op. cit.*, 228–237.

[6] Mayne, *op. cit.*, 236.

[7] Information from M. Robert Rothschild (Ambassador of Belgium in France); Snoy, *op. cit.*, 8.

[8] Information from M. Spaak.

[9] J. H. Huizinga: *Mr. Europe: a political biography of P.-H. Spaak* (London, 1961), 240, 242.

[10] Huizinga, 26.

[11] See p. 23.

[12] Ibid., II, 69.

[13] Spaak, II, 73.

[14] Nora Beloff, 74.

[15] Spaak, II, 84.

[16] Information from M. Spaak.

[17] Mayne: *Recovery of Europe*, 23.

[18] Ibid., II, 72.

[19] Comité Intergouvernemental créé par la Conférence de Messine: Rapport des Chefs de Délégation aux Ministres des Affaires Etrangères (Brussels, 21.4.56) [Spaak Report], 14–19.

[20] Anthony Nutting: *Europe Will Not Wait* (London, 1960), 87.

[21] 24.9.56, from Brussels (Private collection).

[22] Franz Etzel, Vice-President of the High Authority of ECSC, later German Minister of Finance.

[23] Arrangements were shortly concluded to restore the Saar to Germany on 1 January 1956.

[24] Nutting, 88.

[25] Ibid., 87.

[26] Spaak, II, 93.

[27] Ibid., II, 95.

[28] André Siegfried in *l'Année Politique*, 1957.

[29] Preamble to Treaty of Rome.

[30] See p. 63.

[31] Miriam Camps: *Britain and the European Community 1955–1963* (London, 1964), 61–2.

[32] Ibid., 89.

[33] JO (Débats, Assemblée), 5.7.57, 3299, 3304.

[34] Ibid., 6.7.57, 3374.

15

Britain, the Free Trade Area and the European Economic Community

The Treaty of Rome came into force at New Year 1958. Euratom started its operations, which were complemented rather than duplicated by the setting up by OEEC of its European Nuclear Energy Agency. Much more difficult to settle was the relation of OEEC itself to the European Economic Community.

1958 was a preparatory year for EEC. Its organs—the Commission, Council of Ministers, secretariat, etc.—began their formal functioning, but the initiation of the Common Market was only due to begin in January 1959 with the first round of tariff cuts for the Six, leading towards an eventual common tariff. They were also due to remodel the quota system of the Six in a way which would favour imports from each other, and which would therefore be discriminatory against the outside world.

This was worrying for the eleven other OEEC countries, and particularly for Britain, whose economy was afflicted by low productivity and a balance-of-payments problem which, like a grumbling appendix, always threatened to become acute. As long as OEEC remained the major economic organ for Europe, with Britain in a dominating position in it, there was a chance that Britain could continue a strategy which would cushion her as far as possible against too powerful competition by rivals or the onset of a recession.

The prospect of the Six forming a much closer economic unit than Britain had allowed OEEC to become, and from which she would be excluded, made it necessary for some hard thinking to be done. Action was necessary, it was pointed out, in view of disquieting trends which were gradually making Britain's economy less competitive in relation to the rest of the world. The very success of OEEC and the European Payments Union had led to sterling becoming convertible, in most circumstances, into dollars and other currencies, and this deprived Britain of those sterling area restrictions which had given her 'an exceptional degree of preference' and had secured for her markets for half her exports.[1] In particular her position was worsening relatively to that of her continental neighbours, whose vigorous expansion was attracting capital investment on a greater scale.

Warning notes were being sounded by the middle of 1956,[2] and these became louder in the following year, when it was clear that the Common Market was becoming an established fact. Underlining again Britain's failure to attain a high level of capital investment, and the decline of British trade relative to that of the rest of the world, the Economist Intelligence Unit pointed out the probable effect upon her, not only in economic but also political terms, especially if the Six moved towards a federation. 'It may seem absurd to suppose that the United Kingdom, with 300 years of great power status behind it, could become nothing more than another small country. But it took only a hundred years for the Spanish Empire to decay, yet it was, in relation to the world of its day, more formidable than Britain at the height of its nineteenth-century greatness'.[3]

The Englishman who at this time played a leading role in shaping his country's policy was Harold Macmillan. A man of ideals with a liberal outlook, Macmillan had been a strong supporter of the European Movement in the forties and early fifties. He was given the Foreign Office in Sir Anthony Eden's government in April 1955, and was moved to the Exchequer at the re-shuffle of December of that year. As Foreign Secretary he approved the appointment of a representative to take part in the Spaak Committee after the Messina Conference of June 1955,[4] though it was indicative of his failure to appreciate the political importance of these developments that he agreed that the representative concerned should be from the Board of Trade and not the Foreign Office. At that time he was still thinking in terms of strengthening the Council of Europe and Western European Union,[5] with the eventual objective of some kind of confederation. Viewing the aims of the Messina powers as economic, he regarded them as within the area dealt with by OEEC—in agreeing to send a representative to the Spaak Committee he expressed a caution as to duplicating OEEC unnecessarily. In the sphere—that of the Council of Europe and WEU—which he considered as possible for the development of a confederation, he thought of such a development primarily in terms of constructing a framework which would limit the pretensions of a resurgent Germany.[6] Even this enlightened and intelligent statesman had failed to grasp, any more than most of his countrymen, the rationale of the 'community' approach as a means of creating an inner unity among as many countries as would join, with institutions for fostering harmonious growth on all levels, political as well as economic.

In Britain the possibilities of the ECSC as a pilot scheme for such a development were ignored. Instead it was regarded as a moderately useful economic arrangement with which it would be worth while for Britain to associate and a treaty of association between Britain and the ECSC was in fact ratified in February 1955. The idea still persisted that if further arrangements were worked out among the Six, Britain could gain whatever benefits were going by this method of association. In any case, after the failure of EDC, there was considerable scepticism as to whether the Six could succeed in bringing off any further development at all—official circles cherished 'a confident expectation that nothing would come out of Messina'.[7]

Macmillan, however, by early 1956 was worried lest the Six would succeed after all, and create a combination dominated by Germany. Spaak at that time was equally worried, but for the opposite reason—that the negotiations might fail: without Britain it could be EDC all over again. He begged Macmillan to bring Britain into the negotiations of the Six and take the lead before it was too late, as it was, in his view, the last moment for uniting Western Europe.[8]

Such requests strengthened the view in London that Britain was in a strong enough position to impose her own plan on her OEEC partners, including the Six—that if she held out the Six would be obliged to adjust their plans in a way which would suit her. But whereas France was in a position to let herself be wooed by the other five, and could therefore hold out for her own terms of entry into the projected communities, Britain was, in reality, in no such position—her attitude would not be decisive in making or breaking the venture. At the very moment that Spaak was expressing his anxieties to Macmillan the situation was changing:

the coming to power in France of Mollet with his Socialists, mostly committed to the European developments in coalition with the 'European'-minded M.R.P., made continued and stronger French support for the project certain and reduced the need to look for help elsewhere.

Macmillan's calculation was that Britain still had enough weight in OEEC to launch a complementary project open to the eleven non-Messina members. The challenge of the Six with their customs union and internal free trade had to be met on the assumption that they might succeed. On the economic plane the challenge was to Britain's high-tariff régime which protected her against competition from her neighbours (Commonwealth countries had easier access through preferences, and Britain had preferences for her exports to them). To meet the threat of discrimination by the Six, once they had erected their common tariff, it would be necessary for the remaining OEEC countries, including Britain, to offer to dismantle their tariffs on industrial goods, on condition that the Six breached the common tariff in their favour. A free trade area would thus be created for industrial goods, each member, including the Community of the Six, having zero (or merely revenue) tariffs in respect of each other's products while maintaining its own tariffs against the outside world.

It was something that the challenge of the Six impelled Britain to consider lowering her tariffs (it took time for some of Macmillan's colleagues to be convinced of the necessity for this). It could be accepted that the freeing of trade would bring advantages and Britain's initiative in this respect was encouraged by the low-tariff countries in OEEC: where she was open to criticism, and was in a minority of one in the OEEC, was in excluding agricultural products. It seemed that Britain was simply trying to get the best of both worlds—duty-free access for her exports to the continent, while continuing to maintain her cheap food and raw materials imports from the Commonwealth.

When the Free Trade Area was first proposed the Six were ready to accept the scheme as supplementary to EEC, once the latter had been established. Spaak requested that it should not be pushed, since, as a looser arrangement, it might prove more attractive than EEC, especially to the Germans and Dutch. Accordingly the plan was not given a full airing on the Continent until the Treaty of

Rome had been ratified. Spaak was convinced from the start that the French would never accept it,[9] and certainly the more the French looked at it the less they liked it. Though Erhard gave it the strongest support he was overruled by Adenauer who, for the sake of the new-found understanding with France, was prepared to defer to her in this matter.

Partly the French saw in the British move a challenge to the privileged position they had acquired in EEC, partly the employers were not prepared to accept the chill blast of greater competition from the British after nerving themselves to abandon, at least eventually, their protective devices against the Germans. They saw no reason—and others in the Six agreed with them on this—why Britain should have the advantages of a larger market without taking on the obligation of working the institutions and abiding by the rules which made true competition possible. Why should Britain behave like a man who wouldn't marry the girl, it was asked, while expecting to enjoy her favours without the obligations her husband had undertaken?[10]

There was an obvious objection to Britain gaining an unfair advantage over the Six for her exports, and there was the danger of trade distortions if each country or grouping maintained varying levels of tariffs against the outside world (since goods would tend to enter the area through the member with the lowest tariffs, despite schemes to counter this based on certificates of origin of imports). To many on the Continent, Britain's tactics seemed like another attempt to apply the time-worn methods of divide and dominate. They were asking whether Britain's new-found enthusiasm for Europe 'really stems from a humble awareness that the only future for the weak nations of Europe lies together, or merely from a passing wish to bolster a weakened position of national interest'.[11] If Britain really believed in getting together, ran the logic of the 'Europeans', she should be prepared to accept the whole institutional apparatus which was necessary to bring about an integrated multi-national economy, with free movement of labour and capital, in which common policies could be worked out for needy regions and the under-developed world.

The difference in concepts and philosophy which underlay Britain's approach and that of the Community was fundamental.

The federal objective was not specifically mentioned in the Treaty of Rome, and the supranational element in the institutions was played down. But implicit in the arrangements of the Treaty was a pattern of co-operation arising from the ideas on which it was based.

The 'institutional market', as Jacques Rueff dubbed it, differed from the old Cobdenite free trade world after which it seemed the British were hankering. Progressives on the Continent were ready to accept it—but had the British even understood what it was? It was not a matter of 'liberating' trade by merely removing obstacles and letting it return to a state of nature. If such an attempt were made it would fail, as it had failed before, because private interests would conspire to distort the market by gaining protected outlets for themselves. Hence the need for institutions and rules to prevent this, whereby a system of greater equality and justice would be initiated—a plan appealing equally to liberals and socialists. In this light the Common Market was the crowning achievement of twenty years of fresh liberal thought. 'For the neo-liberal ... liberty is the fruit, slowly obtained and constantly threatened, of an institutional evolution founded on millennia of sad experiences, and of religious, moral, political and social developments'.[12]

It was because Macmillan and his colleagues could not accept in principle such institutional arrangements that Britain had taken no further part in the negotiations at Brussels after the publication of the Spaak Report.[13] Whatever sympathies existed among the Six for the Free Trade Area as a supplement to the Common Market, none of them agreed with the British view, constantly reiterated in the post-Messina phase, that virtually no new machinery in addition to OEEC was required, and that most of the objectives of the Six could be attained by simply strengthening OEEC.[14]

A sense of frustration in regard to Britain was growing on the Continent. Actions such as Britain's reducing the strength of the Rhine army shortly after pledging herself to keep her existing forces there shook the confidence of her Western Union partners. Nevertheless support for the FTA as an eventual and complementary development persisted among the Six, despite mistrust engendered by actions such as the circulation of a statement by the Foreign Office at the end of 1955, opposing 'the formation of a limited Common Market on an exclusive rather than an inclusive basis'.[15] This had occasioned indignation among Spaak and his colleagues of the Six. However much Macmillan tried to smooth the matter over, the circular expressed a settled view—if the Market could not be widened it must be opposed. Eighteen months later Macmillan sent a minute to Peter Thorneycroft, now Chancellor of the Exchequer, fulminating with threats against the Six if 'their movement . . . were to take the form of anything that was prejudicial to our interests'.

> We must not be bullied . . . We could if we were driven to it, fight their movement . . . Economically, with the Commonwealth and other friends, including the Scandinavians, we could stand aside from a narrow Common Market. We also have some politico-military weapons.

> What the above amounts to is this: that we must take positive action in this field, to ensure that the wider Free Trade Area is more attractive than the narrower Common Market of the Six. We must take the lead, either in widening their project or, if they will not co-operate with us, in opposing it.[16]

Specifically, Macmillan was ready to make some concessions to 'the strong desire of many European countries for some form of closer *political* association'. The yearning for supranationalism in some quarters might be satisfied by a name, even if the reality were somewhat lacking. 'The management of a European Free Trade Area should be left to a European managing board. This might well be called a 'supranational' institution. But does it matter?'[17] He envisaged a Council of Ministers in which majority voting on 'a limited field of decision' could take place as providing an institutional framework for holding together both the Six and the Eleven.

Such proposals might not have been fruitless had they come at an earlier date. The Spaak Report itself had stated that the possibility was not ruled out of superimposing on the Common Market a free trade area with other countries in certain circumstances which were specified, and it recommended negotiations for finding 'what particularly close form of association could be developed'.[18] When detailed negotiations eventually started the British began to realise the difficulties of linking the Six with the Eleven without taking over far more of the institutional arrangements devised by the Six. The exclusion of agricultural products also ceased to be a dogma, and discussions moved towards a compromise in this field.

By this time Reginald Maudling had been appointed by Macmillan to drive the negotiations through (July 1957). But the concessions which he was authorised to make, over agricultural products and institutional arrangements, did not go far enough. By 1958 time was running against the British. In mid-April, with the fall of Félix Gaillard's government, France's long crisis of régime began, not to be resolved until de Gaulle assumed power on the 1st June. During this period further negotiations were virtually impracticable. De Gaulle's own attitude, originally hostile to the Community projects, took time to crystallise in the new situation where the EEC was a *fait accompli*, and where he had more pressing matters, such as the Algerian revolt, for his attention. Despite his fair words to Macmillan, it was clear that, once the negotiations were properly resumed, France's hardening line was to be continued. It was unfortunate that when at length the British were prepared to make concessions, they were deliberately pushed by the French beyond the point where agreement was possible.[19]

By late 1958 both de Gaulle and the convinced 'Europeans' among the French had decided against the Free Trade Area, but for different reasons. For the latter the dynamic effects of EEC had to be sustained, and a new spirit fostered, both of which might have been threatened if the Community was to be dissolved in the FTA, as they feared, 'like a lump of sugar in an English cup of tea'.[20] They did not wish to risk weakening the new institutions which they saw as a means of regenerating not only the economy of their countries but also their political life.[21] By comparison the FTA plan had little to offer economically and even less politically.

The idealists looked to the creation of a new spirit, arising from working together for a common purpose. A new outlook, almost a new view of life, had to be formed, 'a new soul had to be moulded'[22]. Already 'an admirable enthusiasm' was manifest at Brussels, shared alike by the Community's 'idealists and techni-

149

cians'.[23] But to the development of this spirit the Free Trade Association could contribute nothing.

As for de Gaulle, he was weighing up the situation in the light of his aims for regaining for France the leadership of Europe, and so finding for herself a status independent of the superpowers. In his view France had long been a client state, or at least dependent on others only to be let down by them at crucial moments (as by America and Britain after the First World War, and by Britain again at the time of Hitler's occupation of the Rhineland and rape of Czechoslovakia). How to break this 'longue accoutumance à l'état de satellite'? Certainly not by subordinating France to a structure composed of technocrats in the name of 'Europe', who, together with the parliamentarians forming a legislature would be mostly foreigners; nor by placing her security at the discretion of others in an Atlantic organisation.[24] The unity of Europe had to be pursued, but not by way of a fusion of peoples, only by bringing them closer together, which might be through the Economic Community, moving towards a Confederation. A 'concert' of European states was what de Gaulle liked talking about, with echoes of the nineteenth-century 'Concert of Europe' and Congresses of bygone days. France's chosen partner would be Germany, with whom a network of preferential links would be woven.[25]

The fact that de Gaulle had accepted the EEC as a going concern was an important point, but he soon became clear that Britain should not be involved by way of the Free Trade Association, which he regarded as an attempt on her part to nullify or dissolve the EEC in 'a vast free-trade area'.[26] In his view, Britain's geographical position and history made it impossible for her to accept being shut into the enclosure of a common continental tariff, or to accept an agricultural policy which would mean buying food dear in Europe instead of cheap from the Commonwealth. Even if Britain tried to enter the Community it could only be to destroy it from within, and to draw it westwards towards an Atlantic system which would be incompatible with a 'European Europe'.[27]

At his first meeting with Adenauer, at Colombey-les-deux-Églises, on 14 September 1958, he gained assent to his proposition of developing close and special relations between France and

Germany, of which the benefit to Germany would be support over issues such as Berlin, the restoration of her dignity as a sovereign state, and the completion of Franco-German reconciliation. It marked the forging of what was shortly to be known as the Paris-Bonn axis, for which Adenauer had to pay a price: accepting de Gaulle's concept of 'Europe of the states' instead of the supra-national objectives of the Monnet-Schuman schemes. It also entailed supporting the imposition of a French-oriented common agricultural policy on France's partners in the Community, and the exclusion of Britain from it. The Chancellor pointed out that his people wanted Britain in, and that they did not like the CAP.—but he accepted the General's demands.

At their next meeting, this time in Germany, they agreed to end the Maudling negotiations (26 November 1958). Khruschev's re-opening of the Berlin crisis on 10 November made it more than ever necessary for the German government to have solid support from de Gaulle, and Adenauer had to swallow his anger over the General's bid to put France in a special class among the continental nations by proposing a three-power directorate of the USA Britain and France for heading the Atlantic Alliance—a proposal which the General had made to America and Britain shortly after his first meeting with Adenauer at Colombey, but without telling the Chancellor about it. Macmillan's failure to support this scheme may have been one reason for de Gaulle's decision to stop the FTA negotiations.

By this time de Gaulle had in fact virtually ended the negotiations unilaterally. On 14 November he instructed Jacques Soustelle, his Minister of Information to announce to the Maudling Committee that 'it is apparent to France that it was not possible to form a free trade area as had been wished by the British, that is to say by having free trade between the six countries of the Common Market and the eleven other countries of the OEEC, without a common external tariff embracing the seventeen countries and without harmonisation in the economic and social spheres'.[28]

When the British tried to keep the talks going, and even made threats of retaliation against France if they did not, Couve de Murville walked out of the meeting saying that France would not negotiate under duress. Britain's threats were revealed as baseless, particularly as they merely had the effect of strengthening the unity of the Six, despite the high-handed way in which the decision had been made by France to end the negotiations without prior agreement with her partners. Whereas France's partners had been critical, they now felt they had to stand together. After some delay Britain took the course, which was generally regarded as a second best, to set up the European Free Trade Association (EFTA) with six of the other OEEC countries which had not entered the Community—Norway, Denmark, Sweden, Switzerland, Austria and Portugal (20 November 1959). Free trade was to be in industrial goods only, though some adjustments in the British tariff were made to favour Danish foodstuffs. As for OEEC, it had now been superseded, and was turned into a research and advisory body, the Organisation for Economic Co-operation and Development, with a wider membership including the USA and Canada.

REFERENCES

[1] *New Statesman*, 30.3.57 (T. Balogh).
[2] e.g. *Barclays Bank Quarterly Review*, quoted in *The Financial Times*, 1.6.56.
[3] 'Britain and Europe' (London, 1957), 63.
[4] See p. 130.
[5] See p. 127.
[6] Harold Macmillan: *Riding the Storm* (London, 1971), 67–8.
[7] Ibid., 73.
[8] Ibid., 70.
[9] Nutting, *op. cit.*, 90.
[10] *New York Herald Tribune*, 18.12.58.
[11] *The Economist*, 1.5.57.
[12] *Revue d'Economie Politique*, special number on 'Le Marché Commun et ses problèmes', 1958, J. Rueff: 'Le Marche Institutionnel', 8. See also *Le Monde*, 9.2.58, J. Rueff: 'Le marché institutionnel des Communautés européennes'.
[13] See above, 134–5.
[14] Camps, *op. cit.*, 40.
[15] Macmillan, 73.
[16] Ibid., 437.
[17] Ibid., 436.
[18] *Spaak Report*, 22.
[19] Ibid., 162.
[20] Mayne, 252.
[21] *The Economist*, 10.1.59.
[22] *Combat*, 1.1.58.
[23] *The Times*, 30.12.58.

[24] Charles de Gaulle: *Mémoires d'Espoir, le Renouveau 1958–1962* (Paris, 1970), 178–9.

[25] Ibid., 182–3.

[26] Ibid., 199.

[27] Ibid., 182.

[28] Camps, 165; *L'Année Politique*, 1958, p. 482.

16

De Gaulle's No

The sixties are a period when three conceptions of Europe struggled for mastery: the Europe of the 'Community method', the Europe of de Gaulle, and the Europe of those British who, like Harold Macmillan, thought it was time for Britain to come in. The clash of these rival concepts threatened the life of the new-born EEC. The threat was averted, though the infant Community was weakened by the crises through which it passed. Something of its essential spirit was lost, and a moment came, in the mid-sixties, when it seemed that its further development might be arrested altogether.

What was this 'Community method'—sometimes regarded not so much as a method, rather a way of life? Monnet's description of it is worth quoting:

> In Europe, an open society looking to the future is replacing a defensive one regretting the past. This profound change is being made possible essentially by the new method of common action which is the core of the European Community. After a period of trial and error, this method has become a permanent dialogue between a single European body responsible for expressing the view of the general interest of the Community and the national governments expressing the national views.
>
> The resulting procedure for collective decisions is something quite new and, as far as I know, has no analogy in any traditional system.
>
> It is not federal because there is no central government; the nations take their decisions together in the Council of Ministers. On the other hand, the independent European body proposes policies, and the common element is further underlined by the European Parliament and the European Court of Justice.
>
> This system ... leads to a completely changed approach to common action. In the past, the nations felt no irrevocable commitment. Their responsibility was strictly to themselves, not to any common interest. . . .

But in the European communities, common rules applied by joint institutions give each a responsibility for the effective working of the Community as a whole. This leads the nations within the disciplines of the Community to see a solution to the problems themselves instead of trading temporary advantages. It is this method which has caused a silent revolution in men's attitudes.

In short, Europe has overcome the attitude of domination which ruled state policies for many centuries. . . . It is obvious that countries and peoples who are overcoming this state of mind between themselves will bring the same mentality to their relations with others, outside Europe.

The new method of action developed in Europe replaces the efforts at domination of nation states by a constant process of collective adaptation to new conditions, a chain reaction, a ferment where one change induces another. When people become convinced a change is taking place, that creates a new situation, they act on the revised estimate before that situation is established. . . . Unity in Europe does not produce a new kind of great power; it is a method for introducing change in Europe and consequently in the world. . . . Europeans have built up the European Community precisely in order to find a way out of the conflicts to which the nineteenth century power philosophy gave rise. . . . We already see this sense of world responsibilities developing as unity in Europe begins to affect Britain, America, and even many other countries of the world. European unity is not a blue-print, it is not a theory. It is a process that has already begun, of bringing peoples and nations together to adapt themselves jointly to changing circumstances.

European unity is the most important event in the West since the war, not because it is a great power, but because the new institutional method it introduces is permanently modifying relations between nations and men. Human nature does not change, but when nations and men accept the same rules and the same institutions to make sure that they are applied, their behaviour towards each other changes. This is the process of civilisation itself.[1]

These were large claims. The hitherto impracticable was being realised through, as Uri put it, 'a profoundly realistic inspiration . . . . The idea of supranational community has done more to transform the relations between the countries of Europe than all other international institutions put together'. One of the most original inventions of the Treaty of Rome, he pointed out, was to have foreseen an evolutionary process: the need for unanimity on the Council of Ministers, for instance, would disappear after a period of time, which would vary according to the kind of issues involved.[2]

Monnet and Uri were putting into words a vision which, during these years 1959–62, seemed to be in process of realisation. Visitors to Brussels had the same impression. They were struck by the 'European' spirit and dynamism of the 'multi-lingual tough-minded' officials, mostly aged 35–40, comprising the Commission's staff. There was no ganging-up on a national basis. Even those who might have been angry young men in their adolescence were now Europe's 'sanguine Young Men', convinced they were doing something worth while.[3] This secretariat, 1,846 strong in 1961, served the nine Commissioners who, though appointed by the member governments, were entirely independent—no more than two of them, according to the Treaty of Rome, could have the same nationality. They presided over the nine divisions of the Community: external relations, finance, the internal market, competition, labour, agriculture, transport, overseas development, and administration. Care was taken to vary the nationalities of the officials holding the first three grades under the Commissioner in each division, and everyone belonging to these higher echelons of the administration (Grade A) had to be proficient in at least one other language besides their native tongue.

Among the French who had reservations about these developments, few had been more outspoken than General de Gaulle. If now he came to accept the Community as an accomplished fact, he did not welcome it in the spirit of Monnet. De Gaulle's view of affairs differed from that of almost everybody else. It stood out like a rock in a current, it was said, 'in lapidary constrast to the view of friends and foes alike'.[4]

His views were of a piece with the distinctive role which he believed he had to play. While still a comparatively unknown officer in France's peace-time army, he regarded himself as a man of destiny, born to command—a man accordingly who had to remain aloof from his fellows, friendless (except for his immediate family) and enigmatic.

Such a man, he wrote at that time, 'is passionately anxious to exert his own will, to make his own mind ... He embraces action with the pride of a master; for if he takes a hand in it, it will become his, and he is ready to enjoy success on condition that it really is *his own* ... He is a jealous lover and will share with no one the prizes or the pains that may be his as a result of trying to overcome obstacles . . . This passion for self-reliance is obviously accompanied by some roughness in method. The man of character incorporates in his own person the serenity inherent in his effort . . . He must accept the loneliness which, according to Faguet, is the "wretchedness of superior beings" '.[5]

In de Gaulle the arts of the politician and the other qualities needful for his role were highly developed. Hence the ambiguities of his utterances; but behind these lay ideas which were plain and simple: the restoration of the greatness of France, and the construction of a power-bloc under French hegemony able to speak on equal terms with Russia and the United States. The Suez affair had shown once again the folly of dependence on the Anglo-Saxons. France had to stand on her own feet, even if it meant paying for a nuclear deterrent (whose origins dated back to the last government of the IVth Republic) as an expensive piece of symbolism.

De Gaulle poured scorn on 'the chorus of those who want Europe to be a federation, even without a federator'.[6] If there were a federator to bring this 'type of hybrid' into being, 'the federator would not be European'—in other words, America would take on this federating role. Monnet pointed out that the process leading towards federation was already taking place—the real federator was the community method itself.[7] The Treaty of Rome laid down a process as much as a set of relationships, and this process (for example the stages whereby the Common Market was to be set up), together with the dynamic forces released and the changed attitude of the participants, would lead the countries involved to a closer unity, and eventually perhaps to a federation.

The last word, however, could not be with Monnet and the idealists of Brussels. The situation was not unlike that in which the Frankfurt Assembly had found itself over a hundred years before, in 1848, when it prepared a federal constitution, even set up a shadow federal government, but because power remained with the German states its decisions were ignored when the crunch came in 1849. So now the Brussels Commission might propose, but the governments disposed. Such was the criticism which de Gaulle made of the kind of supranationalism which existed. Even when he wanted to congratulate the Commission on doing a good job in helping to get through the agricultural negotiation as required by France in December 1963, he made it quite clear as to what were the limitations on the Commission's freedom of action. 'No matter how important the studies and advice of the Brussels Commission have been and should continue to be, it is to be clearly seen that the powers and duty of the executive belong only to the governments'. To apply the word 'executive' to what was only a gathering of experts was improper and tendentious.[8] Despite his support of the Community during his first few years of power, de Gaulle soon demonstrated unmistakably the realities of the situation in his rejection of the British application in 1963.

At the start of his relations with de Gaulle during the late fifties, Macmillan was under some illusions. As British Minister resident in North Africa during the war, he believed he had gained de Gaulle's friendship, and mistakenly assumed that their differences could be resolved by personal consultations. There were also illusions of a historical kind.

De Gaulle was something of a Bonaparte—with a role nearer that of Napoleon III than his greater uncle. Macmillan, who also hankered after greatness, saw himself as opposing this atavistic trend, but he too was thinking in terms of the Napoleonic era. When Macmillan was trying to push through the free trade area in June 1958, he had expostulated with de Gaulle. 'The Common Market is the continental system!'—so ran de Gaulle's somewhat dramatised version—'Britain can't accept it. Give it up, I beg you! Otherwise we shall find ourselves in a war which doubtless will be economic at the start, but which runs the risk of extending later into other spheres'.[9] Similar threats leaked from talks which Macmillan had in Washington at the end of March 1960—the economic split between the Six and the rest was menacing the political unity between them and their NATO partners. In the short run there might be reprisals of an economic kind—and the USA too would suffer because Britain would have to cut her dollar imports. In the long run there could be a revival of the Anglo-Russian alliance which had brought Napoleon to his knees. . . .[10] Macmillan, a product of Balliol and shortly to be Chancellor of Oxford University, was letting his academic imagination run riot.

In fact de Gaulle held by far the stronger hand. Good though Macmillan's personal relations were with Eisenhower, and also with Kennedy who took over from him as President at the end of 1960, the United States Government was not prepared to back Britain against the Six. The 'special relationship' which had flourished so strongly during the war and its aftermath was now patently waning. While still regarding Britain as a supporter in many areas of the world, America was now increasingly looking to a consolidated Western Europe, with or without—though preferably with—Britain, 'as an equal partner in the achievement of our common endeavours'.[11] Possibly the Americans had learnt some wisdom from the negative results of pressing the Six too hard over EDC. In any event, while originally welcoming Macmillan's proposal for a free trade area superimposed on EEC, the American Government soon adopted a position of complete detachment over the issue. Douglas Dillon, as Under-Secretary, and later Secretary of State, used his influence in opposition to the scheme. The ill effects politically of the economic division of Western Europe were discounted, alongside the political advantages of the consolidated Six. He was backed by another powerful figure in the State Department, George Ball, long a friend of Monnet and formerly one of his legal advisers. These men were as opposed to 'bridge-building' and tariff agreements between the Six and the Seven, as they had been to the FTA.

Placed in an awkward position of growing isolation from the thriving Community on one side and from America on the other, it was not surprising that Britain began to edge slowly towards the big decision of applying for membership. Although the economic considerations for joining EEC were important—for the Community's economic growth was going up two and half times as fast as that of Britain[12]—the reasons for taking this step were primarily political. Such were the conclusions of the high-powered committee set up under Sir Frank Lee in January 1960. After viewing all the issues and the alternative lines of action, the Committee's conclusions could be summarised in the old axiom, 'if you can't beat 'em, join 'em'. EEC, the Committee decided, was good for the free world, and since the USA was looking to it for partnership, entry by Britain was necessary if she was to regain some of her lost influence in world affairs.[13]

Like putting one toe in the water preparatory to taking the plunge, the Government by June of the following year was intimating that it might be possible for Britain to think of joining the ECSC and Euratom—only to be reminded by Monnet that nothing less than joining 'the whole procession' was feasible. When at last on 31 July 1961 Macmillan made the announcement that Britain would apply for membership of EEC, it was in a flat and uninspired manner, and though a few days later in the debate in Parliament he showed somewhat greater warmth, he took care to play down the political aspects of the decision. 'I must remind the House', he said, 'that the EEC is an economic community, not a defence alliance, or a foreign policy community or a cultural community. It is an economic community, and the region where collective decisions are taken is related to the sphere covered by the Treaty, economic tariffs, markets and all the rest'.[14] *Le Monde* noted his lack of enthusiasm, and—slightly varying the metaphor of the reluctant swimmer—compared him to one who 'arrived at the end of the springboard could not do otherwise than throw himself into the water'. Neither the Prime Minister nor his audience (except for the Liberal leader Jo Grimond) showed any European 'flame', while Hugh Gaitskell, speaking for Labour, was negative.[15] 'The tragedy is', commented *The Observer* on his first statement, 'that by failing to make a warm positive assertion of his belief in the need for European unity, the Prime Minister has once again laid the British policy wide open to the criticism that it is merely a selfish attempt to safeguard Britain's commercial interests'.[16]

Not only did Macmillan's approach make it seem that Britain was merely confronting a disagreeable necessity—he tried to do so by placing the emphasis falsely on the economic instead of the political aspects of the decision. Whatever the economic advantages of going in (about which British economists have always contradicted each other), the decision was made for political reasons, among which were fears that Britain would be left out of the combination which de Gaulle was trying to create.

While coming down in favour of the economic integration of the Six, at least up to a certain point, de Gaulle rejected political integration of the kind which had been proposed for EDC, pushing instead his personal scheme for a revived Congress System of early nineteenth-century type in which France would play the dominant role. Economic integration could benefit France, especially by providing an outlet for her agricultural surpluses, while her position within the EEC gave de Gaulle a chance of swaying the other member-states towards political ends which he favoured. De Gaulle's attempt to use them for achieving his objectives through a structure which he could dominate blocked the development of the Community along the lines favoured by its founders. An incident in the pursuit of this strategy was his veto on British entry.

De Gaulle's opening bid for a tri-partite nuclear directorate with Britain and the USA served notice that France was claiming world power status: it was scarcely likely that de Gaulle imagined that his demand could be accepted. America's refusal was not outright (just before he died in 1959 John Foster Dulles, as Secretary of State, suggested that France could have a say in the deployment of nuclear weapons on the continent)[17], but a refusal it could only be. The way was now clear for de Gaulle to follow another path to the objective of world power: building a third force bloc independent of 'the Anglo-Saxons', as the leader of which France could take up an arbitral position between East and West, encouraging when timely a détente which could bring at least some of the states now under Russian control into the orbit of 'European Europe'.

The rest of de Gaulle's policy flowed from these central ideas—the withdrawal from NATO command of the Mediterranean fleet and eventually France's entire withdrawal from NATO; the decision to build the *force de frappe*, and the refusal to accept nuclear aid from America—however much more credible it would make France's deterrent—if it meant moving back again into dependence on her. Towards Britain de Gaulle showed some ambivalence, in the main taking a negative attitude towards her participating in his continental bloc, since her presence would both dilute French leadership and serve as a channel (or Trojan horse) for American influence; though on the other hand if Britain were ready to cut her special ties with America and share her expertise in building a nuclear European third force in partnership with France, her inclusion was not definitely ruled out. France's obligations, said de Gaulle early in 1962, were 'to build Western Europe into an organized union of states so that gradually there may be established on both sides of the Rhine, the Alps, and perhaps the

Channel, the most powerful, prosperous and influential political, economic, cultural and military complex in the world'.[18]

To begin with, the Germany of Adenauer seemed a preferable partner, because one more easily dominated. From the first meeting between de Gaulle and Adenauer in September 1958 when the two elderly statesman 'discovered each other', it seemed possible for de Gaulle to exploit the relationship to this end. This he succeeded in doing, despite setbacks such as Adenauer's indignation over de Gaulle's failure to inform him of the demand for a tripartite directorate (in which Germany was to have no part), by playing upon the Chancellor's eagerness to seal his life's work by a lasting reconciliation between France and Germany. On many points the views of both converged. They shared a common mistrust of Germany, at least the Prussian-dominated Germany, which Adenauer no more than de Gaulle wished to see restored[19], and they agreed in disapproving the tendencies of the Commission to encroach on the spheres of the responsible governments.[20]

Regarding the European Community as an instrument of policy, de Gaulle had to adapt it to his aims. This meant preventing its evolution in a federal direction by playing down or obstructing its still embryonic supranational features, and by constructing a political organ for the Six detached from the Community system.

In moving on the second point de Gaulle made a good start, as it seemed, in June 1959, with a proposal to the Germans and Italians for regular meetings of the government leaders, for which continuity would be aided by a small secretariat. When it came to enlarging this design by including the Benelux countries, the Dutch at once objected: for any such political scheme the British, they said, would have to be included too. Nonetheless in November an agreement was reached for the Foreign Ministers of the Six to meet every six months, and this led up to the General's disclosure of his plans for 'an organised concert':[21] a Council of Heads of Governments meeting every three months, with a permanent secretariat and four commissions dealing with political, economic, cultural and defence matters. None of his partners however was ready to agree on the merits of this plan. He had a hard time in July 1960 at Rambouillet persuading Adenauer to accept it, the Chancellor being unenthusiastic for a scheme which would weaken NATO and alienate the Americans. As for the opposition of the Belgians and the Dutch, de Gaulle dismissed scornfully the views of the 'little powers always on their guard against the "great" ones of the Continent, shore-dwellers of the North Sea traditionally protected by the British navy, now to be relieved by that of the Americans'.[22]

Despite this opposition de Gaulle pressed forward with his plan. Adenauer had been hauled over the coals by his government and party for accepting it,[23] but meeting de Gaulle in February 1961 Adenauer was persuaded that the General's plan would not affect as adversely as had originally appeared either NATO or EEC. The meeting was immediately followed by a 'little summit' with leaders of the other four Common Market countries, but no agreement could be reached owing to the opposition of Joseph Luns, the Netherlands Foreign Minister, who argued—logically enough —that as supranationalism was being abandoned as a feature of the political structure the British could have no objections to participating, and that indeed they should be invited to join the discussions before they went any further.

There was something of 'heads I win tails you lose' about Luns' intervention—either stick to a Brussels-type supranational arrangement if Britain was not in, or have Britain in, in which case a Gaullist-style scheme would be acceptable. Luns was using the supranational argument to get Britain in—a constant objective of Dutch policy (the Belgians were more flexible)—but both alternatives were equally objectionable to de Gaulle. Adenauer, having gone so far along the road to meet the General's wishes, felt if anything more aggrieved than de Gaulle at the wrecking of the scheme. However bitter he felt, de Gaulle admitted that the obstinacy of the Dutch made them rate as one of the few nations of Europe (had not the Netherlands stood out against Louis XIV?), and he respected their six-foot representative who was able not only physically but morally to look him in the eye. 'You love France, you are pro-French', he said to Luns, 'but why have you become an agent of the British?[24]

Although Luns had little support, his objections held up further developments. A committee under Christian Fouchet was appointed to formulate proposals for another meeting at Bonn in July, which seemed to mark a further advance to a common position, but in fact this was never achieved. Had de Gaulle been ready to make some concession to the principle of supranationalism in the political arrangements which he proposed, he might well have secured the kind of leadership at which he was aiming—but on a point of principle he would not budge.[25] The nearest de Gaulle got to realising his 'Holy Alliance on foreign policy between Europe's Grand Old Men'[26] was in the Franco-German Treaty of Friendship of January 1963, in which some of his proposals for a political framework were applied—but as they were applied only between two (and the two most powerful) countries of the Six, it was generally regarded by 'Europeans' as a step back towards the alliance system of an earlier age.

In 1961 however the stage which these developments had reached was encouraging for the British. In the debate early in August on Britain's application to join the Communities, Macmillan praised de Gaulle's concept of a confederation, which he construed as a 'commonwealth, if hon. Members would like to call it that', while making it clear that he thought those who were aiming at a federation were on the wrong track.[27] But however much de Gaulle's ideas had appeal for those who wished to restrict supranationalism to the narrowest field, the implications of his refusal to allow the British to join the discussions about them indicated his doubts about letting the British participate in any such arrangements at all. If Macmillan had inklings of this they were too unpalatable to express.

At the time it seemed that de Gaulle was prepared to let the British application to join the Communities go through. Words by the French Foreign Minister, Couve de Murville, at the Council of Europe's Assembly meeting at Strasbourg, seemed to invite the application.

> Our partners in the Common Market and we ourselves have always said that the Common Market was, and always remained, open to any other European country which wished to join it ... We persist in hoping, furthermore, that certain refusals, although repeated, will not be maintained.[28]

Whether or not there was a shift in the General's position is uncertain. Was he cautiously beckoning Britain with a view to her help in constructing the political institutions which his more federal-minded colleagues of the Six opposed—perhaps just as a tactical move which could be negated later by a turn in the opposite direction? Conducting diplomacy as a continuation of war, the General believed in keeping all his options open.

France's veto on British membership was for the time being suspended, available to be used at any point in the negotiations for entry, if de Gaulle felt this to be desirable. Meanwhile, in case it seemed politic for the negotiations ultimately to succeed, de Gaulle attempted—though vainly—to press his political plans to a conclusion, and also to complete the agricultural policy of the Community before the date of Britain's entry and so confront her with a *fait accompli*. On the latter issue he succeeded.

As de Gaulle saw it, the common agricultural policy was a necessity for France, involving the fixing of prices for farm products at a level higher than world prices, but lower than those in Germany: the common external tariff (which de Gaulle pressed to have applied in 1960) would be completed by levies on agricultural imports which would bring their prices up to the level of French products, while the prices in Germany (and elsewhere in the Community where they were higher than those in France) would come down to the French level. The extinguishing of internal tariffs, which was the complement of setting up the common external tariff, would consequently open up the German market for the French farm surpluses.

De Gaulle pushed the policy through despite opposition from the Dutch, whose previously low agricultural prices had enabled them to undercut the French, and even stronger opposition from the Germans ('our principal contradictors'). For him it was a question of now or never, the moment for playing for the highest stakes—in such matter of capital interest for France 'we are ready for the rupture if what is necessary is not done'. A letter and telegram to Adenauer helped to shift the Germans. The clock was stopped at midnight on 31 December 1961, and in one of those marathon sessions (another aspect of the 'Community method' with which the world was becoming familiar) the first stage of the common agricultural policy was finally agreed on the night of 13–14 January 1962, 'after 137 hours of discussion, with 214 hours in sub-committee; 582,000 pages of documents; 3 heart attacks'—a staggering record.[29] The Germans agreed first, to reduce their grain prices towards the French level, until by 1 January 1970

165

there would be the same 'target' price for grain throughout the Community; secondly, that there should be a levy on grain imports from outside the Community which would bring their price to a level which would give Community grain a preference—all this to the benefit of France as a net exporter. What remained to be settled were the ultimate target price and the 'financial regulation' governing the way in which the levies, to be paid into the common agricultural fund, should be used. In any case the way was now cleared, according to the procedural arrangements of the Treaty of Rome, for moving into the second phase of developing the Community.

Since the arrangements for agriculture were crucial for Britain, dependent as she was on cheap agricultural imports at world prices, especially from the Commonwealth, the hope at Whitehall had been that these questions would have been left over until after Britain's entry had been negotiated—but from France's point of view this could have been disastrous, since the Germans and British, as the two largest food-importers, could have ganged up together against her. The fact that such complex negotiations were going on at the same time as the equally complex ones for British entry put the British team, headed by Edward Heath, in the position of negotiating 'on a moving staircase'.

France was in a strong position to press on with the stages which were moving the EEC towards an economic union. No longer the invalid of Western Europe sheltering behind her tariffs, she was enjoying robust health, thanks to the years of development, particularly of the infrastructure of her economy, which had been carried on since the war under the Monnet Plan, and more recently to the $17\frac{1}{2}$ per cent devaluation put through in December 1958. With this fillip to exports, French industrialists were pleasantly surprised to find how competitive their goods had become with those of their partners in the Six, and could take in their stride the progressive lowering of tariffs which the stages of the Treaty of Rome procedure involved.

This strengthening of France's economic position gave added weight to de Gaulle's dominating leadership of the Six. He arranged that in addition to the 'moving staircase' complications mentioned above, the negotiations would take place by the most cumbrous machinery possible. This was partly a matter of principle: he preferred that the negotiations should be carried out, according to the formula of *L'Europe des états,* by the six states negotiating through their Ministers, not as a more or less homogeneous Council of Ministers but as representatives of their governments. There was no question of the Commission negotiating on their behalf—in fact, de Gaulle wished to have the Commission excluded altogether from the negotiations, though eventually it was agreed that its members should be present as observers. It played in the event a far greater role than this status suggested, and really to the advantage of the French 'in urging the rest of the Six to reject British proposals which, if adopted, might have stretched the Treaty of Rome or strained the cohesion of the Community'.[30]

There had been hopes that the methods used so successfully in negotiating the Treaty of Rome would have been applied, with the appointment of a strong political personality as Chairman to carry the negotiations through. Spaak was eager to take on again this exacting role, but de Gaulle opposed his appointment. The French laid it down that the Six must together come to an agreed position on every question before taking it up with the British.[31] This meant that at every stage of the negotiations much of the time on each question was spent by representatives of the Six thrashing out a common position together (only made possible by the presence of the Commission to provide guidance and expertise), while Heath and his colleagues remained kicking their heels outside. It almost seemed as if the French were not anxious for the negotiations to succeed.

The British were disappointed that, in the negotiations, it would not be a case of the seven governments working in concert as the Six had done while drafting the Rome Treaty. Britain negotiating, in fact bargaining, with the Six was a step away from Community method at its best. Her negotiators were not to be allowed much leeway, as there was to be no 'interpreting' or stretching of the Treaty in her interests, and the transition period which she was to be allowed, if accepted as a member, was to be literally a transition to the new situation and not a period of grace.[32] Britain had to face the uncomfortable position of not only abandoning her preferences with Commonwealth countries, but, in some cases, putting up reverse preferences which favoured trade with the Six instead. She had naturally to do her best for the Commonwealth, and this involved immensely complicated negotiations, dealing with Commonwealth products one by one; and she also had obligations to her EFTA partners, two of whom (Denmark and Norway) wanted to enter the Community with her (Ireland, not a member of EFTA, was seeking entry at the same time).

Had Britain negotiated as a founder-member of EEC in 1955–57 she would almost certainly have got the kind of arrangements she wanted for the Commonwealth and agriculture. Now the Community's position, stiffened by the French, had hardened, and Heath found himself conducting 'the biggest, most complicated, and most difficult negotiation of modern times'.[33] This he did with great ability, quickly getting on good terms with Hallstein and winning golden opinions for his grasp and patience. He was supported by an extremely able team, and though the British did not achieve quite the skill which the French had shown in negotiating from weakness, they showed far more sensitivity to the 'European' viewpoint and awareness of the limitations of their bargaining position than they had during the FTA negotiations.[34]

Macmillan had done well to place Heath at the head of the negotiating team since he was a man of conviction in regard to the European experiment. He had a real understanding of the principles on which it was based, and had told fellow-Tories at the previous party conference that the Six saw the Community not only as a means of economic expansion, but 'as a chance of developing a new spirit', and that Britain would be involved with something that was 'almost a way of life'.[35] It was not entirely his fault that the British tried for too much at the start and held on too long to untenable positions. Had they made concessions at earlier stages it is possible that the negotiations might have succeeded. On the other hand the deterioration of the former Community spirit, in which each party treated its partners' problems (and in this case its future partners') as 'matters of common concern',[36] told against the British. The verdict of a close observer was that 'the Six were far less understanding of Mr. Macmillan's political problems than they had been of each other's difficulties during the Rome negotiations'.[37]

The slowness with which the negotiations got under way put a successful conclusion in jeopardy. The meetings of autumn 1961 were little more than a taking up of positions on both sides. The nub of the negotiations was not reached until the French had forced through the settlement of the common agricultural policy in January 1962 and the Community had entered the second phase of its development as laid down by the Treaty of Rome. The most fruitful period of the negotiations lasted from April to July of that year, during which time matters such as industrial imports from the developed Commonweath countries and imports (largely non-industrial) from the Asian Commonwealth were agreed, together with association or alternatively trade agreements for the African Commonwealth countries. The question of temperate zone imports, of particular importance to New Zealand, Australia and Canada, was discussed and in part dealt with item by item, but never finally settled. At the end of July and beginning of August a situation of some strain developed, since the British wanted the negotiations to reach a point where they could present the Commonwealth Prime Ministers' conference, due to meet on 10 September, with a clear outline of the package which Britain would have to accept—at least as it affected the Commonwealth, if she was to enter the EEC.

Failure to achieve this meant that too many loose ends were left for the autumn session, when in any case further time was wasted over what proved the most difficult question, whether to let Britain have special transitional arrangements in bringing her agriculture into the Community agricultural system (abandoning deficiency payments in favour of price-support by levies on imported foodstuffs), or whether she should move straight into the transitional regime adopted by the Six. Instead of seeking a consensus solution in the best Community spirit, the atmosphere deteriorated so far that at one time the delegates were wasting hours in scoring debating points off each other.[38] All this was grist to the mill of those who did not want the negotiations to succeed. Even before Britain's application was in, it was realised the longer drawn out the negotiations were the greater would be the chance of the opponents of Britain's entry to sabotage them, especially since at the beginning there were few well-informed people who would give them more than a fifty-fifty chance of success.[39]

De Gaulle eventually vetoed British entry at a press conference on 14 January 1963. This was not because the negotiations had stalled. They were in fact just getting going again after the Christmas recess with good chances of success. Sicco Mansholt of the Netherlands, the Commission's Vice-President responsible for Agriculture, had been left with the task of preparing a memorandum for solving the outstanding issues in agriculture: since mid-December he had been chairing a Committee of Ministers of Agriculture of Britain and the Six, exploring the practical implications for British agriculture of the change-over to the common agricultural policy, and their findings and recommendations were due to be discussed on the 15th January, the day after the General's announcement.

De Gaulle in fact ended the negotiations because they were near success. At the time, the meeting of de Gaulle and Macmillan at the Château de Champs on the 1st and 2nd June 1962 seemed to indicate that the two men were coming close together, and this augured well for the negotiations. Macmillan told de Gaulle that he fully agreed with him on the confederal development for Western Europe, as opposed to the supranational, and made it clear how strongly committed Britain had now become to entering the Community. There were dangers in the apparent congruence of views on political organisation, since issues which lay at the heart of any real political agreement, those on defence, were skirted. While Britain seemed to be moving nearer to France in the matter of the superstructure which had to be built for Europe, France was moving away into the realms of self-sufficient defence, severing her links with NATO, and building her nuclear deterrent and the *force de frappe* to deliver it.

The implications of Britain coming in with these issues unresolved were clear to the General. Britain in defence matters would still be closely linked with America, so that from the General's point of view, even if Britain came into the political structure he was trying to create, 'the road led equally well to a protectorate by Washington'.[40] Now that it was brought home to him that Britain would go far to gain entrance to the Community, the political consequences could be seen as disturbing to his whole strategy.

At what point the General decided to keep Britain out is hard to say. He had only grudgingly accepted Britain's candidature in the first place because of his partners' pressure on him to do so. Not long after the Château de Champs meeting with Macmillan he still seemed to regard British entry as a disagreeable necessity. 'I would rather have Europe than NATO, and among all the forms of Europe I like that of the Six best. But the five others wish absolutely to bring Britain in'.[41] Preferring to exclude Britain, yet without making a breach with the other five, the strategy was clearly to make the terms so tough that Britain would herself renounce her application. But until the last moment the General could afford to keep an option open, for if Britain were to accept the harsh terms offered her, it would mean her virtually abandoning the Commonwealth (in his view), and so being cut down to a size equivalent to that of France, while French agriculture would further benefit through the British market being opened to it on French terms, together with the advantages accruing from the large levies on her non-Community imports which Britain would be obliged to pay, and of which—if France had her way over the 'financial regulation', the lion's share would come to her. He had also to watch how far the French themselves supported British entry: the signs were that many were opposed.[42]

If however the British neither abandoned the terms which they felt to be fair for the Commonwealth, nor themselves withdrew in frustration from the negotiations, de Gaulle had to be prepared to use the veto, but he could only take the risk of thus antagonising his partners when he had become strong enough to do so with impunity. Sir Pierson Dixon, Britain's Ambassador to France and head of the delegation at official level, felt certain from the start of the negotiations that de Gaulle was only playing for time until he was strong enough to pronounce his veto. Hence the complicated mode of the negotiations and the tactics of France's chief negotiator, Couve de Murville, stalling first on Britain's demand for 'comparable outlets' for Commonwealth agriculture in the Community (to compensate for those that would be lost in Britain), and when that line was blocked stalling on the alternative policy of making 'world-wide agreements' in regard to the products of temperate zone agriculture which could be imported into the Community. Though less advantageous than the 'comparable outlets' approach, agreements along these lines would have benefited Commonwealth producers—but again they were held up since the

French kept long-drawn negotiations going on each individual item. When these tactics proved insufficient for playing out time long enough, Couve switched to the financial regulation. This, he said, had to be decided first before the price-levels could be agreed at which temperate products would enter the Community. Either France's interpretation of the common agricultural policy as agreed in January had to be accepted (that levies paid by the importing countries, mainly Britain and Germany, should be used to subsidise the exporting countries, mainly France), or France would refuse to go on discussing the problems of Commonwealth exports.[43] This is not to say that the game as played by Couve was deliberately carried on with a view to the eventual climax of the veto. In his mind the Government needed this accession of strength, completed eventually by the legislative elections at the end of November, in order to bring sufficient pressure to bear on the new candidate to accept the terms which France prescribed. But whatever the motives for the 'stretch-out' technique, he applied it in masterly fashion.[44]

Such tactics pursued relentlessly carried France through the months of negotiation without the final crucial decisions being taken—it took her through the Evian agreements which in March 1962 got the Algerian question out of the way, while Couve's raising of the financial regulation issue at the end of the summer session produced a crisis in the negotiations from 25 July onwards which prevented the decisions being reached, as desired by Britain, before the negotiations were suspended for the holidays in August. Since Continental holidays made it impracticable to resume serious negotiations much before October, it became possible to continue deferring decisions until the French referendum on 28 October, on introducing universal suffrage for electing the President. De Gaulle had not wanted to go to the polls as a declared Anglophobe,[45] which could have lost him votes, but as in the event he won the referendum, and the subsequent general election returned a majority of his supporters, his position was sufficiently strengthened to pronounce his veto no matter how outraged were his partners.

Mid-January 1963 was the moment for the General to act. There were signs that by New Year he had made his decision to do so, in consequence of the talks between Macmillan and Kennedy at

Nassau. He needed to forestall the agreement which might come over outstanding agricultural issues through the report of the Mansholt Committee, due in the middle of the month, and to put an end to the negotiations in Brussels before Adenauer came to Paris on 20 January to sign the Franco-German Treaty of Friendship.

For de Gaulle the Cuba crisis in October 1962 had underlined further the point he had been making: in the face of a direct nuclear threat America would take her own decisions, with little time or thought for consulting with her European allies. 'Europe' (i.e. the Europe of the Six) had to be in a like position in the event of being similarly threatened, independent of any yea or nay from America in any decision that might have to be made. Yet British policy was making Britain more, not less dependent on America. To maintain her credibility as a nuclear power Britain had made a deal for buying from America Skybolt air-to-ground rockets, which could have given her ageing force of V-bombers another lease of life. When Skybolt failed at the tests America offered Britain Polaris missiles, which could be fitted with British nuclear warheads and launched from British-built nuclear submarines.

This arrangement was made at the Nassau conference between Kennedy and Macmillan on 18–21 December 1962. A plan was also mooted on the same occasion by the Americans, to strengthen the ties between the NATO allies through the formation of a 'multilateral' nuclear naval force centred around the American and British Polaris-carrying submarines[46]—a force in which not only would vessels of various nations serve, but in which further integration would take place, it was hoped, through mixed-manning. However nice it was for the British to be granted continued membership of the nuclear club in this way, the whole project was of a kind to be anathema to de Gaulle. He had already forbidden the siting of nuclear weapons under NATO command on French soil.

Looked at from this point of view the Nassau agreement made it more than ever impossible for de Gaulle to accept Britain, as a nuclear client of America, in the European Community. It made no difference that Macmillan met him at Rambouillet on 15 December, just before proceeding to Nassau, and told him that he would be asking for help from the Americans in place of Skybolt.[47] There was one possible way of retreat for Macmillan, but not one which he was prepared to take—to begin cutting his ties with America and instead offer to come into a nuclear partnership with France: de Gaulle may indeed have been 'holding out a perch' to Macmillan with this in view, but he could not possibly alight on it.[48] It was not surprising, therefore, when Common Market entry was raised, that de Gaulle queried Macmillan's protestations that Britain was no longer given to the splendid isolation of Victorian days, and asked whether the British were really ready to shut themselves up with the Continentals behind a common external tariff, abandoning their importation of cheap Commonwealth food. Were they ready to join the 'European Europe' of de Gaulle's vision, abandon their privileged ties with America, and stop trying to drown the Community in a sea of 'Atlanticism'?[49] When, a few days later, news of the Nassau agreement came through, followed by an offer of Polaris missiles to the French on the same terms as to the British, provided they committed the *force de frappe* to NATO, de Gaulle could flatter himself that France had now come on far enough under his tutelage to be offered membership of the Anglo-American nuclear club—which he courteously refused—while being strengthened in his conviction that Britain was not yet ready to enter 'Europe'.

He made the point again in his broadcast for New Year 1963, referring to the way in which the union of Western Europe was 'establishing the balance with the United States'—a union which was 'ready to receive in the future an England which could and would wish to join them definitely and without reserve'.[50] To the perceptive it was a negative answer to the question whether he would allow Britain into the Community. De Gaulle could afford to take this line—he and France were riding high. Much of his speech was in a tone of self-assurance and congratulation, with the promise of a great France of 100 m. souls by the time the century ended.

At this point a whole stable of Trojan horses began to be mentioned in the French press. Not only was Britain risking being a Trojan horse for America, by seeking to enter the Community at the same time as integrating completely her system of defence in that of America,[51] but American capital investment in Europe, already on a scale to make planning on the government level difficult, was playing a similar role.[52] It was almost as if a *mot d'ordre* had come from the General.

While doubts were increasing (except apparently among the British) as to whether the negotiations could still succeed, de Gaulle on the 14th January held the press-conference which was their death-warrant. What angered his partners—with the exception of Adenauer who was now ready to accept anything as long as the Franco-German Treaty was signed—was the fact that he took the decision to torpedo the negotiations without consulting them, and announced it unilaterally as a personal ukaze in direct opposition to their wills. 'With a brutality without example in the history of the European Community, manifesting utter scorn for those with whom he was negotiating, allies or adversaries, he stopped the negotiations which he had undertaken in complete agreement with his partners, while invoking pretexts whose brittleness was only too obvious ... Never more could the confidence and the spirit of co-operation which had prevailed during the early years exist in the same way'.[53]

Heath and the representatives of the five tried to ignore the General's directive, and continued with their discussions on the Mansholt Committee's report as if nothing had happened—if there was to be a break, they felt, the onus must be put squarely on the General for making it. On the 16th Couve told Luns that an end must be made 'of all this nonsense', and at a meeting of ministers the following day made it clear to his colleagues that the negotiations would have to stop. 'The rumpus was indescribable. All the ministers lost their tempers, none with more zest than M. Spaak'.[54] With the Commission standing firm alongside the other Foreign Ministers the French were completely isolated. Even so the General's will had to be done, and the negotiations were finally ended on 29 January 1963.

Whatever de Gaulle's reasons, the pretext for his action had been provided by the half-hearted way in which Macmillan and his associates (with exceptions such as Heath) had explained to their countrymen the need for British entry as they saw it, and by the vacillating attitude of the Labour opposition, culminating in Gaitskell's outright rejection of the proposal after first accepting it in principle. It was 'not only de Gaulle and the Gaullists, but other more Anglophile Europeans, [who] observed this apparent lack of commitment' on the part of Macmillan, while it was easy enough for de Gaulle to exploit the doubts raised by Gaitskell and his colleagues at the Labour Party Conference in October 1962. The ardently nationalist tone of the speeches on that occasion, the contempt for what was called 'the two faces of Europe', the assertions that Britain would become merely 'a province of Europe' and as such could no longer fulfil her duties as mother country of the Commonwealth[55]—all this gave colour to the view that Britain was not ready to enter the Community. A further practical point was not overlooked by the General. Macmillan, he believed, was on the way out : there was little sense in doing further business with him when a prospective Labour Government would relegate the whole question of Britain's entry to the Greek Calends.[56]

'You will see', the General said to Luns à propos of his recently pronounced veto, 'the Conservatives will be defeated at the next election. Labour will make such a mess of it that the Conservatives will win the following election—then England may be ready to enter the Community'. By that time, in his view, England would be weak enough.[57]

REFERENCES

[1] Speech at Second World Congress of Man-made Fibres, London, 1.5.62.
[2] Le Monde, 15.1.61.
[3] Economist, 29.7.61.
[4] Ibid., 4.11.61.
[5] Charles de Gaulle: The Edge of the Sword (first published 1932—English edition, London, 1960), 40, 41, 62.
[6] Charles de Gaulle: Mémoires d'Espoir: Le Renouveau, 194.
[7] Camps, 426–7.
[8] Alfred Grosser: La Politique Extérieure de la Ve République (Paris, 1965), 114.
[9] Mémoires d'Espoir: Le Renouveau, 199.
[10] Guardian, 1.4.60; Financial Times, 4.4.60.
[11] George Ball (speech of 8.2.62), quoted in M. Beloff, 114.
[12] Hansard, Vol. 640, 17.5.61 (Heath).
[13] Camps, 281.
[14] Hansard, Vol. 645, col. 1490; Anthony Sampson: Macmillan (London, 1967), 212.
[15] Le Monde, 2.8.61.
[16] The Observer, 1.8.61.
[17] John Newhouse: De Gaulle and the Anglo-Saxons (London, 1970), 82.
[18] Ibid., 168.
[19] Ibid., 68.

[20] Maurice Couve de Murville: *Une Politique Etrangère 1958–1969* (Paris, 1971), 245.

[21] *Le Renouveau*, 205.

[22] Ibid., 207.

[23] Grosser, 86.

[24] Information from Dr. Luns.

[25] Anthony Hartley: *Gaullism* (London, 1971), 243.

[26] *Economist*, 9.12.61.

[27] *Hansard*, Vol. 645, col. 1491; Camps, 360.

[28] Camps, 334.

[29] Walter Hallstein: *United Europe* (Havard, 1962), 55.

[30] Camps, 376.

[31] Ibid., 375; Spaak II, 398–9.

[32] Camps, 372.

[33] Edward Heath: *Old World, New Horizons* (London, 1970), 31.

[34] Camps, 371, 373.

[35] *The Times*, 14.10.60; *Economist*, 31.12.60.

[36] Hallstein, 47.

[37] Camps, 462.

[38] Mayne: *Recovery of Europe*, 271.

[39] *The Observer*, 14.5.61; *Guardian*, 27.7.61.

[40] *Le Renouveau*, 212.

[41] At an Elysée reception, reported in *The Times*, 29.6.62; see also Couve de Murville, *op. cit.*, 411.

[42] Hartley, 221.

[43] Piers Dixon: *Double Diploma: The Life of Sir Pierson Dixon* (London, 1968), 285, 291.

[44] Newhouse, 175.

[45] Ibid., 281.

[46] Elisabeth Barker: *Britain in a divided Europe 1946–1970* (London, 1971), 175.

[47] Dixon, 300.

[48] N. Beloff, 158; Newhouse, 207.

[49] De Gaulle: *Le Renouveau*, 230–32; Barker, 183.

[50] *Observer Foreign News Service*, 1.1.63 (Nora Beloff).

[51] *Le Monde*, 10.1.63 (André Fontaine).

[52] *Le Monde*, 10.1.63 (Maurice Duverger).

[53] Spaak, II, 401, 406.

[54] N. Beloff, 167.

[55] Ibid., 140.

[56] Ibid., 156.

[57] Information from Dr. Luns.

17

The Crisis of 1965

By January 1965 de Gaulle had in effect shot his bolt. His veto on British membership threw his colleagues of the Six temporarily into confusion. French power had been asserted, and the battle-line clearly set with the Anglo-Saxons.[1] The special relationship with the German Federal Republic was apparently secured, crowned by the Franco-German Treaty of Friendship, which Adenauer (braving criticism in his own ranks) came to sign in Paris a few days after the veto.

In reality this treaty set the seal upon an epoch which was ending. The special relationship which the General had fostered with Adenauer had failed the year before, though only just, to achieve the objective of a political structure for 'European Europe', wrecked on the granitic obstinacy of the Dutch. With Adenauer's retirement from the Chancellorship in October 1963 the situation changed. Ludwig Erhard and his Foreign Minister Gerhard Schroeder were not disposed to play along with de Gaulle —if they had to make a choice between France and America, they would come down in favour of America. Nor did the German public wish to change this state of affairs. When Kennedy visited Germany in 1963 the ovations were as warm as those accorded to de Gaulle a year before.[2] Only in a negative sense had de Gaulle achieved something, by bringing Kennedy's policy of partnership with a united Western Europe to a halt. Beyond that he could not go. He had regarded the British as a Trojan horse for America in Europe (a concept remote from American thinking)—but he had 'mistaken the horse'. This turned out to be Germany rather than Britain.[3]

The next years saw frustration in the Franco-German relationship. There were the arrangements for regular meetings and consultation at various levels, but on general lines of policy there was little meeting of minds. In Community affairs the common effort at co-ordinated policies, to achieve a consensus by 'Community spirit', evaporated. Schroeder brought back bargaining, virtually horse-trading of the old diplomatic kind, by his proposals for a 'synchronised working programme', initially for supporting the French desire for completing the common agricultural policy in exchange for their approval for bringing the Community into the Kennedy round of tariff-cutting.

The Kennedy Round had been proposed by the United States with a view to reducing the effects of the Community's common tariff as an obstacle to their trade. Erhard's faith was in free trade policies, but there were Gaullist fears that the Kennedy Round might be the prelude to some kind of economic association between Europe and America, an Atlantic community in which Britain would play a major part. If Germany pushed her partners towards accepting a re-vamped version of the Free Trade Area, 'Europe' would again be in danger of dissolution in it.

This bogey of 'Atlantisme' was not so alarming as to stop France from exacting the uttermost in rewards from the common agricultural policy, but it put a strain on Community relations. The other danger of supranationalism within the Community de Gaulle was determined to scotch, no less since the Commission's President, with his supranational ambitions, was a German backed in his policies by the Federal Republic.

Walter Hallstein was a man of considerable experience when he became President of the Commission. In addition to war-time service and an American prison camp, he had reached the highest honours in his profession, of Law, had become Rector of Frankfurt University, head of the German Foreign Office, and his country's principal negotiator in the setting up of the Coal and Steel Community at the Messina and Brussels conferences. As President of the Commission he had conducted affairs with a mixture of boldness and prudence, handling issues with especial delicacy on which the French felt strongly. But if it had been possible to accuse him of being pro-French, as some had been ready to do, he set himself on a collision course with them in 1965 by trying for too much too quickly.

France's acceptance of Hallstein as President of the Commission in January 1958 had been hailed as an important sign of the extent to which the hatchet had been buried between France and Germany. Whether de Gaulle shared these feelings at the time is unlikely (he had not yet returned to power), but he expressed himself unfavourably about Hallstein later. 'He ardently espouses the superstate', de Gaulle wrote. He did not like Hallstein assuming the trappings of the head of a sovereign state, 'disposing of several thousand officials ... receiving letters of credence from foreign ambassadors, aspiring to great honours on his official visits'. He regarded him as a sincere European, but first and foremost as 'a German ambitious for his country' (nationalism for de Gaulle was the prime motive wherever he looked). Hallstein's Europeanism, in his view, 'provided a framework in which his country could freely find again respectability and equality of rights ... then acquire the preponderant weight necessary ... to bring it about that the quarrel over its frontiers and unity should be assumed by a powerful group'.[4]

Hallstein, in other words, wanted to use the EEC for Germany's national ends, whereas he, de Gaulle, was determined to use it for France's—and if he failed in his claim to a monopoly in this matter, he was prepared to limit the Community to a low level of function, and if necessary to destroy it.

For the time being it was showing renewed vitality, though with less Community spirit, which waned as 'synchronisation' increased, with all the partners insisting that immediate payment should be made for concessions. The difficulties in negotiations were becoming greater, partly because the Community was moving into a new phase. The Treaty of Rome had initiated a process and laid down guide-lines, and it had been a question of lowering and adjusting tariffs, and putting in place the bits of machinery for making a customs union. Now the next phase was on the way, an economic union, and after that would come 'the third stage of the rocket', as Hallstein called it, political union, which for him meant federation.[5]

Meanwhile some important steps were taken. In December 1963 a package covering many agricultural items was got through after a typical marathon session complete with all-night sitting, thus clearing the way for starting the Kennedy Round. Pressure had been great to complete this deal, since de Gaulle had threatened that the Community would 'disappear' if the deadlines for the settlement of these agricultural issues were not met, and the relief at this achievement was correspondingly great. A year later when there were even more anxieties over the December package, the rejoicing was greater and expectations for the future more euphoric; and in April 1965 another large step was taken, bringing about the fusion of the institutions of the three Communities. But, such moods apart, there was a feeling that the EEC was getting through a time of testing, that the process of integration was proving irreversible, and that prospects were reasonably bright. 'The *élan*, the romanticism and the sense of urgency of earlier days was missing, but there was a feeling of commitment to the Economic Community that ran deeper than the differences between France and the rest'.[6]

There was therefore little reason for forebodings as the Community moved into 1965, a decade after the 're-launch' of Messina which had brought it into being. Yet its existence was jeopardised by the attempt of Hallstein to move farther and faster than was wise towards the still distant goal of federalism, which was countered—inevitably—by the intransigent opposition of the General.

Early in 1965 Hallstein, strongly supported by Mansholt, prepared a package along synchronisation lines, which was approved by his colleagues on the Commission though not without warnings and objections from the Frenchman, Robert Marjolin. It was designed to complete the business which the French had much at heart, the payments to the fund which financed matters such as export rebates and modernisation schemes under the common agricultural policy. The Commission's plan was that the levies on food imports from outside the Community should be paid direct into the fund, together with the duties accruing from the common external tariff on industrial goods; and this tariff it was expected would be in place by 1 July 1967, the same date as common prices for agricultural products within the Community were to come into force.

Since France would be the greatest beneficiary of the fund, she had an immediate interest in completing these arrangements. For the time being, until 1 July 1967, the current arrangements for financing the fund would continue, i.e. each country would make contributions to the fund in accordance with a 'key' which had been previously negotiated. The French themselves had seemed ready for the change of system which would give the Community, under the Commission's direction, its 'own resources'.

This strengthening of the Commission, making it somewhat more independent, ran counter to de Gaulle's policy of limiting the supranational elements in the Community, but it was hoped that no objections would come from that quarter since the assuming of its 'own resources' by the Community had been foreseen by the Treaty of Rome, and was a logical outcome of the agricultural policy for which France had so stoutly battled. It might be expected that the throwing in of the proceeds of the industrial tariffs could also be allowed to pass, together with the putting forward of the date when this enhancement of the Commission's powers would take effect to July 1967 instead of 1 January 1970, originally foreseen as the date when the transition to the customs union would be complete.

What was perhaps more open to question was the third element in the Commission's package, the strengthening of the powers of control by the European Assembly over the Community budget. This, Hallstein could claim, was a logical step since, with the ending of national contributions to the Fund one means of democratic control over the spending powers of the Community would disappear, that effected by the national parliaments. It was important therefore to increase the control which the European Parliament (or Assembly, by whichever name it was called) could have over it. Under the Treaty of Rome it was only able to propose amendments to the budget, and it was left to the Council, after consultation with the Commission, whether or not to accept them. Under the modified version of the relevant article of the Treaty (Article 203), amendments supported by the Commission had to be accepted unless they were overruled by the Council with a five-sixths majority.

A further measure of control by the Parliament in financial matters was also proposed: if the Commission needed to increase its 'own resources' above the amount which tariffs and levies would bring in, e.g. by a Community tax, and if the Parliament supported these proposals by a two-thirds majority, the Council could adopt them by a qualified majority vote. This procedure would mean that a government could no longer veto financial proposals supported by both the Commission and the Parliament, if there was the stated majority on the Council in favour of them. Even in the case of the budget being amended by the Parliament and the amendments not being accepted as they stood by the Commission, but modified by it, a four-sixths majority of the Council would be enough to pass it.[7]

When Hallstein publicised his plan in a speech to the Parliament in March 1965 he received from that body the strongest support—and this may have been the moment when de Gaulle determined to dig his toes in. First, French policy was switched from supporting the Commission's proposals that levies should be paid direct into the Agricultural Fund when the single-price system came into effect for the main agricultural commodities in July 1967. Instead, Couve de Murville argued that, since under the Treaty of Rome the single-market stage was not due to come into effect until 1970, the Fund could continue to be financed until then by national contributions. This would mean that the question of control over the levies and related finance by the European Parliament would not arise, since they would continue to be in the purview of the national parliaments. At the same time and with less logic (but in the interest of French farmers), France would continue to support the proposal that the single-price system for the main agricultural products should come into effect on 1 July 1967.

Disposing thus of the possibility that the Community would get its 'own resources' by 1967, the French maintained that the current method of financing the Agricultural Fund by national contributions should continue until 1970, and that all the Council had to do during this period was to confirm the existing arrangements. It was over this point that the rift between Couve, who was Chairman of the Council at the time, and his colleagues really developed, since other countries, and particularly Italy and Germany, were dissatisfied at the way things worked out according to the 'key', or scales, which determined the amount of the national contributions. When the scales were originally determined in 1962 the Italians thought that they, like the French, would be beneficiaries from the system, in that Italy was a net exporter of agricultural produce, so that they would get more from the export rebates paid out from the fund than they would lose from the contribution they had to make to it. But since then Italy had prospered, the standard of living had gone up, and Italy had become a net im-

G   183

porter of produce from outside the Community. There was an obvious injustice in the Italians paying so high a contribution, and though an adjustment was made in 1964 reducing their contribution, they still considered the system disadvantageous to themselves. The Germans took a similar view, since the Federal Republic was also a net importer of foodstuffs, so that they naturally tended to range themselves against France, who was by a long way the chief beneficiary of the system.

The Germans too had their particular grievances, for the French had pressed them strongly in 1964 to accept a standard price for cereals (in the single-price system due to take effect in July 1967) below that which German farmers had been getting—though it was a good price for the French peasants. Erhard had accepted this in December 1964 in the face of de Gaulle's threats that otherwise the Community might 'dissolve', although, with an election coming on in 1965, it meant a hazard for the Government at the polls.

This was just one of many disagreements between the French and Germans which had cropped up since the signing of the Franco-German Treaty of Friendship in January 1963. It was unsatisfactory in practice for the Germans to be tied in with the French, at a time when de Gaulle was trying to make his French-dominated 'European Europe' viable by pressing the Germans to finance his costly nuclear deterrent and for good measure abandon their support for Kennedy's proposal of a NATO Multi-Lateral Force (MLF), which President Johnson, after Kennedy's assassination in November 1963, continued with for a time. By yielding on the cereals price issue in December 1964, and so turning aside de Gaulle's threat about the dissolution of the Community, Erhard hoped that, as a *quid pro quo*, the French would not cavil at his pro-NATO policy (at a moment when de Gaulle was planning to take France out of NATO), and that the way would be open for another stage in the evolution of the Community towards a federation, which was the form of political union favoured by the Germans. Further, having given way over the cereals issue the Germans were not prepared to give way easily to the French over other issues, such as the financing of the Agricultural Fund, on which they had divergent views.

Hence the line-up at Brussels in June 1965, when the French insisted that according to the time-table previously agreed by the Six, the matter of financing the Agricultural Fund had to be settled by the end of the month. The usual threats were made that if it was not so settled a grave situation would arise, though it was not until the Council's meeting on 30 June that the French unwillingness to compromise became clear. Until then the Five had assumed that, although it would be necessary to give way to the French in accepting that the system of financing the Fund by national contributions would continue after July 1967, it would be possible to bargain over the question as to how long after 1967 that system would continue, and that as part of the final package the French would agree to a time-table for considering the Commission's related proposals regarding the Community's 'own resources' and a move towards European parliamentary control.

As the discussions went on under Couve's chairmanship during the afternoon and evening of 30 June a compromise seemed on the way, especially after the French proposed revised scales for contributions to the Fund which favoured the Italians, hitherto their most articulate opponents. At the same time Couve tried to narrow the discussions down to the sole question of renewing the system of financing the Fund until 1970, dismissing all other elements of the Commission's proposals as irrelevant. While Spaak was prepared to support the French, no doubt sensing the danger of a rupture, German opposition in support of the Dutch and Italians hardened. The French were particularly incensed when Dr Schroeder 'ostentatiously drew from his pocket a Bundestag resolution adopted a few hours earlier expressing strong support for an increase in the powers of the European Parliament. This gesture was interpreted as a warning to the French that some concession on the parliamentary point would have to be made'.[8]

Whether this incident had any effect on subsequent developments is doubtful, since de Gaulle had determined that unless France's partners yielded fully on the issue as presented to them by Couve he would seize the opportunity to break the negotiations and challenge the course towards integration on which the Community was set. Instructions to this effect apparently came through from the Elysée during the evening, and although the Five were ready to continue the discussions, or to adjourn them on the stop-the-clock system after the midnight deadline had expired, at 2 a.m.

on 1 July, Couve abruptly declared that it was impossible to reach agreement and therewith ended the session. Next day he stated that since solemn undertakings had not been fulfilled (for settling the financial arrangements by 30 June) there was no point in further discussions and 'each government must draw the consequences'.[9] This was underlined by a statement from the French cabinet, in which the General's hand was to be seen, that because of this lack of respect for engagements taken, 'everything was at dead point', and France would not take part in any further meetings at Brussels. 'One of the most discouraging conclusions that one can draw from the rupture', as *Le Monde* pointed out, 'is the disappearance of the Community spirit to which the Common Market has owed its greatest successes'.[10]

For a time it seemed as if the whole system might come to a halt. On 5 July the French Permanent Representative was withdrawn from Brussels, and a boycott began of meetings of the Council and of all but committees dealing with routine discussions or administration such as the review of farm prices. The French firmly refused to take part in any committee work which could lead to new projects or decisions—'a difficult but inevitable decision', as Couve described it, 'without which the Common Market would have been irrevocably committed to a course of enfeeblement and impotence, and the agricultural policy on which France counted would have been in effect doomed'.[11]

The other Five were determined to stick it out, despite the empty seat at Council and other meetings, but—guided by Spaak and Emilio Colombo of Italy—their policy was to do this in as conciliatory a manner as possible, not attempting new projects but working out mandates arising from previous decisions, and aiding the Commission to elaborate a compromise over the issues which were the immediate cause of the deadlock. This compromise was along the lines which appeared to have been emerging in the meeting of 30 June—1 July before the French broke it off, and leant heavily towards satisfying the French.

One view was that de Gaulle was bluffing, and that he would not press matters to a breakdown of the Common Market—French agriculture had too much to lose. This was soon evident from the storm of protest which came from the farmers' organisations, accompanied by equally strong disapproval from the industrialists[12]

—indeed there was no section of French opinion, apart from the Gaullists, who did not deprecate the General's action, as was shown by the spectrum of speakers at the 1000-strong Extraordinary Congress of the European Movement at Cannes in October.[13]

Meanwhile de Gaulle made it clear that he was prepared to forego his entente with the Germans, since he was now pursuing a policy of rapprochement with Russia which implied weakening on Berlin. He had lost interest in 'European Europe' and was concerned only with 'independence'—for France. The crisis was, in his view, inevitable, and could only be resolved by rectifying certain 'mistakes or ambiguities' in the Treaty of Rome, notably the provisions for the transition to majority voting in the Council and to a strengthened role for the Commission. If 'this embryonic technocracy. for the most part foreign' had its way, 'France would be exposed to the possibility of being overruled in any economic matter whatsoever, and therefore in social and sometimes political matters. . . . One can see where such a subordinate position could lead us, if we allowed ourselves to deny at one and the same time our freedom of action [i.e. give up the right of veto] and our Constitution, which lays down that "'French sovereignty resides in the French people, which exercises it through its representatives and by means of referenda without making any sort of exception at all." '[14]

As the December elections drew near the pro-European and consequently anti-Government pronouncements of farmers, *patronat* and trades unions became stronger.[15] When de Gaulle failed to obtain a clear majority on the first ballot conclusions began to be drawn: it seemed that the Europeans would have to be conciliated. De Gaulle got home on the run-off, but a switch in policy was indicated. Before long the Government accepted a plan, proposed by Spaak, for the Council (including France) to meet—but without the Commission, to consider the situation.

At meetings of the Council at Luxembourg on 17–18 January and 28 January 1966, and at the intervening meetings of the Permanent Representatives—again including the French—at Brussels, a compromise was thrashed out, or rather, on the key issue of majority voting, an agreement to differ. There was general agreement that on 'issues very important to one or more member countries' the Council should try to reach unanimity. The Five

187

accepted that the French view be recorded that, over such issues 'the discussion must be continued until unanimous agreement is reached', while the third paragraph recorded that a divergence of views existed 'on what should be done in the event of a failure to reach complete agreement'. Nevertheless, stated the fourth paragraph, this difference of view would not prevent the Council from resuming its work in accordance with the 'normal procedure'.[16] The French merely made it explicit that there might be another crisis if they found themselves put in a minority on a matter where they deemed that their vital interests were at stake.

As for the other issues, the Commission's wings were slightly clipped. It had to accept a rather stricter procedure for preparing its proposals through consultations with the Permanent Representatives, in order to ensure better contact with the member governments, but its all-important right of initiative was specifically safeguarded. A time-table was also agreed along lines proposed by the French, for settling outstanding issues such as the regulation for financing the Agricultural Fund. The fact that the Five gave so little ground and that the Treaty of Rome was preserved was due in large part to the leadership assumed by Dr. Schroeder—the first time in the history of the Community that Germany had been ready to offer such leadership in confrontation with France, and that the remaining Four had been ready to accept it. This uniting of the Five into a cohesive body under German leadership may well have been a reason as weighty as the alienation of pro-European opinion in France for de Gaulle's abandonment of the attempt at 'settling accounts once and for all with a supranational Europe'.[17]

A scapegoat, or rather victim, was found in Hallstein, the renewal of whose Presidency of the Commission was blocked by France, except—after protestations by Germany—for a one-year term. As such an arrangement would have been a breach of the Treaty, Hallstein took the dignified course of retiring.

REFERENCES

[1] Couve de Murville, 257.
[2] Hartley, 225.
[3] Grosser, 99.
[4] De Gaulle: *Le Renouveau*, 195.
[5] Walter Hallstein: *1963—Year of Trial* (address at annual meeting of German newspaper publishers, 4.7.63), 3–5.

[6] Miriam Camps: *What Kind of Europe?* (London, 1965), 33.
[7] Miriam Camps: *European Unification in the Sixties* (London, 1967), 43–45.
[8] Camps, *op. cit.*, 67.
[9] Ibid., 69; Couve de Murville, *op. cit.*, 334.
[10] *Le Monde*, 2.7.65 (Roger Massip).
[11] Couve, 334.
[12] *The Times*, 3.7.65.
[13] *Le Monde*, 3–4.10.65.
[14] Speech of 9.7.65, quoted in Camps: *European Unification in the Sixties*, 81–2.
[15] Camps, 96.
[16] Ibid., 112.
[17] Hartley, 229.

18

The EEC since the Luxembourg Compromise

The return of France to normal membership of the Community was a victory, even if a qualified one, for the Commission. Since then decisions in the Council have sometimes been reached by majority vote, but complex moves and systems of consultation have been developed, and have to be worked through, before major matters involving decisions are even brought before the Council.

The main bodies operating this system are, first, the President and members of the Commission. The Commission's primary role is that of initiator. In a similar way to that in which Monnet's Commission of the Plan operated in France, but now on a supranational basis, it has to identify what are the common interests of the Six—basically in terms of economic adjustment and development; and, after consulting the Permanent Representatives, the European Parliament, the Economic and Social Council, as well as governments, pressure groups and other interested parties, it has to make proposals as to how these interests can best be forwarded —proposals which may take the form of broad lines of policy as well as detailed and highly complex measures.

In this respect the Commission has the functions of a secretariat, and at meetings of the Council, where its views are presented by the President or others, it has something of the role of a chairman, though the President never in fact takes the chair.[1] It has to mediate between the conflicting views of the member governments, to find a consensus and effect compromises.

Besides these initiating and mediatory roles it has supervisory and even executive functions. It has to keep a watch on the way the Community's policies and regulations are carried out, and where they are not being observed it has to bring such breaches to the attention of governments or individual firms, and, if necessary, bring them before the Court of Justice. But as an executive its powers are circumscribed since a far larger share of executive powers in the sense of the ability to take decisions, is in the hands of the Council. In so far as these powers 'are prescribed and defined by the Treaties or by the Community rules laid down by the Council, "executant" would be as appropriate a term for them as "executive". Only in a limited sense does the Commission have the margin of decision in changing circumstances that is normally the prerogative of the executive branch of government'.[2]

The Council is the body where ultimate power lies. It is composed of the Foreign Ministers of the member countries, or other Ministers as deputed, and meets monthly or at other times as necessary. Its powers are restricted by the fact that it is dependent on the Commission's initiatives for making any policy whatever, and that it has to be unanimous if it is to amend the Commission's proposals—though by a qualified majority it can reject them. 'As a forum for decision-making the Council is certainly the Community's supreme legislative institution',[3] yet it only has time to consider a limited number of issues presented by the Commission. The rest are dealt with by the third body to play a part in the process, the Committee of Permanent Representatives of the member states.

The need for such a body became clear in the early days of the workings of the ECSC, though this had not been foreseen by the Treaty of Paris. A committee was created by the Council of Ministers in February 1953 'to co-ordinate the elements' of its work, and 'to assure to the sessions of the Council an appropriate preparation, in such a way as to facilitate its work by the examination and advanced study of the questions on its agenda'.[4] The utility of this body was such that a provision for creating 'a committee formed out of the representatives of the member states', of which the Council was to determine the role and competence, was set up by Article 151 of the Treaty of Rome.

The Permanent Representatives forming this committee are of ambassadorial status, and perform two functions, 1. representing their countries in dealing with the Commission, and 2. preparing the briefs for their respective Ministers on the Council, while settling among themselves all questions which can be appropriately dealt with (i.e. all minor questions and those without political connotations). Agreements in the latter cases are filed on List A, which the Council formally validates without examination (though it is open to a Minister to challenge the decisions of the Committee). Only the more important or controversial questions are relegated to List B for the personal consideration of the Ministers.

Much of the work in preparing the agreements, and also for the briefing of the Ministers on the more controversial issues, is of a highly technical nature, and is carried out by groups of experts working with or under the assistants of the Representatives who compose their staff or 'cabinets'. There are ten or so of these 'groupes de travail'. These are not to be confused with other working-groups set up directly by the Council for special purposes, such as that for agriculture.[5]

All this activity is enmeshed with that of the Commission by the fact that the full Committee of Permanent Representatives meets with the Commission at least weekly, and that its task is to work out the practical application of the initiatives proposed by the Commission; further, it meets most days with one or another member of the Commission. All these meetings and the numerous social contacts, both with the Commission members and with each other, do much to temper the national stance of the committee members, who can be regarded as the hinge between Commission and Council—though they also (and this applies particularly to the French Representative) appear at times to the Commission more in the nature of an opposing element.[6]

The fourth element is composed of the Commission's secretariat. This has evolved from that of the High Authority for the ECSC, which was created by Monnet on the lines of his Commission for the Plan in France, and was directed by him in the same highly personal manner and with the same flair for developing team-work in unconventional ways which he had previously shown. There was much improvisation, little respect for protocol, practically no grades or ranks—everyone participating fully in what each regarded as a common enterprise.

As in the French Commission of the Plan,[7] so in the Authority, Monnet hoped to keep the numbers of officials small, a mere 60 or so—but inevitably these increased. Heads of Divisions were appointed and grades were introduced. Nevertheless relations between officials in the different grades remained close and friendly, and most had a sense of participating in a satisfactory way. The tone was set by Monnet's way of conducting the Authority's meetings: when national feelings were aroused over whatever issue among the supposedly supranational members, Monnet would bang the table—'We must remember we are *Europeans*!'[8] But 'le style Monnet' could not be continued indefinitely in conditions where a relatively large bureaucracy was concerned; a certain cheerful anarchy was acceptable when the situation was fresh and fluid, not when it meant leaving a Head of Division waiting for two or three hours to be seen.

After Monnet resigned in 1954 his successor, René Mayer, kept the machine going as well as possible, instituting regular meetings for his immediate colleagues on the Authority and making other necessary arrangements. A new stage was reached with the creation of the EEC after the ratification of the Treaty of Rome in 1957, and the establishment of its Commission at Brussels. Over a quarter of the officials came from the ECSC at Luxembourg permanently, and others were seconded temporarily to help start the organisation off, but with the influx of new officials what was left of the spirit and methods of the Monnet days was gradually eroded. Hallstein introduced an almost hierarchic stratification of the officials, and punctilio and protocol became increasingly important. After the fusion of the ECSC and Euratom with EEC became effective in 1967, a small number of officials were left at Luxembourg to maintain ancillary services, the rest joining those at Brussels to make up the five or six thousand who now work in the vast and airless 'Bâtiment Berlaymont' and other neighbouring buildings.

It is perhaps symbolical of this situation that only the windows of the top floor of the Berlaymont open, bringing a breath of fresh air and freedom to the Commissioners and those attending the Council whose meeting place is there. The other officials, immured in their glass and concrete boxes, complain, and even strike, on account of the unbreathable atmosphere, but the malaise is as much psychological as physical. Many officials feel frustrated because too little Community spirit exists in the organisation itself: the very word Community is belied by the lack of this quality as felt by members of the 'Eurocrats' themselves.

This is largely the problem of any big organisation—difficulties of communication, a failure of the sense of participation, promotions and appointments made for reasons other than the efficiency of the institution, and in consequence a growing preoccupation about career and a tendency to politicking on the part of the officials in general.

The continued existence of a fund of enthusiasm and idealism among some of the officials is however still noticeable. This was indicated by the demonstration at the time of The Hague Conference in December 1969, when officials through their union organisations joined the Mouvement Fédéral Européen to come in their hundreds to 'defend the European idea'. Several thousand, including the Directors-General, signed a manifesto which was delivered to the Chairman of the Conference, the Prime Minister of Holland.

The cry for greater participation is a familiar one since the student riots and other happenings—'the events'—of May 1968. The officials may be right: if there is to be a real community in Europe, the officials of the Community, the whole way in which the business is done, could well set the pattern. With Britain and her associates members, this may be one of the levels where her greatest contribution could be made. The esteem with which British administration is regarded on the Continent is a pointer in this direction. British entry could in fact help to improve the workings of what may otherwise develop into an even more cumbrous machine, provided that the British officials at all levels have the personality, tact, imagination and various other qualities to help break down the rigidities which have been developing.

Despite the increasingly complex nature of the negotiations which have to be pursued in the formulation of policy, progress could still be satisfactory if the will, or the 'Community spirit', were to exist in sufficient strength. The customs union for industrial goods was effected in 1968, two years before the end of the transition period envisaged by the Treaty of Rome; the common market in agriculture was also completed; and the Commission carried out a successful negotiation with the Americans, on behalf of the Six, in the tariff-cutting procedure of the Kennedy Round. Further, with de Gaulle's resignation in 1969, it became possible to take steps for bringing about the entry of Britain, Denmark, Norway and Ireland.

On the other hand the effects of de Gaulle's attempt to substitute nationalism for Community spirit in the operations of the EEC are difficult to assess. The Commission's cautious and appeasing policy towards France after the fiasco of the abortive 1965 package deal was no doubt necessary to bring her back to a reasonable degree of co-operation without too much loss of face. Besides the forced retirement of Hallstein from the Commission, Etienne Hirsch, a committed 'European' and one of Monnet's former brains-trust, had also been obliged to vacate the presidency of the Euratom Commission in favour of a Gaullist nominee. Officials have been increasingly appointed as nationals of particular countries or as representatives of interested groups who have to be kept in line, rather than *engagés* of the European idea.

In other words, what is threatening the Commission is bureaucracy at its worst, inefficient, rigid and uncreative, its appointments dependent on patronage, and lacking the stimulus and control which a democratically elected parliament might provide. Instead of identifying the best course of action to pursue in given circumstances, there is a tendency towards a cautious balancing approach for effecting a compromise at a level acceptable to all: policy tends 'to be based on the sum of the member countries' protectionisms rather than on a rational conception of the Community as a whole'.[9] Fear of another confrontation such as that of 1965 between the Five and the French has made for immobility. It is clear that no automatic process has been set in motion for bringing the Commission to the point where it would acquire sovereign control over decisive areas and so achieve what has been called 'a benign conspiracy to create a federal Europe behind the backs of the Governments'.[10]

However many sectors of the economy are brought under the Commission's control, there is still a leap to be made from this 'functionalist' accruing of specialised powers to the full-scale sovereignty implied in authority in its widest political sense, i.e. over the armed forces and those areas where the threat of armed might can make itself felt, foreign affairs. Whatever may be the future of the European experiment, de Gaulle's intervention was decisive in precluding the Commission from becoming the executive of a federal Europe.

REFERENCES

[1] Richard Mayne: *The Institutions of the European Community* (London, 1968), 29.

[2] Ibid., 28.

[3] Ibid., 29.

[4] W. J. Ganshof van der Meersch (ed.): *Les Novelles: Droit des Communités Européennes* (Brussels, 1969).

[5] Ibid., 245–6. For a full analysis of the working of the Committee of Permanent Representatives and its relation with other committees (eg. the important Medium-Term Economic Policy Committee), see *Government and Opposition*, Vol. 6, no. 4, Autumn 1971, pp. 417 ff., or Ghita Ionescu: *The New Politics of European Integration* (London, 1972).

[6] Ibid., 249, 250. Information from M. J. V. M. van der Meulen and M. Jean Rey.

[7] See above, p. 61 *seq.*

[8] Information from Mr. Tony Rollman.

[9] John Pinder: 'Positive and Negative Integration', *The World Today*, vol. 24, No. 3, March 1968, 100, cited in David Coombes: *Politics and Bureaucracy in the European Community* (London, 1970), 303.

[10] Andrew Shonfield: 'Journey to an unknown destination' (Reith Lecture, 1972).

19

British Entry and the Prospects for Europe

De Gaulle's intervention in favour of 'Europe des états' may not have precluded an eventual move to federation: it certainly slowed it up, and the sign of this was the downgrading of the pretensions to represent a sovereign body on the part of the President of the Commission, when the practice initiated by Hallstein of receiving Ambassadors to the Community in the manner of the head of a state was discontinued. This blow to the federal idea was however pleasing to those, especially in Britain, who wished to gain the benefits of membership of the Community without the sacrifice of sovereign status which would result from federation. In the Labour Party particularly waverers who belonged to its old strongly anti-federalist core could be won to support entry to the Common Market.

Though a certain amount of Labour support developed at the time of Macmillan's bid for entry to the Communities, this was negated by Macmillan's making the question more of a party matter than he need have done, and by the half-heartedness of Gaitskell's support at its strongest and his turning against British entry before he died in January 1963. The issue of British entry was 'a dead duck' at the election in October 1964, but soon after its victory at the polls Labour was forced to re-think its attitude.

The development of EFTA had no attractive political possibilities; even as a small free-trade area in industrial goods it was treated cavalierly by the British Government when, without consultation with its members or any other warning, a 15 per cent surcharge was slapped on imports—which particularly hit the EFTA countries—soon after Labour achieved power. 'The fact that the EFTA countries received no better treatment than the other European countries ... made a mockery of the frequent assertions by Labour leaders that, unlike the Conservatives, they took the EFTA seriously and intended to make it a more important instrument'.[1] In practice they found that EFTA was in no way a substitute for EEC, especially if the question concerned the regaining of Britain's political influence in Europe. Eventually, after skirting round the problem for some time and going through motions similar to those of the Conservatives a few years before—yearning for 'co-operation' of the OEEC type, hoping for 'bridge-building' between the Six and the Seven—for anything short of actually entering the EEC—enough Labour leaders became convinced that entrance into the Community was the price Britain would have to pay if she was to achieve political influence abroad and economic viability at home.

It was now all too obvious that the nation-state had become too narrow a context within which to build socialism in one country. What the Attlee Government had attempted, not without some success, in the immediate post-war years, with all the apparatus of war-time controls at its disposal, was quite impracticable in the nineteen-sixties. With the extension of the welfare state and the complex management of the economy, the civil service had greatly swollen and government had become more expensive. This, together with rising standards and the need to maintain economic growth, produced a situation in which Keynsian policies on a national basis could not work—though Keynes as far back as the twenties had been advocating wide free-trade areas. The overheads of the system could not be absorbed when the economic base was a population of only some 55 million.

What the Benelux countries had realised in the nineteen-thirties and the Six in the fifties had now become stark reality for Britain in the sixties. The limits of sovereignty on a political and economic level had been demonstrated by the speed with which a disapproving America had brought the Suez venture—undertaken by Western Europe's two strongest powers—to a halt. Now, when Harold Wilson took over the government the impossibility of proceeding to extend the welfare state in accordance with electoral promises, was swiftly revealed. The last months of the 'never-had-it-so-good' Conservative Government had already run down the reserves to danger-point, and on the morrow of Labour's accession to power the Bank of England, through its Governor Lord Cromer, warned that a policy of 'stop' instead of 'go' was imperative.[2]

From then on the Government was hag-ridden by its balance of payments difficulties. Britain was soon deeply in debt, having borrowed all she could from the International Monetary Fund and the governments and banks of available countries. Her budgets in the years immediately after devaluation were checked by an IMF team,[3] and though, under Roy Jenkins as Chancellor of the Exchequer, Britain after devaluation in 1967 came back again into the black, her financial and monetary difficulties made the Group of Ten or the 'Gnomes of Zürich' powerful factors in the determination of policies. Rather than continue with such *ad hoc* truncating of sovereignty, involving a passive role for Britain vis-à-vis the bankers and international agencies, it was clearly far better for Britain to enter a structured system where, by pooling sovereignty and sharing in the decision-making, she could both give and take.

Once committed, Labour made its attempt. Wilson told the Assembly of the Council of Europe in January 1967 that Britain would join the Community so that it could 'speak from strength to our Atlantic partners', and would not be left out of the new political unity that would be forged within the next twenty years. 'History and the young generation', he said, 'will condemn, beyond any power of ours to defend or excuse, the failure to seize what so many of us can clearly see now as a swirling, urgent tide in man's affairs.'[4] He gave special responsibilities for Europe to two strong pro-Marketeers, George Brown and George Thomson, and with Brown toured the capitals of the Six to investigate the possibilities and terms for British entry. Support was duly given by the Five, and though de Gaulle was not absolutely discouraging, he eventually vetoed the negotiations in November 1967.

Nonetheless there were signs that the General's attitude towards British entry was changing, connected with a reassessment on his part of the strategy needed to secure Europe's independence from America. Jean Rey was convinced that the successful negotiation of the Kennedy Round by the Commission, concluded in 1967, had started a shift in his thinking, for without the governments of the Six giving full powers to a single negotiator—on that occasion Jean Rey himself—it would have been impossible for the great weight of the Community to have counted, enabling it to stand as an equal negotiator confronting the enormous power of America.

The bargaining on that occasion had been tough. Before his

death in 1963 Kennedy had proposed that a 50 per cent tariff cut should be made by all the countries which had signed the General Agreement on Tariffs and Trade (GATT), but since America's tariffs were so high, in some cases twice as high as those of the EEC, America would still have been left with an undue trading advantage if the Kennedy formula had been directly applied. A strong negotiator was needed on behalf of the Community, to bring American tariffs down to something nearer the European level as the price for easing admittance of American goods to the European market. Jean Rey as chief negotiator for the Community found his hands almost tied by the necessity of constantly referring back to the governments of the Six or their representatives, whose deliberations were slowed by the bickering amongst them. After days of deadlock at Geneva, and unable to wait for a meeting of the Council of Ministers, Rey phoned the French and German governments for authorisation to act as a plenipotentiary—an arrangement in which the other Four concurred—and was able to bring the negotiations to a triumphant conclusion.[5]

Rey believed that this spectacle of the European Community acting as a unity and on equal terms in a large negotiation with America revealed to de Gaulle possibilities of the role it might play which he had not appreciated before. At the same time, disillusioned with the special relationship with the German Federal Republic as a means of securing French hegemony, de Gaulle seemed more disposed to look to Britain. But, though Britain 'had evolved much' from the position she used to take vis-à-vis America, as he told Wilson in January 1967, and now 'really wished to moor herself alongside the Continent',[6] the process had not gone far enough. He was still afraid that British entry would lead to the creation of a free trade zone in Western Europe pending an Atlantic one, and thought it best to wait until the British should 'achieve the profound economic and political transformation which would enable them to join the Six continentals'.[7]

It was true that Britain, or at least the Labour Party, had apparently much evolved. The White Paper put up by the Wilson Government in favour of applying for entry was approved in the House of Commons by 488 votes against 62—'the biggest majority on a contested vote on a matter of public policy for almost a century', as Wilson pointed out.[8] Though this did not stop de Gaulle from re-imposing his veto, it seemed that he had evolved further himself after the unnerving experience of the students' revolt and subsequent 'events' in the spring and summer of 1968. In February 1969 he told the recently appointed British Ambassador, Christopher Soames, that, while British entry would still change the character of the Common Market, he was now prepared to accept such a change, which he foresaw would be into a loose form of free trade area, within which Britain was to join with France, Germany and Italy as one of an ill-defined directorate. His suggestion of secret bilateral talks to resolve differences between the British and French views fell to the ground however when the Foreign Office informed Germany and the other Community partners about the démarche lest they should get the impression of something going on behind their backs, which left de Gaulle and his government feeling that their confidence had been betrayed.[10]

The General's understandable annoyance at this response to his olive-branch might have held up further advance indefinitely but for his resignation the following May. His successor, Georges Pompidou, trimming his sails to the wind, called a meeting of the Six at The Hague that December (1st–2nd) in order to bring the whole Community project on to a new course. There, after a rather half-hearted speech in which Pompidou seemed to suggest that France was likely to proceed with the tactics of 1962–63, Willi Brandt, the new German Chancellor, appearing as 'the real leader of the European Community',[9] called for a clear commitment to enlarging it, and for a deadline for opening negotiations with Britain and the other candidates. His people, he said, expected him to return from the conference with 'concrete arrangements for the Community's enlargement'. Pompidou's response was positive. Negotiations were fixed to begin with Britain the following midsummer. They were opened by the Conservative Government led by Heath shortly after replacing Labour at the election of June 1970.

The condition for progress, Pompidou said, was completing the financial regulation for agriculture. After that, along with the enlargement of the Community, steps could be taken towards monetary and eventually economic union. It was a big programme, to be achieved, he later proposed, by 1980. Europe was again on the move.

The French abandonment of the veto on British entry was the decisive factor in this development. Its precondition was the change in Britain's world position and sense of priorities, away from the Commonwealth (whose economic and political importance to Britain had greatly diminished by comparison with the early fifties), and towards a Western Europe with which her trade had greatly increased despite the barrier of the common tariff around the Six. Economic necessity had prompted Britain's abandonment of any serious world-role east of Suez, and her presence in the Persian Gulf was nearing its end. Yet Britain was a country used to counting as a power, and a great one, in the world. Having lost an empire, in Dean Acheson's phrase, and no longer enjoying a special relationship with America, she could only find a role commensurate in some degree with that of her past by close association with her continental neighbours.

For France the moment was convenient. With the completion of the financial regulation the common agricultural policy was now fully in place. Britain's readiness to accept the Treaty of Rome in its entirely meant that she would not contest the common agricultural policy (CAP), so that the French agricultural surplus, over and above that part of it which she disposed of to the Five, could henceforth flow into the British market. But even more important were the political aspects. Britain was now needed as a balancing factor against the increasing political and economic strength of the Federal Republic. Since Brandt's accession to power as Chancellor in October 1969, it was clear that he would carry on the Ostpolitik of détente with Russia, Poland and East Germany which he had already embarked upon as Foreign Minister, taking over the role in Eastern Europe which de Gaulle had conceived for France. In economic and monetary matters she could no longer be swayed by France as in the days of the Adenauer-de Gaulle honeymoon. This was shown by the German refusal to revalue the mark and so help the weakening franc in the autumn of 1968, and by the decision to float the mark two years later, putting an almost intolerable strain on the financing of the CAP, dependent as this was on fixed parities between the member states.

Another part of the price for France's readiness to accept Britain and the other applicants was agreement on confederation as the political form for the developing Community. Pompidou as much as de Gaulle regarded supranationalism as anathema. At this meeting with Pompidou in May 1971 Heath apparently concurred in this attitude, the more readily since the majority of his compatriots were opposed to entering the Community partly on grounds of the supposed loss of sovereignty involved. By accepting the situation of the Luxembourg compromise sovereignty could be assumed to be less affected than would be the case if Britain had to accept federation.

How far did this agreement tally with the realities of the case? Were the statesmen fooling themselves or their electorates? It was hard to see how the march towards monetary and economic union could take place without a form of political union much closer than that which is understood by confederation. And to the objectives of monetary and economic union the statesmen were now as much committed as to the enlargement of the Community. The object for which France had fought so tenaciously, the establishment of the common agricultural policy—the greatest Community achievement to date, and the one which had determined the continued existence of the Community—involved the maintenance of fixed parities. But this could only be achieved by a common monetary policy, and for this it scarcely needed the example of Benelux (instructive though this was) to realise that a common economic policy was essential. In fact it was doubtful, as the monetary chaos of the late sixties and early seventies showed, whether monetary union could be achieved without first taking a long step towards economic union. The question would one day—and perhaps fairly soon—have to be faced whether the complex intermeshing decisions involved in commercial agreements, development programmes, regional policies, company law, aid and trade for the Third World, and the strategy for dealing with the American economic colossus (leaving aside that for Japan, China and the Soviet Union), could ever be undertaken except in a unified structure where majority voting would operate.

If there were a logical development as to means, unavoidable if the agreed ends were to be pursued, it was still uncertain as the seventies proceeded as to how the ultimate structures would be shaped. While some, like Jean Rey as a former President of the Commission, still believed that the locus of power in an embryonic federation would move to the Commission, the general feeling was that the Council was bound to continue in its decision-making role. Those who foresaw federation as the goal believed that qualified majority voting would have to become the rule in the Council with its enlarged membership if it was to carry out its tasks, while it yet remained unclear whether the Committee of Permanent Representatives would usurp or share the Commission's functions as an initiating body in relation to it. Especially when it came to dealing with the Americans it seemed that a more unified system was needed: in the early seventies high visiting officials, like Nathaniel Samuels of the American Department of Economic Affairs, were calling on the Permanent Representatives as well as the Commission, which they did not do before.

Instead of this dispersal of power and influence, there was much hope among believers in the Community idea that Britain's entry would lead to a focussing of effort, so that development could go forward in the way they approved. The fact that Britain appointed men of weight to the Commission, Sir Christopher Soames and George Thomson, was considered as a good augury, and it was believed that British administrative flair would bring new life to the Commission and its officials as a whole. Futhermore, it was felt that the British could hardly allow the European Parliament to continue for long as an ineffective talking-shop. Now more than ever since the completed agricultural regulation had brought the Community's 'own resources' (the income of which it disposed) up to a considerable sum, it was necessary to have its budgetary and other policies watched over and validated properly, and this should be the function of the Parliament. The strengthening of the Parliament and the ultimate election of its members (instead of their nomination by governments from the national parliaments) was something that Britain was likely to pursue.

The British Government was already in 1972 blowing coldly on a revived Fouchet Plan[11] put forward by Pompidou for political union, which would have its secretariat at Paris instead of Brussels. The objection was to the site rather than the structure, though implicit in the proposal was a choice for an inter-governmental directorate to replace the Council with its potentially supranational implications. A postponement of decision on this matter had the advantage of not prejudging the future, which British pragmatism would rather see evolve than be determined by imposing a pattern, possibly prematurely, on a system whose aims and functions were not yet clearly defined. Whether the 'unknown destination' to which the Community was proceeding was to be a federation or something short of it, the Benelux model, limited in scale as it was, suggested that a high degree of economic and monetary unity, and close political co-operation, were possible without formal pooling of sovereignty to the extent that might be expected in a federal system.

REFERENCES

[1] Camps: *Britain and the European Community*, 142.

[2] Harold Wilson: *The Labour Government 1964–1970* (London, 1971), 34–5.

[3] Watson, 105.

[4] Pierre Uri (ed.): *From Commonwealth to Common Market*; Nora Beloff: What happened in Britain after the General said No (London, 1968), 73.

[5] Information from M. Rey; Alan Watson: *Europe at Risk* (London, 1972), 205.

[6] Wilson, 340.

[7] Ibid., 393.

[8] Ibid., 390.

[9] *The Times*, 2.12.69.

[10] For the Soames Affair and the change in French policy leading to the Summit at The Hague, see Uwe Kitzinger: *Diplomacy and Persuasion, How Britain Joined the Common Market* (London, 1973), Chapter 1, pp. 35 *seq*.

[11] See p. 163.

Benelux could work with a 'Collège d'Impulsion' roughly analagous to the EEC Commission, but much of its business was naturally done through the Community which greatly increased the means, both formal and informal, for close consultation on matters economic or political. For the Community too there was much to be said for other ways of reaching decisions than through the formal Council and Commission. Two committees, set up after the Summit at The Hague of 1969, had been meeting to examine means of creating an economic and political union. While the parallel Werner Committee recommended steps to bring about economic and monetary union by 1980, the Davignon Committee counselled little more than periodic meetings of the Foreign Ministers, for 'better mutual comprehension of the major problems of international politics . . . and, where it seems possible and desirable, common action'.[1] Professor Ralf Dahrendorf, the Member of the Commission in charge of external affairs, compared favourably the Foreign Ministers' meetings held under the Davignon formula, where real political issues were discussed such as a common attitude to the Middle East conflict, with the near-paralysis of the Council, as illustrated by its meeting in December 1970, when trying to implement the objectives of the Werner Report.[2] Yet could this essentially inter-governmental approach go much further than consultations? To apply policies which could lead to the desired objectives, was not a greater power of centralised decision-making required?

Aims would determine means, and so the Community's ultimate structure. But these aims were not confined to the nature of the Community: the aims of the Community itself, its rationale in the world, were not yet determined. The decision had to be made whether the Community would be inward-looking, developing Western Europe to capacity as a rich man's club, or whether it would be outward-looking, to build up a global system which would cut the gap between the rich and the poor countries, and help the latter to the point of take-off.

The choice had not been made as to the basic orientation of the Community because its role in the world had not been adequately considered. The first Community, for Coal and Steel, had been brought into being to save a crumbling Western Europe, to reconcile those who had been fighting each other, and to create a framework within which France and Germany together could initiate an era of peaceful co-operation. It was a decision to enable Germany, as she recovered her strength, to share the economic benefits instead of making them the basis of another attempt at conquest or hegemony. All this had been well begun in the early fifties. Civilisation had been saved—thanks as much to American support and generosity as to the efforts of Europeans themselves—and the re-launch of the mid-fifties had taken place to apply the lessons of the pilot-scheme to a larger sphere, and so bring the countries involved 'ever closer together', while building an economy on a sufficient scale to be autonomous and self-directing in relation to that of the United States and the rest of the world. In fact for such autonomy to be attained the economy of the Six was too small: Britain's adhesion was needed to complete it.

None of these aims could be regarded as ultimate. To bring the West European countries closer together and to build an economy which could vie with America's in wealth, research and development, were limited aims. Their fulfilment might mean just another America. If no further decision were made as to the orientation of this enormously potential organism, materialism would take over and it would be America at its worst.

If another decision was possible, it was because among the ideas of those who created the Community were some which promised a better *world*. This was inherent in that amalgam of Christianity, socialism, liberalism and humanist pragmatism which was the Community's ideological basis.[3]

Robert Schuman, among the founders of the European Communities, gave the strongest lead in terms of Christian inspiration. After resigning as Foreign Minister in January 1953, he devoted himself to creating the moral and spiritual climate in which could be built the Europe of his vision. This role went far beyond anything he had envisaged for himself as a political leader: he had not been concerned, according to Dean Acheson, with ways of influencing public opinion at the grass-roots level,[4] but in a conversation with Frank Buchman (October 1949) he indicated the task which he later undertook until his death in 1963. 'Statesmen can propose far-reaching plans', he said, 'but they cannot put them into effect without far-reaching change in the hearts of people—this is your work, and it is the kind of job I would like to do myself for the rest of my life'.[5]

During these last years of travelling and public speaking, scarcely interrupted by his appointment as Minister of Justice in 1955, he became known as 'the Pilgrim of Europe'. A speech of 1955 at Augsburg shows his faith in a Europe growing from its original Christian roots, whose lineaments could be discerned as far back as the time of Charlemagne in 'a community based on the equality of rights of each confederate state under a common authority and discipline'. The Christian recognition of the fundamental equality of men could point the way towards political understanding, and though pressure for this had been enormously increased by the threat of nuclear disaster the need was still acute for 'psychological preparation ... putting aside all the accumulated inflammable matter of hatred, jealousy and mistrust'. Europe, called 'to live in community', opening up hitherto undreamed of perspectives through her scientific discoveries and technical conquests, must not abandon 'her noble primacy' and yield to others, 'less prepared than herself, the great role and all the responsibilities decreed by Providence ... She must strengthen herself inwardly, not in her own interest but for the sake of humanity'.[6]

In André Philip, Christianity and socialism blended, and it was Philip who in his latter years, until his death in 1970, spelt out most clearly this concern for Europe's role in bringing something new to the rest of the world. A man for whom the words 'Christian' and 'revolutionary' were synonymous,[7] he saw no short cut to building an ideal civilisation, but believed in moving society towards a condition 'which would present no obstacles to the free action of the spirit'. This modestly expressed aim sprang from his conviction that Christianity is the essential element in European civilisation whose values are based on the idea that 'the word became flesh': a faith impelling men to know the world, to love it and to change it.[8] Logically, in applying this faith, Europe must move towards realising in the Third World the same values of justice and freedom, however incomplete and provisional the resulting changes and structures might be.[9] In this conviction Philip devoted himself increasingly from 1955 onwards to the problems of the developing countries, and in 1967 became President of the Centre of Development of the Organisation for Economic Cooperation and Development (OECD).

After The Hague Conference of December 1969 he made an urgent appeal to the countries concerned to fill up the gap which had been left in the conference agenda concerning the developing world.

'The European idea, on the morrow of the liberation', he said, 'aroused the enthusiasm of the masses, particularly of the youth, because it was linked with the idea of the search for a new type of civilisation. But, in the era of concrete realisations, this idea has been lost in technicalities and it no longer stirs the public imagination. Further progress ... can only be achieved if it is sustained by the public opinion of our countries, and if a new enthusiasm is aroused by a new dynamic mystique. That can only be the idea of an independent Europe, capable in the face of the two super-powers of making a third voice heard, and opening a third way, that of a new project of civilisation, of a responsible society administered at all levels by responsible men, thanks to the fullest participation by the public, and devoted to the service of the least fortunate and the disinherited of the earth. Europe at the service of the Third World—that should be the new idea which alone can give our efforts meaning and creative value'.[10]

This line of thought had an appeal to all socialists, indeed to all men who realised that the typical modern manifestation of the class war had become the pressure for increasing affluence among the developed nations at the expense of the poorer ones, a veiled conflict which often erupted in racial forms. For most socialists in the countries of the Six, however, their strongest convictions about the value of the Community arose from their experience of the full employment and rising incomes which it brought. Real net incomes had doubled since 1958—in manufacturing the real hourly earnings rose by 90 per cent between 1958 and 1968, matching a growth rate for average gross national product running at 5.2 per cent at the end of the decade (in Britain, it must be said, such evidence convinced only some socialists of its value, despite the fact that there the real hourly increase had been at less than half the rate—40 per cent—and the rise in g.n.p. only 2.5 per cent).[11]

Among the liberal-humanist founders of the Community, men like Monnet, Beyen and Spaak (who was nominally a socialist), down-to-earth pragmatism mingled with far-sighted idealism. These pioneers of the 'Community method' had been ready to subordinate doctrine to the changing economic and political needs of the evolving situation. This philosophy implied that 'the institutions of the Community ... are not instruments designed by a unique and irreversible act of will to carry out a clear-cut common purpose, but rather the expression of a set of common circumstances continuously shaping the societies of all the member nations'.[12]

Was this 'ideology of integration'[13] powerful enough to carry the Community through the next phase of its development towards a goal which, logically, seemed nothing less than global? Could statesmen, inspired by this idea and supported by an effective body of public opinion, realise in practice those aims prescribed by Monnet—not to bring into being another great power, as had happened with the Zollverein in the 19th century, no new system of domination, but a community with a sense of responsibility for the world, expressing itself in a way which could transform relationships on a global scale?[14] One of Monnet's collaborators, Max Kohnstamm, spoke of 'the practical application of a method, a process of bringing peoples and nations together so that they can adapt themselves jointly and peacefully to constantly changing circumstances. The natural next step would be the creation of an organised partnership between this growing European community and the United States ... Atlantic partnership might eventually move towards the establishment of common rules and common institutions between East and West'.[15]

In gaining the co-operation of America for a policy directed towards helping the Third World as much through trade as aid, another move along the lines of the Kennedy Round was becoming due. This technique of tariff-cutting had worked well on industrial tariffs, since according to the rules of GATT the major negotiating partners had been obliged to generalise their mutual reductions to all other signatories on the most-favoured-nation principle. But the benefits to the exporters of primary products had not been great, and the less developed countries had been disappointed by the lack of progress made, both then and at the subsequent UNCTAD conferences.[16]

A new start was needed if the Kennedy Round was not to mark the last real advance in trade liberalisation. The effort in this direction initiated by Cordell Hull in 1934 was running out of steam. America's mounting adverse trade balance at the end of the decade had impelled the government to take the drastic, though temporary step of import surcharges. An agreement with Saudi Arabia secured preferential access for her companies to the oil of that country, and there were endless opportunities with the Latin American states for maintaining them as a dependent clientèle.

The Community too seemed on the way to bringing trade liberalisation to an end. It was doing what most great trading states or empires had done in the past, throwing out a protective glacis behind which it could shelter against adverse fluctuations, whether of trade or production, exporting its unemployment and other problems in order to maintain the living-standards of its own citizens. At the same time, apart from the advantages accorded by the Yaounde Conventions in respect of mainly tropical products (in temperate products New Zealand's butter exports were in a special category under the British Treaty of Accession), the system of levies on agricultural imports under the common agricultural policy discriminated severely against exporters of primary products, both from the Third World and the United States.

In cases where the countries associated with the Community were obliged, through reverse preferences, to accept industrial products at low or zero tariffs from it, their own industrial development was inhibited. But whether or not the Community's preferential system was harmful to the less developed countries concerned, the United States could not view with equanimity the creation of what amounted to a protected region covering the former EFTA countries and the Mediterranean, with extensions into Africa, making a nonsense of much of GATT's most-favoured-nation system.

Not only were imports kept out of the Common Market by this system, but the agricultural products of the Community were in some cases exported in direct competition with those originating much more cheaply from elsewhere. To maintain the relatively high price level of Community farm products, a system of market intervention was being operated whereby goods produced in excess of those which could be sold at this level were either bought up and stockpiled or exported with rebates financed from Community resources.[17] The cost of this policy was, in 1968-9, $956m. in excess of the funds accruing from the import levies, which meant that exports of Community agricultural products were being financed to that extent from taxes paid by the non-agricultural majority of the population, on top of what they were already paying by way of the difference between world food prices and those within the Community.

Despite these exports there was a continued tendency for the mountain of butter and other products to grow, while the farmers in whose interests the CAP was supposed to exist remained in many cases dissatisfied, complaining that the prices they were getting were too low, and even demonstrating in Brussels or pouring milk into rivers. It was not only German grain producers who had been discriminated against when the CAP was being set up,[18] and who had to be given deficiency payments, despite the doctrine of the CAP against this procedure: in the case of the French farmers the smaller peasants were left badly off by comparison with the bigger and richer ones. An attempt was being made under the Mansholt Plan for the 'structural reform' of agriculture to deal with rural poverty coexisting with excess production (of milk in particular), by financial grants to peasants for leaving the land, for retirement or for retraining in industry, but the money available was limited by the high cost of market support and export rebates. Rural poverty, it seemed, was in its way as intractable as that of the Third World: despite the constant movement of country folk to the towns it continued to exist in pockets, as among hill farmers, or in wide areas, as in Italy. In fact Italy, with the highest agricultural population and the lowest income per head of any country in the Community, was making disproportionately high payments to the agricultural fund since—just before the initiation of the CAP—she had become a net importer of food. Britain, as a major importer of food, was obliged to make a contribution of £125 m. to the Community budget in her year of entry.

Though not the cause of the rapid inflation from which the Six were suffering (for the British rate of inflation was just as bad, or worse), it was clear that the CAP was an aggravating factor, and that the high cost of feed-grains in particular was bound to maintain the soaring prices of meat. Dissatisfaction with the policy both in its impact on Community members and on the outside world, notably the USA and suppliers from developing countries, made it seem possible that a radical revision of the policy might take place before the seventies were out—perhaps accelerated by difficulties in solving that other problem of maintaining stable monetary rates without which the complicated price and support policies could hardly be kept intact.

Had the CAP outlived its role? To bring it into being a whole policy had been necessary extending over several years, a programme which supplemented that (mainly concerning the setting up of the common industrial tariff) laid down for the first phases of the Community's life by the Treaty of Rome. This programme had closely involved France, and without the CAP it was possible that France under de Gaulle would either have withdrawn from the Community or have wrecked it. The CAP had been the Community's child, concern for which had kept the Community moving together during a critical phase of its development—a problem child, but 'a well-loved problem child' whose future was now in doubt.[19]

In his article (under a nom-de-plume) in *Die Zeit* of August 1971, Dr. Dahrendorf had asserted that nothing less than 'a re-nationalisation of agricultural policy' was on the way . . .

'In 1969 France gladly seized the opportunity of its devaluation to free her agricultural market a little from the Common Market for the benefit of her own farmers; the Federal Republic of Germany no less eagerly did likewise, first in 1969 and again in 1971; and Mr. Geoffrey Rippon has already announced a small option on the common non-Community in favour of his hill-farmers. Strictly speaking, for years past only the Common Agricultural *Fund* has existed, but not the Common Agricultural *Market*. Ineffective common agricultural price agreements exist, but no common agricultural policy. To put it bluntly, those who are not Frenchmen or EEC Europeans of the heroic old days will shed no tears over this development, but will rather wish for its moderate but deliberate continuation'.[20]

Evidently the British, on the point of entering the Community, could shed no tears about this. In any case their policy was moving nearer that of the CAP, with the beginning of a change-over from deficiency payments to a system of levies on imports in 1971.

The concession on imports of New Zealand butter represented another hole punched in the CAP. The political will favouring British entry on the part of the Six (and most decisively France), made it possible to subordinate the economic questions involved, though from the economic point of view flexibility about butter may have been in part the consequence of a realisation that milk production at existing levels within the Community might not be maintained. With the death or pensioning off of the ageing continental farmers (average age 57), it was thought that fewer of the coming generation would be ready to rise early for milking and doing the other disagreeable chores which often made a cowhand seem like 'a combination of waiter and lavatory attendant to a lot of dumb animals'.[21] On the other hand milk production showed continued elasticity upwards: the fact that Community producers secured an 8 per cent increase in price for their butter in March 1972 resulted at once in a 17 per cent increase in production, and the swelling of the butter mountain to 320,000 tonnes.[22] In the same way in Britain the industrialisation of the milk-producing process, with 'cotels' on the lines of the battery system of rearing chickens, tended to produce ever greater quantities of milk, with fewer workers employed.

The question of dairying was a crucial one for the seventies. Excess milk could be disposed of by manufacturing butter, cheese and powdered milk. A good deal of these products were being sold within the Community at a cheap rate—deep-frozen butter and cheap grades of cheese selling at prices equivalent to those for New Zealand butter and cheese in Britain, especially to the forces and welfare institutions, but also to housewives who could not afford the price of fresh 'luxury' butter as an alternative to margarine. The remainder, mostly milk-powder, was going overseas as famine relief or aid for developing countries. There were however limits to the latter method of disposal.

'The use of food surpluses to relieve the immediate crises of famine commands universal support. The notion that they should be deliberately produced in order to provide a permanent element in the food supplies of poorer countries must be questioned ... Far from providing a secure supply of appropriate food products, it is likely to be erratic, offering food when local supplies are abundant and failing to provide aid when shortages in developing countries are most acute. If, however, the under-lying goal is permanently to improve the condition of life of those people who at present have inadequate diets, then what is needed is the transfer of capital and skills. Should the disposal of food products, resulting from mistaken farm policies in developed countries, form an excuse for not providing the type of aid and the conditions of trade which could make a much greater long-run contribution to the alleviation of hunger and poverty, then food aid might well damage the interests of the third world'.[23]

From another aspect the CAP had adverse effects of planetary significance, in stimulating production, especially by factory-farm methods, which brought profits to large-scale farmers and food processers. Since laissez-faire still ruled within the managed market framework of the CAP, those with capital naturally put it into the most profitable lines for investment, no matter how damaging to the environment these might be, or how wasteful of limited resources.

These aberrations were not greatly discouraged by the Mansholt Plan for the structural reform of agriculture (1968), with the aim of taking farmers off the land, increasing productivity and raising farm incomes to the levels obtaining in industry; for it was clear that removal of peasants from the land tended, at least in the short-run, towards increases of productivity on a scale which more than offset the drop in production resulting from the smaller work-force. As for the environmental hazard which often resulted, Mansholt himself made the first significant statement by a Com-munity leader, just before taking office as President of the Commission in March 1972, in calling on the Community to abandon the doctrine of constantly increasing the gross national product, and give a lead in developing non-polluting production methods. This was a start, though it would be some time before public opinion could be brought to act, through the Community framework or any other, on what was rapidly becoming—along with the plight of the Third World—the major challenge to the complacent inward-looking materialist outlook of the 'never-had-it-so-good' affluent one-third of the Earth's population.

Could this one-third begin to face its responsibilities, both as regards the under-privileged two-thirds of humanity, and for the environmental hazards and over-exploitation of scarce resources resulting from its industrial and technological revolutions? No one country, not even the United States, nor a group like the enlarged Community, could be strong enough to take on these tasks alone. These problems could only be tackled adequately if the advanced countries took them on together—a united approach which would have to become normal in the 'Planetary Age'[24] into which history was moving.

The Community might at least set the pattern for this development. In his Reith Lectures Andrew Shonfield suggested that one of the fields within which the Community could most rapidly advance was in its relationship with the underdeveloped countries, and to manage the joint external commercial policy which this would involve he proposed 'an executive merger' of the agencies and instruments through which the member-states have carried out such policies to date.

'If we did that, the appearance of substantial embassies of the European Community in more than half the capitals of the world would itself be a visible demonstration of Western Europe's identity as a new factor in international relations ... The establishment of joint control over the external commercial relations of the Community countries, which is now imminent, should be complemented by a common European development policy'.[25]

Capital, whether invested by individuals, companies, states or associations of states, is expected in the ordinary way to make a profit, and this applies to its investment in backward or declining regions as in developing countries overseas—in both cases lack of infrastructure, services, communications and accessibility to the main economic centres has to be counted on the debit side. Could other criteria than securing the maximum return on capital apply in the new epoch 'in which our means of communication, by bringing people closer together, will eventually enable man to regard all mankind as his neighbour?'[26] At the Summit Conference of the Nine in October 1972 a new will was shown for devising an adequate social and regional policy within the Community. The next step could well be the elaboration of policies for the developing world, related to a scaling down of the demands of the developed countries for scarce resources.

An agreement carried out by the European Jute Industry under the leadership of its President, Robert Carmichael[27] of France, during the sixties had demonstrated how, working with Community and UN bodies like the Food and Agriculture Organisation (FAO), it was possible to guarantee fair and stable prices to the primary producers in India and Pakistan. This arrangement was, naturally, dependent on political stability in the Indian sub-continent, and also on a stand by governments and responsible individuals against extortionate practices by the big buyers and middlemen, and the corruption which these practices involved. By his personal commitment to bringing change of motives to men and nations, Carmichael carried his fight for fair shares for the cultivator to the very heart of the matter.

Global planning based on change in obdurate human ways and attitudes came to the fore as an ever more urgent need for the seventies—not only 'world-strategies to permit developing countries to earn the needed capital to secure the extra skills', nor merely a revision of 'the constructed world order of technological innovation, investment flows and commercial exchanges' in a way that would 'recognise the interdependence of nations and the underlying community of the species, man'.[28] These were great and necessary aims, but their fulfilment presupposed a profound moral change, a re-orientation of approach on the part of those of mankind who had both power and responsibility through membership of the developed nations. To begin to supply the needs of the Third World and safeguard the environment at the same time there had to be a readiness not merely to contribute 1 per cent of gross national product to aid, as André Philip proposed in 1964 (or the more modest target of 0.7 per cent of g.n.p. subsequently proposed by the United Nations), or to generalise preferences or scale down tariffs so that trade, going alongside of aid, could provide the momentum for growth in the Third World. The richer countries had to be prepared to curtail growth, or to go for the kind of growth which neither deprives the poorer countries nor threatens the environment: to create a world in which no longer 'developed' animal pets have the chance of a better diet than all too many 'developing' babies, nor where such anomalies exist as the diversion of at least 50 per cent of the world's fish meal for pigs and chickens in the richer lands, instead of helping feed the Third World's hungry children 'at an annual cost of no more than $8 a child'.[29]

Despite the discrepancy between needs and policies adequate to meet them, the Community at least promised progress.

'By 1970 the Six were providing a rather bigger export market for the third world than Britain and the United States combined ... The EEC, though its exports to these countries have nearly doubled in 10 years, has increased its imports from them so much faster that its deficit rose to $4.8 billion in 1970. This allowed these countries to finance their imports from the United States (with which they had a $2.5 billion deficit) and other foreign payments out of their surplus earnings in trade with the Six'.[30]

In the face of such needs, the limitations of policies for controlling and directing capital, like nationalisation, were apparent—policies which had been formulated in an earlier industrial age. 'Archaic socialism' necessarily found itself in alliance with nationalism.[31] What was needed was a way of mobilising and directing capital, not primarily on the national but international scale in accordance with 'a new form of constructive ... non-materialistic thinking'.[32]

A key question in Europe in the seventies was certainly the deployment of capital, and in particular the investments of multi-national companies. These were operating, not only in Europe but throughout the world, on a scale and in a manner which made nonsense of frontiers and governmental controls. This new market economy which they were creating could not be properly subjected to national taxation systems, nor could it be constrained or directed in other ways by governments, whether for providing capital for backward regions or for maintaining full employment in a country.

Within the Community, promoters had been inhibited in creating their own transnational companies after failure to work out and promulgate a European company law; but the American companies could operate safely from their home bases either by building subsidiaries in Europe or taking over and merging existing companies. They could also command capital in the form of Eurodollars and Eurobonds, despite the fact that these represented American indebtedness rather than American credit—an endless stream of IOU's originating in the sixties when America's strong balance of payments had turned into a deficit. This Midas-touch was due to the fact that these companies could market products of the most advanced technology, such as computers and the goods made by computer-based industry, in a quantity and with a degree of sophistication which could not easily be rivalled, thanks to the economies of scale which were possible in the United States, and to the extent of government-supported research at the technological growth-points.

The Gaullist reaction of prohibiting or making difficulties for American-based companies had failed: they had merely directed their enterprise elsewhere, until falling investments prompted the French government to a change of policy. Could the Europe of the Nine do better? Could America and Japan be brought into a development plan, initiated by the Community but global in its scope?

Such a policy could be nothing less than global in its scope—a planetary policy for a planetary age. The nations of Western Europe, realising that most of the important problems could no longer be tackled on a national basis, have moved towards pooling sovereignty on an increasing range of questions. 'The huge concentrations of corporate power in the hands of international businesses, taken together, demand the establishment of a new dimension of international public power'.[33] By associating various countries with them, and by drawing the former EFTA members who have not entered the Community into a free trade area along with it (an arrangement like that to which de Gaulle gave his original uncompromising No), the Community, by far the world's greatest trading bloc, is building economic relationships of power and resilience throughout the world. It even attracts countries within the Soviet orbit (Rumania has asked to have the benefit of the Community's generalised preferences) despite Russian opposition to the Community.

The Community has performed much better than Comecon, which suggests that as a capitalist organisation it has advantages which its Soviet-inspired counterpart lacks. Yugoslavia, a 'People's Democracy' (though not oriented to Moscow), has realised the advantages of an agreement with the Community, while Franco's Spain also builds as many links as it can. The Italian and French Communists have come to accept it—the Italians with a measure of enthusiasm. With such powers of attraction for East as well as

West, left as well as right, and the leverage throughout the world given by its 40 per cent share of world trade, and its system of generalised preferences, the Community could be in a strong enough position to call the tune for policies concerning growth, the environment and the developing world, and so avert the disaster which otherwise is threatened, as the century closes, by the current demographic and economic trends.

What are the chances for the generating of a public opinion which can demand policies adequate to this challenge, and for the self-denial on the part of people in the richer lands which that implies? The Community, imaginatively led, could create one of the building blocks of an effectively managed world economy,[34] bringing to this task all the experience of applying on a planetary scale common rules and common institutions, creating the consensus which makes possible the institutional market, and—ending distortions of trade and other injustices—providing where they are needed capital, work, opportunity and a rising standard of living. Together with America and Japan, the Community along with the rest of the Group of 21 can make a start with a monetary policy which will ensure stability with trade expansion throughout the world.

What has to be created are 'the energies, the psychic force, the profound commitment'[35] needed for the wider loyalties and the global vision. Recognition of our 'environmental interdependence' can doubtless help to give us that sense of community on a world scale, 'of belonging and living together, without which no human society can be built up, survive and prosper',[36] but we equally need those 'teams' who can play the part of a 'general staff for Europe's renewal' and for 'transforming human societies and attitudes'.[37] We need to seize the opportunity to which Robert Schuman pointed for 'creating a moral climate in which true brotherly unity can flourish ... by bringing people together in public assemblies and personal encounters', and so providing 'teams of trained men, ready for the service of the state, apostles of reconciliation and builders of a new world ... the beginning of a far-reaching transformation of society in which ... the first steps have already been taken'.[37]

For a few this may mean work as officials of the Community, but for everyone there is an equally important role in whatever

220

sphere their calling lies, applying in practice those values and that style of working together which have been both the best and the most distinctive marks of European civilisation, and so fulfilling on an ever wider plane what Schuman called 'the universal law of love and charity which has made every man our neighbour'.

REFERENCES

[1] Watson, 193.

[2] 'Wieland Europa': 'From the First to the Second Europe', in *Die Zeit,* 1.8.71, translated in *Encounter,* April 1972, 87, 88 *seq.*

[3] G. de Carmoy: *The Foreign Policies of France 1944–1968* (Chicago, 1970), 116.

[4] *Sketches from Life,* 60.

[5] Information from Mr. John Caulfeild.

[6] *La Documentation Catholique,* no. 1208, 18.9.55, pp. 1158 *seq.*

[7] *André Philip par Lui-même,* 9.

[8] Ibid., 66–70.

[9] Ibid., 211–212.

[10] *Le Monde,* 6.12.61.

[11] *The Times,* 25.2.71. For the doubling of the standard of living in the Community between 1959 and 1971 see *Fifth General Report on the Activities of the Communities,* 1971 (Brussels/Luxembourg, Feb. 1972), 133.

[12] Andrew Shonfield: 'Journey to an unknown destination' (Reith Lecture), *The Listener,* 9.11.72.

[13] De Carmoy, 116.

[14] See above, Chapter 17.

[15] *Frontier,* Spring 1967, quoted in *Christians and the Common Market: report presented to the British Council of Churches* (SCM Broadsheet, London, 1967), 44.

[16] *Fifth General Report . . . of the Communities,* 1971, 331.

[17] John Marsh and Pierre Uri: 'Europe's Food Balance', in Richard Mayne (ed.): *Europe Tomorrow* (London, 1972), 109–110. See also *The World Today,* May 1972, Trevor Parfitt: 'Farm Prices and Parity in the EEC'.

[18] See above, p. 165.

[19] *Encounter,* April 1972, pp. 84 *seq.*

[20] *Idem.*

[21] Arthur Street, quoted in Clifford Selly: *Ill fares the Land* (London, 1972), 85.

[22] *30 Jours d'Europe,* no. 171, October 1972, 16.

[23] *Europe Tomorrow,* 108–9.

[24] Louis Armand and Michael Drancourt: *The European Challenge* (London, 1970), 124.

[25] *The Listener,* 14.12.72.

[26] Armand and Drancourt, 234

[27] M. Carmichael's papers, and reports of the European Jute Industries Association of which M. Carmichael was President.

[28] Barbara Ward and René Dubos: *Only One Earth* (London, 1972), 285.

[29] Ibid., 276. See 201–202, also *The World Today,* Jan. 1971, Vanya Walker-Leigh: 'The generalised system of preferences'.

[30] *The Times*, 2.7.71 (Uwe Kitzinger).
[31] Armand and Drancourt, 97–102.
[32] Ibid., 142.
[33] *The Listener*, 9.11.72. See also *The World Today*, April 1972. John Pinder: 'The enlarged community, the U.S. and others', and October 1971 C. F. G. Ransom: 'The Future of EEC-COMECON Relations'.
[34] François Duchêne: 'The Uncertainties of Independence' in Max Kohnstamm and Wolfgang Hager (eds.): *A Nation Writ Large? Foreign Policy Problems Before the European Community* (London, 1973).
[35] Ward and Dubos, 96.
[36] Ibid., 297.
[37] Armand and Drancourt, 207, 237.
[38] Buchman, *op. cit.*, 348 (see above, p. 52).

Select Bibliography

The references at the end of each chapter indicate the sources which I have found useful. Some of the books have appeared, since the time I was using them, in English translations, e.g. Konrad Adenauer: *Erinnerungen*, P.-H. Spaak: *Combats Inachevés*, and General de Gaulle: *Mémoires d'Espoir: Le Renouveau*.

The following is a list of works, selected somewhat arbitrarily without any claim to completeness, which in some cases are to be found in the references and in others supplement them.

Works of reference:

L'Année Politique
The Annual Register
Keesings' Contemporary Archives
Dictionary of International Biography (London)
International Who's Who (London)
Who's Who in Europe (Brussels)
Statesman's Year Book
Sweet and Maxwell (publishers): *European Community Treaties* (London, 1972)
Paul Reuter and André Gros: *Traités et documents diplomatiques* (Paris, 1960)

Political and economic background

Geoffrey Barraclough: *An Introduction to Contemporary History* (London, 1967 ed.)
Peter Calvocoressi: *World Politics since 1945* (London, 1971)
Leslie James: *Europe* (vol I of World Affairs since 1939) (Oxford, 1965)
W. Knapp: *Unity and Nationalism in Europe since 1945* (London, 1969)
Walter Laqueur: *Europe since Hitler* (London, 1970)
Roger Morgan: *West European Politics since 1945, the Shaping of the European Community* (London, 1972)
R. C. Mowat: *Ruin and Resurgence, Europe 1939–1965* (London, 1966)
M. M. Postan: *An Economic History of Western Europe 1945–1964* (London, 1967)
Anthony Sampson: *The New Europeans* (London, 1968)
Michael Stewart: *Keynes and After* (London, 1967)
J. M. Roberts: *Europe 1880–1945* (London, 1967)
D. W. Urwin: *Western Europe since 1945* (London, 1968)

The European Economic Community

Henri Brugmans: *L'Idée européenne 1918–1965* (Bruges, 1965)

C. A. Cosgrove and K. J. Twitchett: *The New International Actors: the United Nations and the European Economic Community* (London, 1970)

G. R. Denton (ed.): *Economic Integration in Europe* (London, 1969)

Louis Armand and Michel Drancourt: *The European Challenge* (London, 1970)

Pierre Drouin: *L'Europe du Marché Commun* (Paris, 1963)

W. O. Henderson: *The Genesis of the Common Market* (London, 1962)

Ghita Ionescu: *The New Politics of European Integration* (London, 1972)

Finn B. Jensen: *The Common Market* (Philadephia, 1965)

W. R. Lewis: *Rome or Brussels?* (London, 1971)

L. N. Lindberg: *The Political Dynamics of European Integration* (Stanford, 1963)

Richard Mayne: *The Recovery of Europe* (London, 1970); *The Institutions of the European Community* (London, 1968); (ed.) *Europe Tomorrow* (London, 1972)

J. E. Meade *et al*: *Case Studies in European Economic Union* (Oxford, 1962); *Negotiations for Benelux* (Princeton, 1957)

Anthony Nutting: *Europe will not wait* (London, 1960)

John Pinder (ed.): *The Economics of Europe* (London, 1971)

Roy Pryce: *The Political Future of the European Community* (London, 1962)

Ivor Richard *et al*: *Europe and the Open Sea* (London, 1971)

S. C. M. Broadsheet: *Christians and the Common Market* (London, 1967)

Altiero Spinelli: *The Eurocrats* (Johns Hopkins, 1966)

Dennis Swann: *The Economics of the Common Market* (London, 1970)

British and French aspects

Miriam Camps: *Britain and the European Community* (London, 1964); *European Unification in the Sixties* (London, 1967)

Maurice Couve de Murville: *Une Politique Étrangère 1958–1969* (Paris, 1971)

Georgette Elgey: *Histoire de la IVe. République: Vol. 1, La République des Illusions* (Paris, 1965), *Vol. 2, La République des Contradictions* (Paris, 1968)

Lord Gladwyn: *De Gaulle's Europe, or why the General says No* (London, 1969); *The European Idea* (London, 1967)

A. Grosser: *La IVe République et sa politique extérieure* (Paris, 1961); *La politique extérieure de la Ve. République* (Paris, 1965)
Anthony Hartley: *Gaullism* (London, 1972)
Uwe Kitzinger: *The Challenge of the Common Market* (Oxford, 1961); (ed.): *The Second Try, Labour and the EEC* (London, 1968); *Diplomacy and Persuasion, how Britain joined the Common Market* (London, 1973)
John Lambert: *Britain in a Federal Europe* (London, 1968)
R. J. Lieber: *British Politics and European Unity* (Berkeley, 1970)
Vera Lutz: *Central Planning for the Market Economy, an analysis of the French theory and experience* (London, 1965)
John Newhouse: *Collision in Brussels* (London, 1967)
Clifford Selly: *Ill Fares the Land* (London, 1972)
David Spanier: *Europe our Europe, the inside story of the Common Market negotiations* (London, 1972)

Euro-American relations and the developing world

E. H. van der Bergel: *From Marshall Aid to Atlantic Partnership* (Amsterdam, 1966)
Kurt Birrenbach: *The Future of Atlantic Community* (New York, 1963)
Alistair Buchan (ed.): *Europe's Futures, Europe's Choices* (London, 1969)
R. N. Gardner: *Sterling-Dollar Diplomacy* (New York, 1969)
R. N. Gardner and M. F. Millikan: *The Global Partnership: International Agencies and Economic Development* (New York, 1968)
H. G. Johnson: *Trade Strategy for Rich and Poor Countries* (London, 1971)
H. A. Kissinger: *The Troubled Partnership* (New York, 1965)
Max Kohnstamm and Wolfgang Hager (eds.); *A Nation Writ Large? Foreign Affairs Problems before the European Community* (London, 1973)
J. R. Mitchell: *The United States and Canada* (*vol. 2 of World Affairs since 1939.*) (Oxford, 1968)
Sir Eric Roll: *The World After Keynes* (London, 1968)
J. J. Servan-Schreiber: *The American Challenge* (London, 1969)
Franz-Joseph Strauss: *Challenge and Response—a Programme for Europe* (London, 1969)
Raymond Vernon: *Sovereignty at Bay, the Multinational Spread of United States Enterprises* (London, 1971)

Reviews

Journal of Common Market Studies, Government and Opposition, International Affairs, The World Today, Europa Archiv, Le Monde weekly review, etc.

SELECT BIBLIOGRAPHY

Publications by the Commission of the European Communities (a selection)
General Reports (annual)
Bulletin of the European Communities (with supplements)
European Community (popular edition of the Bulletin)
Europe Documents (Agence Internationale d'information pour la presse, Brussels)

Publications of Institutes

Royal Institute of International Affairs (Chatham House), London: *Survey, Documents, International Affairs, The World Today,* Papers published jointly with P.E.P.
Institut Royal des Rélations Internationales, Brussels: *Bulletin*
Collège d'Europe, Bruges
Centre de Recherches Européennes, Lausanne
Graduate Institute of International Studies, Geneva, etc.

Index

227

Observer, The 160
Organisation for Economic Co-operation and Development (OECD) 152, and André Philip 208
Organisation for European Economic Co-operation (OEEC) 41–2, 81, 88, 95, 104, 106–8, 123–4, 129, 131–3, 142–5, 147, 151–2, 198
Orwell, George (Eric Blair) 23
Ostpolitik 202
Ottawa Conference (1932) 12, 104
Oxford University 158
Ouchy, Convention of (1932) 12

Pakistan 217
Pan-European Movement 25
Paris 45, 71–3, 82, 94, 96, 98, 102, 121, 127, 133, 136, 138, 151, 173, 178, 204, Treaty of Paris 118–19, 128, 191, Paris Agreements 127, Summit Conference of the Nine (1972) 217
Parti Démocrate Populaire 47
Paul, St 1
Pearl Harbor 36
Peloponnesian War 34
Pentagon 124
Persian Gulf 202
Perspectives 99
Pétain, Marshal Philippe 47, 49, 72
Philip, André 23–5, 57–8, 61, 67, 72–5, 86–8, 115, 118, 131, 208–9, 217
Pineau, Christian 140
Pius XII 54
Plan for the Modernisation and Equipment of France (*see also* Monnet, Jean) 56–7, 114
Pleven, René 98, 121, Plan 125 (*see also* European Defence Community)
Plowden, Sir Edwin 107
Poincaré, Raymond 18
Poinso-Chapuis decree 69
Poland 9, 58, 202
Polaris missiles 173–4
Policy Planning (Staff) Committee (USA) 38–9, 81
Pollution, *see* Environmental pollution
Pompidou, Georges 201–2, 204
Popular Front (French Government of 1936) 25
Popular Party (Italy) 47
Portugal 152
Potsdam Conference (1945) 70
Poujadists 137–8
Protestantism 2, 23, 32, 51, 54, 80
Prussia 3–5, 16, 44, 162

Quotas 9, 12, 89, 142

Ramadier, Paul 68
Rambouillet 162, 173

Rassemblement du Peuple Français (RPF) 68
Reciprocal Trade Agreements Act (1934) 31, 211
Reformation 2
Renault car factories 67
Republican Party (USA) 36, 40
Resistance movements 21–2, 43, 52–4, 72
Reuter, Professor Paul 78
Rey, Jean 199–200, 203
Reynaud, Paul 47
Rhine 15–20, 78, 91, 161, Rhine Army 147
Rhineland 14–18, 80, 150
Rhöndorf 19
Rippon, Geoffrey 213
Robertson, General Sir Brian 71
Robespierre, Maximilien de 2
Rollman, Tony 88–9, 115
Roman Catholic Church 1
Roman Empire 1
Roman History 49
Rome 127, 129
Rome, Treaty of (1957) 24, 56, 128–42, 145–7, 155–7, 160, 166, 168–9, 190, 182–3, 187–8, 191, 193–4, 202, 213
Roosevelt, Franklin Delano 33–5
Rossi, Ernesto 21
Rougemont, Denis de 25–6
Royal Air Force (RAF) 126
Rueff, Jacques 147
Ruhr 3, 15, 17–18, 20, 71, 73, 75, 80–1, 84, 87, 92–3, 99, 116, 118, International Authority for the Ruhr (Ruhr Statute) 73, 75, 81, 84, 89
Rumania 9, 58, 219
Russia, *see* Union of Soviet Socialist Republics

Saar 16, 71–2, 75, 80–1, 84, 87, 91–3, 100, 127, 136
Salisbury, Third Marquess of 7
Samuels, Nathaniel 204
Saudi Arabia 211
Scandinavia 1, 6, 11, 148
Schleswig-Holstein 3
Schroeder, Dr. Gerhard 178–9, 185, 188
Schumacher, Karl 118–19
Schuman Declaration, *see* Declaration of 9 May
Schuman Plan 15, 18, 30, 43, 56–7, 82, 88, 98–100, 102–3, 105, 107–16, 118, 120–1, 123, 151
Schuman, Robert; and European Movement 28, background 43–9, ideas 49–50, 52, 207–8, 221, Minister

233